REAL PHYSICIANS ✢ REAL FAITH

EDITED BY
BENJAMIN R. DOOLITTLE, MD, MDiv
AND DAVID L. LARSON, MD

The Christian Medical & Dental Associations was founded in 1931 and currently serves more than 13,000 members; coordinates a network of Christian healthcare professionals for personal and professional growth; sponsors student ministries in medical and dental schools; conducts overseas healthcare projects for underserved populations; addresses policies on healthcare, medical ethics and bioethical and human rights issues; distributes educational and inspirational resources; provides missionary healthcare professionals with continuing education resources; and conducts international academic exchange programs.

For more information:
Christian Medical & Dental Associations
P.O. Box 7500
Bristol, TN 37621-7500
888-230-2637
cmda.org • main@cmda.org

Editing by Mandi Morrin.
Cover design and interior layout by Ahaa! Design.

©2025 by Benjamin R. Doolittle, David L. Larson and Christian Medical & Dental Associations
All rights reserved. No part of this publication may be reproduced in any form without written permission from Christian Medical & Dental Associations.

Scripture references marked (ESV) are taken from The ESV® Bible (The Holy Bible, English Standard Version®). ESV® Text Edition: 2016. Copyright © 2001 by Crossway, a publishing ministry of Good News Publishers. All rights reserved.
Scripture references marked (NKJV) are taken from the New King James Version®. Copyright © 1982 by Thomas Nelson. Used by permission.
Scripture references marked (NIV) are taken from THE HOLY BIBLE, NEW INTERNATIONAL VERSION., NIV. Copyright © 1973, 1978, 1984, 2011 by Biblica, Inc. Used by permission. All rights reserved worldwide.
Scripture references marked (NLT) are taken from the Holy Bible, New Living Translation, copyright © 1996, 2004, 2015 by Tyndale House Foundation. Used by permission of Tyndale House Publishers, Inc., Carol Stream, Illinois 60188. All rights reserved.

ISBN #979-8-9921995-0-5

Library of Congress Control Number: 2025934686

Printed in the United States of America

ENDORSEMENTS

"In a world where medicine and faith often seem to belong to separate worlds, *Real Physicians, Real Faith* introduces us to real people in whose lives they are deeply united. Their moving biographical stories point toward a vision of healing that extends comprehensively to both body and spirit."

—S. Mark Heim
Samuel Abbot Professor of Christian Theology
Andover Newton Seminary at Yale Divinity School

"*Real Physicians, Real Faith* is a profoundly inspiring collection of authentic testimonies that beautifully captures the intersection of faith and medicine. Through heartfelt stories of spiritual growth and pivotal moments—whether with patients, colleagues or family members—this book offers a rare glimpse into how physicians navigate their faith in the context of their calling. As I read these testimonies, I was deeply encouraged to reflect on my own faith journey, and was moved to see how so many physicians are living out their faith, shining Christ's light and love as they help their patients pursue better health."

—Gordon Chen, MD
CEO of ThriveWell
Principal and Board Member of ChenMed

TABLE OF CONTENTS

FOREWORD 7
INTRODUCTION 9

THE MISSION FIELD 11
    1. MIKE CHUPP, MD, FACS 13
    2. RUSSELL WHITE, MD 19
    3. AARON BRANCH, MD 25

THE BEDSIDE 33
    4. TRACY A. BALBONI, MD, MPH 35
    5. ANDRE CIPTA, MD 43
    6. KRISTIN COLLIER, MD, FACP 51
    7. AMY HAYTON, MD 57
    8. KIMBELL KORNU, MD, PHD 63
    9. CHRISTINE LIU, MD 69
    10. JANET MA, MD 77
    11. JOHN D. MELLINGER, MD 83
    12. GRACE OEI, MD, MA 89
    13. BARRY J. WU, MD 95

THE CHURCH 101
14. SCOTT MORRIS, MD 103
15. BENJAMIN R. DOOLITTLE, MD MDIV 111
16. MARTA ILLUECA, MD, MDIV, MS, FAAP 117
17. CHARLES HODGES, MD 123

THE ACADEMY 129
18. DEBRA A. SCHWINN, MD 131
19. JEANNETTE E. SOUTH-PAUL, MD 137
20. WARREN KINGHORN, MD, THD 143
21. RICHARD M. ALLMAN, MD 149
22. ANDRE VAN MOL, MD 157
23. SHARON A. FALKENHEIMER, MD, MPH, MA (BIOETHICS), PHD 163
24. JOHN PATRICK, MD 169
25. MICHAEL MILLER, MD 183

APPENDIX 189
YOUR STORY 203

FOREWORD

One of the greatest blessings of my life in my roles as a healthcare missionary, Director of World Medical Mission and CEO of Christian Medical & Dental Associations (CMDA) was getting to know countless Christian physicians who live out their faith daily in their practices and their homes. Hearing their personal stories, seeing their lives and watching their interactions with people were testimonies to me that strengthened my faith and molded my life.

I felt the call to healthcare missions as a senior in high school after my dad took me on a mission trip to Haiti. My dad encouraged me to spend a summer after my junior year at Asbury College, where I was a pre-med student, with Dr. Ernie Steury at Tenwek Hospital in Kenya, Africa. Mom and Dad had supported and prayed for the Steury family since Ernie arrived at Tenwek as its first physician in 1959.

I lived in Ernie's home, ate at his table and followed him day and night around the hospital. He taught me to first assist in surgery and let me deliver my first baby. I saw him pray before he operated, lay a comforting hand on every patient, have family devotions each morning and lead people to Christ at their bedside. He demonstrated to me compassion, patience, love, joy, perseverance and a high level of medical expertise in the face of overwhelming needs and extremely limited resources. He became my role model. I wanted to be just like him as I returned to continue my training. Soon after I got back to the United States, I started the process and then received preliminary appointment to be a missionary with World Gospel Mission when I finished my training. Nine years later I arrived with my family at Tenwek to join Dr. Steury.

He was the first of several physicians whose living testimonies touched my life and soul. Each year, about 40 physicians would come to Tenwek for a month or two through World Medical Mission to help us carry our heavy workload. A number of those visiting physicians stayed in our home. One surgeon from Pennsylvania came every year and brought a student and resident to disciple, teach and introduce them to healthcare missions. The first time he ate at our table he said, "Dave, I know you are working flat out. Can I pick up a couple of your nights of your call this month along with my regular ones?" What a testimony of servanthood! He loved to memorize Scripture. I still remember him quoting an entire book of the New Testament from memory when he spoke at one of our Sunday night services. His passion for knowing God's Word also enhanced my hunger for it. He was one of the humblest men I have ever met, and I still cherish the memory of him 40 years later. His imprint still marks my life.

I could tell you similar stories about other physicians, including those who joined medical relief teams I led into Sudan and Somalia serving in the pressure cooker of civil war, famine and epidemics. Life was hard, patient numbers were overwhelming and the locations was dangerous. In Mogadishu, armed guards always accompanied us. In Sudan, our team was kidnapped and held hostage for a few days. Seeing team members trust in God, watching their compassion for the terrible suffering of our patients and observing their willingness to put their lives in jeopardy to help to share the gospel touched my mind and heart and strengthened my own walk with the Lord.

The number of physicians who became role models for me only increased after I had the privilege of leading CMDA. I could fill pages with their testimonial words and lives. They inspired me as living examples of what God could do through those who were totally committed to serve Him. They inspired me to be more like our Savior as I saw Christ in them.

Nothing is more compelling than an individual's personal testimony who is living life for Jesus. They encourage, teach and help us grow both in our professional lives and in our walk with the Lord. The personal stories contained in *Real Physicians, Real Faith* shared by Christian physicians are compelling. Several of them serve in challenging academic environments and in what I believe is one of the most difficult "mission fields" for healthcare professionals. Their words will encourage, challenge and grow your faith.

I love this book, and so will you. I could hardly put it down. Though I personally have known some of these healthcare professionals as friends and colleagues for years, I got to know them at a deeper level as I read their chapters. Those I didn't know personally left me desiring to meet them.

Whether you are exploring a personal relationship with Christ, are early in your faith walk with your Savior or have been a Christian for a number of years, you have a great read ahead. Read on!

BY DAVID STEVENS, MD, MA (ETHICS)
CEO Emeritus, Christian Medical & Dental Associations

INTRODUCTION

In fall 2024, Ben spent a sabbatical at The Faraday Institute for Science & Religion and St. Edmund's College, University of Cambridge. The Faraday Institute is a welcoming community of keen-minded scholars and good-hearted friends. The place is a beehive of activity. They have programs for undergraduate and graduate students, churches and schools. Their team lectures everywhere from Japan to the United Arab Emirates. They greeted Ben into their midst, hooked him into all the fun Cambridge spots and challenged him with the most provocative ideas.

Several of the Faraday scholars mentioned a deeply influential book, *Real Scientists, Real Faith*, first published in 1991, which is a collection of essays by Christian Oxbridge scientists who reconcile their faith and their science. They are astronomers, biochemists and physicists of the highest rank. At a time when the "New Atheists" are so popular, and the "Nones" are on the rise, this thoughtful collection gives a refreshing perspective: it is possible to be both a scientist and a Christian.

This collection is borne from that tradition; yet, perhaps physicians engage in faith a bit differently than the scientist. A scientist beholds the glory of God in the cosmos, in the chemical reaction and in the microscope. A physician beholds the glory of God in the patient. God's presence is often experienced in the weeping, the suffering, the grind of the work and even, hopefully, the healing. We rejoice when the patient improves, but we also struggle with our burnout and our failures. Sure, we too are scientists, but we are also human. Because medicine is intensely human, we, as Christian physicians, lean into our faith. What else are we to do? As Peter said to Jesus, "Lord, to whom shall we go? You have the words of eternal life. We have come to believe and to know that you are the Holy One of God" (John 6:68b-69, NIV).

This book, *Real Physicians, Real Faith*, germinated in Cambridge and bore fruit through Christian Medical & Dental Associations' (CMDA) Christian Academic Physician and Scientists (CAPS) specialty section. CAPS meets virtually each month to encourage Christian faculty members and equip them in leadership ministry (Luke 4:18).

Among CAPS' activities is the CAPS Writing Lab, which was initiated by a chance conversation between Ben and Andre Cipta, MD, the first recipient of the CAPS Faith and Medicine Research Sponsorship. They attended Dr. Harold Koenig's annual course on religion, spirituality and health at Duke University and launched the CAPS Writing Lab for CAPS members to brainstorm ideas, make goals and support one another in their academic work. When Ben returned from Cambridge, he pitched this project to the lab group that immediately rallied. David reached out to CMDA CEO Dr. Mike Chupp, who enthusiastically gave a green light. This collection, we believe, is both the joy of those conversations and the fruit of the Spirit.

Ben, Andre, David and Mike invited a variety of Christian physicians from different pathways to write a thoughtful, personal essay about how their faith and medical practice intertwined. Perhaps they were influenced by a patient? A tragic moment in their lives? A grace-imbued rescue? A conflict difficult to resolve? They are a diverse group—surgeons, primary care doctors, missionaries, academics, researchers and even a flight surgeon!

And so, the book has a diversity of stories. Some are intensely personal. Dr. Christine Liu shares about her son who was born with hydrocephalus. Dr. Kimbell Kornu writes about his sister who died from Chronic Lymphocytic Leukemia. Other stories are more harrowing. Dr. Russell White tells the incredible story of a patient who nearly bleeds out from a ruptured aorta. How he saved this man is almost too good to be true, but you will have to read Chapter 2 to find out the rest of this unbelievable story. Stories come from the highest echelon of the academy. Dr. Debra Schwinn is a university president and former medical school dean. Dr. Jeannette South-Paul is a Provost and Executive Vice-President. The authors tell lots of stories of the patients who inspire us, challenge us and deepen our faith. (Please note, any patient name has been changed and details have been altered to preserve confidentiality). Throughout, we share how God has moved in their lives. Dr. John Patrick quotes Anselm of Canterbury, "Credo ut intelligam," (we believe so that we may understand). Perhaps this is the most authentic position. How else can we contend with the suffering of our patients? Our own challenges with grief and trauma?

The co-editors are so grateful for the authentic struggles, deep faith and abiding love of these contributors—and also for receiving their manuscripts in the requested six weeks, a miracle in itself! We are not perfect—far from it. We struggle with our faith. We doubt. We weep. Each of these stories articulates the mystery of God's power to work in our lives. We hope these stories give witness not to us, but to God's grace. We hope these stories encourage those on their own journey, those who ponder how being a Christian and a physician are not contrary to each other but synergistically lead to the flourishing of both.

Blessings and good cheer to all,
Ben and David
Co-editors

THE MISSION FIELD

CHAPTER 1

THE SACRED, OFT SURPRISING AND SOMETIMES SCARY CALL OF GOD

MIKE CHUPP, MD, FACS
CHIEF EXECUTIVE OFFICER, CHRISTIAN MEDICAL & DENTAL ASSOCIATIONS

> *"Calling is the truth that God calls us to Himself so decisively that everything I am, everything I do, and everything I have is invested with a special dynamism and devotion lived out in response to God's summons and service."*
>
> —OS GUINNESS, THE CALL

My knees were visibly shaking, and my mouth went dry. Suddenly, an image of Moses standing before Yahweh at the burning bush came to mind, a former Egyptian prince turned shepherd giving God lame excuses on a rocky Sinai hillside. How often had I considered him a wimp for his reticence to obey Yahweh on that day? My knees had never shaken, not even when managing life-threatening injuries as a missionary surgeon in Kenya, including removing an arrow from a man's beating heart. Yet here I was, sitting across the table from two physicians at the headquarters of Christian Medical & Dental Associations (CMDA) in Bristol, Tennessee. These men, Dr. David Stevens and Dr. Gene Rudd, were my heroes as Christian leaders in healthcare, and they had led CMDA for more than 20 years. Under their leadership, CMDA had experienced remarkable growth as it became a major voice in the public square on some of the most controversial bioethical issues of the 21st century. They were the catalysts in a campaign to challenge Christian healthcare professionals to be about kingdom business in their own practices across America. And now they were asking me (with no forewarning) to consider leaving a 23-year career in clinical surgery and mission hospital leadership to join them in the

United States as the Executive Vice President of CMDA. Dr. Stevens even suggested it was likely I would then be considered by the CMDA Board of Trustees to succeed him as Chief Executive Officer (CEO), as he moved onto his next assignment from God. Okay, Moses, I apologize.

I've told a few people about my path to become CEO of CMDA, including a friend of CMDA and philanthropist, Roger Leonard. After hearing my story, Roger told me that should I ever write a biography, he suggested calling it *Sacred Leadership*. When I asked him why, he told me, "Your story, Mike, exemplifies what I read in my Bible, an obedient and consecrated life results in sacred outcomes. You are clearly living out a consecrated life." His comments took me back to a sacred moment when I was 20 years old, during a six-week, short-term mission experience in Sierra Leone, West Africa. At that time, I was a college pre-med student at Taylor University in Indiana. Not one person in my family was in medicine or nursing to guide me in this journey, but I had felt a keen desire from the age of 16 to become a doctor so I might do ministry the way Jesus did—preaching AND healing. For nearly two weeks, I assisted a single missionary nurse named Geri Gerig in a clinic near a remote village in Sierra Leone called Yifin. Geri's compassion, patience and competent care for these Africans, over more than 15 years, moved me in a powerful way. One evening, after time in God's Word and reflecting on what I had observed, I knelt by my bed in the guestroom of a missionary couple on furlough in the United States. I sincerely told God that if He opened the door for me to get into medical school and eventually become a doctor, I would joyfully serve Africans in the same way Geri was serving. I would say this was the first of several sacred moments of consecration in my life and walk with Christ. Two months later, I was accepted into Indiana University School of Medicine in their first round of accepted students for the next academic year, 1984 to 1985.

Four years later I was back in Africa, this time in Kenya as a fourth-year medical student on an elective at Tenwek Hospital, and I encountered an American general surgeon by the name of Jim Teeter. Dr. Teeter had been serving for a couple of months each year for more than 15 years with World Medical Mission at Tenwek. I just happened to overlap with his time of service in early 1988. I had decided to pursue general surgery and was awaiting match results in March of that year. Dr. Teeter took me aside in the guesthouse, after a few weeks of working together, and told me:

> "Mike, I know you are thinking and praying about how to serve Christ in medical missions. You could choose to volunteer as I have done, a couple of months a year, but I want you to consider a different path. You have now seen the difference career missionaries, including Dr. Ernie Steury, have made here at Tenwek for almost 40 years. Nearly all the major growth and advancement here has come because of the deep and abiding commitment of a consecrated group of American missionaries and Kenyan national staff. I think that when you finish surgical training, you should join them long term."

During those two months, I met Dr. David Stevens, a family physician and the acting CEO and Medical Superintendent of Tenwek at the time. Dave wrote me a letter when I returned to the U.S. and asked me to consider going "all in, by becoming a career missionary after general surgery training and consider joining us at Tenwek." Receiving that letter and reading Dave's specific comments of his gratitude for the kingdom impact of my service at Tenwek became a *sacred* moment for me. With a newfound resolve, I wanted to complete surgical training and become a medical missionary, *just like Dr. David Stevens*.

My wife Pam and I met at Indianapolis Baptist High School, where her dad was the administrator of the school system. One of the first conversations I remember having with this beautiful 14-year-old blonde girl was the real and moving experience she had in a summer camp the year before. She told me she had sensed a real Holy Spirit "tug" to become a missionary in Africa someday. This conversation preceded my Sierra Leone sacred moment by two years. Pam's own sacred moment of calling and purpose, during a girls' summer camp, would become critical 10 years later, when I asked Pam to marry me on the second date of our renewed romance. We had gone our separate ways when I was a pre-med student at Taylor and had not seen each other for the eight years of my medical school and surgery training. When she said "yes" to my marriage proposal, she cried as I held her hands. I was so touched, thinking her tears were from pure joy. A few years into our marriage, however, she admitted to me those tears came for a different reason. As she accepted my proposal, she knew this would mean a different path for her future; one that would likely mean leaving friends and family behind to answer the call to Africa she knew she would have with me.

After five years of general surgery training and three years in practice in Michigan with Southwestern Medical Clinic, I felt well-prepared to manage a wide array of surgical challenges in a rural Kenyan mission hospital like Tenwek when we arrived in late 1996. I knew I would have to stretch and learn to offer surgical care across the specialties, but little did I know that, over the course of the next four years, my general surgery career would be hijacked by two unmet and yet critical needs: orthopedic surgical care and physician administrative leadership. I will return to the leadership piece, but, first, I was not prepared to manage the huge load of orthopedic surgical care in this established, referral hospital. It came to the point during my first year when I realized I had *to fix the bone or just go home*! My learning curve was shallow, prolonged and, at times, quite frustrating, but some early positive outcomes encouraged me to keep learning by doing. I often felt like a chief resident in orthopedics with only an occasional appearance by an attending short-term orthopedic surgeon to critique my work. While I found joy in making profound differences in these patients' lives, I was finding myself doing orthopedic surgery 24 hours a day, seven days a week, with general surgery taking a backseat. I began fearing my success in managing a growing orthopedic department would mean the end of any future re-entry back into general surgery in the states. I brought my concerns to God:

> *"Lord, I don't want to commit career suicide, but it is obvious you made me for this work, and you are blessing it (much to my amazement). Please provide a real orthopedic surgeon*

for this needed specialty care or give me peace and assurance that I'll be ok, because I know you've got this."

In response to that prayer, He did not bring along a long-term orthopedic surgeon for an entire decade. Instead, He gave me amazing peace that my surgical career was in His hands and He would take care of surgical credentialing back home in the U.S. Over the next 15 years, I returned every three or four years to my home base in St. Joseph, Michigan with a wonderful group of doctors at Southwestern Medical Clinic. Not once was the issue of my clinical focus in Kenya on orthopedics raised by leadership or the hospital credentialing committee. I found myself busy every time I returned to the U.S., where I could perform "bread and butter" general surgery and endoscopy.

I previously mentioned the physician leadership need at Tenwek in 1996. I have often wondered if my life would have turned out differently if I had I stayed in the U.S. and focused solely on a general surgery practice, instead of being thrown into the deep end of performing surgery and managing a large African mission hospital. Just five months after launching my missionary surgical career at Tenwek, I was invited before the Tenwek management team and asked if I would consider taking on the responsibility of being Medical Superintendent as the incumbent leader was heading home on furlough in a few months. As I considered the offer, I realized they had no other choices than me at that time. There would be no other long-term doctor options for at least another nine to 12 months. I had not held any medical leadership roles or healthcare administration responsibilities up to that point in my career—none. I figured they would replace me as soon as someone with any qualifications came along. A year later, I was attending a CMDA conference outside of Nairobi and met the Medical Superintendent of Kijabe Mission Hospital, Dr. Tim Fader. Tim had held that position for several years and had a great reputation. I shared with Tim that serving as the Tenwek "Med Sup" that year had curtailed my time in the operating room. He then told me something I'll never forget: "Mike, our hospitals can recruit missionary surgeons, and they come in large numbers, both long-term and short-term. That's the easy part out here in Kenya, but to find someone who is willing and gifted to handle hospital administration, that is golden." From that moment on, I stopped complaining and committed to being a better physician leader. I did not love surgery any less, but Tim's perspective helped me understand how God may have called, and planned, for me to be a part of something surprising and special as the Medical Superintendent of Tenwek Hospital. It was 17 years later, after an amazing journey of serving the missionary and national staff of this rapidly growing ministry, that Dr. David Stevens knocked on my door and my knees shook at the thought of taking his place at CMDA.

The process of becoming a surgeon is marked by personal sacrifice, grueling hours and accepting the reality that mistakes on the job can result in significant morbidity, or even mortality, for patients. The life of a missionary doctor also comes with some necessary sacrifices and struggles, both professionally and personally. However, those sacrifices and their associated pain pale in comparison to the suffering endured by anyone who carries and then is crucified on a cross. The Lord Jesus told His disciples, "If anyone would come after me, let him deny himself and take up his cross daily and follow me" (Luke 9:23b, ESV). When Dr. Stevens asked me to consider leaving Tenwek Hospital to join him at CMDA, he made it clear that if I said "yes," this would be the end of my clinical career in surgery. Surgical skills have a shelf life, of sorts, and this move would likely take me out of the operating room for good. It was a scary proposition for me, following my 25 years as a surgeon in the U.S. and Kenya and a mission hospital leader at Tenwek. Apparently, cross-bearing is part of our daily job description until Jesus comes back or takes us home. Jesus' own view of what He would endure led Him to admit His own angst in John 12:27-28, "Now my soul is troubled, and what shall I say? 'Father, save me from this hour'? No, it was for this very reason I came to this hour. Father, glorify your name!" (NIV). Two chapters later, He instructs the disciples, "Do not let your hearts be troubled" (John 14:1a, NIV). Clearly, though, what awaited Christ that passion week was troubling to our Lord Jesus. God's call CAN be scary, especially if we come to understand the "how" of fulfilling that call. In a passage of Scripture missiologist Lesslie Newbigin described in *Foolishness to the Greeks* as the central missional text of the New Testament, Paul told the Corinthians, "For we who are alive are always being given over to death for Jesus' sake, so that his life may also be revealed in our mortal body. So then, death is at work in us, but life is at work in you" (2 Corinthians 4:11-12, NIV). The other day, a Christian physician friend of mine shared with me, "Mike, we as doctors, who call ourselves Christians, sometimes believe wrongly that the personal sacrifice required to train for and then practice our specialty means we get a pass on further sacrifice for God's kingdom." He was right. As physicians, we are seasoned experts at delayed gratification and putting patients' needs first; therefore, putting oneself and one's career at risk in obedience to Christ isn't smart or "good stewardship." As a result, I have observed a widespread reticence on the part of Christian healthcare professionals in America to talk openly about their faith in the healthcare workplace. I call it the disturbing disconnect or Christian doctors' dissociative disorder—treating faith as a personal identity accessory that can and must be removed before starting rounds, washing your hands at the scrub sink or sitting in a hospital committee meeting. Dr. Luke made sure future generations of Christian healthcare professionals would know how the Lord Jesus felt about such dissociative behavior: "If anyone is ashamed of me and my message, the Son of Man will be ashamed of that person when he returns in his glory and in the glory of the Father and the holy angels" (Luke 9:26, NLT).

I'll finish my story with a Scripture that has given me courage in responding to the sacred, oft surprising and sometimes scary call of God. I shared this declaration from Isaiah 50:7 at my commissioning service during the 2019 CMDA National Convention in North Carolina, and it remains my personal leadership mantra: "Because the Sovereign Lord helps me, I will not be disgraced. Therefore, I have set my face like a stone, determined to do his will. And I know that I will not be put to shame" (NLT). Leading

CMDA through COVID controversies, the rise of critical race theory and Marxism, the LGBTQ revolution, political turmoil and the abdication of a true Hippocratic ethic by nearly all major professional healthcare associations in America has been challenging, to say the least. It's a good thing we don't know all the details of our future when we say "yes" to God or His representatives in our lives, like Dr. David Stevens. It is certainly one unique aspect of our Lord Jesus Christ's obedience to His Father that is so remarkable—He DID know all that was coming (John 18:4), and He endured it anyway because of the joy set before Him (Hebrews 12:2). I started this chapter with an Os Guinness quote about the call, so let me finish with another by Os Guinness from *Carpe Diem Redeemed*:

> "Those who respond to God's call, who come to know Him and walk with Him in accomplishing His purposes in the world, are like entrepreneurial partners, junior partners, of course. The meaning of history then is the working out of God's covenantal purposes over time but always far beyond any single generation and always far beyond any human understanding."

In 2016, Dr. Mike Chupp completed 20 years of service as a career missionary surgeon with World Gospel Mission, serving at Tenwek Mission Hospital in Kenya. Dr. David Stevens invited Mike to join the executive leadership team of CMDA in Bristol, Tennessee in mid-2016. Mike joyfully shares, "It has been a great honor to help lead the organization that has had the longest and most profound impact on my professional life as a Christian physician." Dr. Chupp was appointed CEO by the CMDA Board of Trustees in September 2019, as Dr. Stevens' successor. With God's help, CMDA has continued to advance and thrive under Dr. Chupp's leadership, pursuing the vision of "Bringing the hope and healing of Christ to the world through healthcare professionals." Mike has been married to Pam for 32 years, and they have four adult children and one granddaughter.

CHAPTER 2

With God All Things Are Possible... And Yet...

Russell White, MD

"Daktari, please come to casualty to see a 15-year-old boy who has been vomiting blood."

It was 8 p.m. on a Friday night in February 1998. I had just gotten home after a long day in the operating room and was hoping to spend some time with my wife and three young sons, when the phone rang with a call from our emergency department at Tenwek Hospital in southwestern Kenya. I quickly made my way back up the hill to the hospital and found Wesley lying on his side on a stretcher in the emergency room. A bucket was on the floor next to him, and it was filled with blood. The team had started an IV, and he was receiving resuscitative fluids. The rather primitive monitor on the shelf above this thin adolescent boy showed he was tachycardic and hypotensive. The conjunctivae of his eyes were extremely pale, indicating significant anemia, clearly related to the obvious blood loss. "Get some blood flowing into his veins as soon as we have a unit cross-matched, and keep giving the crystalloid resuscitation," I told our young intern caring for the patient. I walked the 20 yards to our operating rooms and spoke with the on-call team to arrange an upper gastrointestinal (GI) endoscopy under general anesthesia as soon as the blood was flowing into the patient.

I started back down the hill the short distance to our house while waiting for the on-call team to get things ready for Wesley. I found myself reflecting on my time at Tenwek thus far. After our arrival six months previously, our family, including three boys aged seven, four and two, was settling into life at Tenwek. Beth and I had spent time at Tenwek five years earlier while I was in my general surgery residency, so we knew what to expect. The work was exciting, challenging and heavier than I had expected when we agreed God was leading us to Tenwek as full-time healthcare missionaries.

I was to join three other general surgeons at Tenwek, looking forward to their camaraderie and the opportunity for my own professional development. Dr. Bob Wesche had been working at Tenwek for more than 30 years and was expected to provide a wealth of learning opportunities for me, as I would encounter the breadth of true "general surgery," which Bob described as including "the skin and its contents." However, in early 1997 when Beth and I set our dates for arrival at Tenwek to be in September of that year, Bob and Dora Wesche took this to be God's leading for them to retire and leave the field just before our arrival. This was a setback, but I knew Dr. Michael Johnson, a surgeon from Philadelphia, Pennsylvania, had been working at Tenwek for 17 years, and I would certainly learn much from him. Michael and I had met previously at a conference in the U.S., and I was sure we could work well together.

Upon arrival in September 1997, as our family drove into the Tenwek compound, we passed a truck packed high with household goods heading out. I recognized Michael Johnson in the passenger seat, and we waved for them to stop. We were only separated by a few feet as we sat conversing through our open windows. However, that distance soon felt like hundreds of miles. "Didn't anyone tell you about our plans?" he asked. I was unaware of any plans for the Johnson family, except that Michael would be working with me in surgery at Tenwek Hospital. "We are moving to Kijabe Hospital so our kids can attend Rift Valley Academy. Sorry about the oversight in not letting you know." My plans of being on call every fourth night and weekend had shrunk to every third night and weekend, and now they were reduced to every other night and weekend. More importantly, the practical knowledge and experience these two seasoned missionary surgeons could have shared with me in the areas of orthopedics, urology, gynecology, neurosurgery and pediatric surgery were sequentially reduced to nothing as I began my surgical career at Tenwek Hospital. The third surgeon, Dr. Mike Chupp, had been at Tenwek for less than one year at that time. Thankfully, the relationship with Mike and his family would grow to be a deep source of professional and personal partnership for me and my family over the next 20 years.

Upon my return to the operating room 45 minutes later, Wesley was asleep on the operating room table with an endotracheal tube in place. As I inserted our old-fashioned direct vision gastroscope into Welsey's esophagus, I thought myself well prepared for GI bleeds with epinephrine injection, heater probe and even a banding device for esophageal varices. At this point in my career at Tenwek, I had performed hundreds of endoscopic procedures, as esophageal cancer and peptic ulcer disease were both extremely common in our area. Proton pump inhibitors were just coming onto the market in Kenya, and their high price put them out of the range of most of our patients. Upon reaching the third portion of the duodenum with my scope, I was dumbfounded to realize there was no sign of bleeding anywhere in Wesley's upper GI tract. How could this be? The bucket in front of him had been full of blood!

I asked for the flexible bronchoscope to evaluate his airway—though it would be highly unusual to have this quantity of blood from the airway. As I got to the bifurcation of the trachea with my scope, I could see a pristine trachea and right main-stem bronchus. The left side, however, was completely obstructed by a large blood clot. I knew enough to leave the clot untouched at this point and not "poke the bear!" I removed the bronchoscope and began to ponder. Wesley had been well resuscitated by now, and his pulse and blood pressure were in the normal range. As I examined him again, I discovered some unusual findings. While the pulses in his upper extremities were bounding, I could not appreciate any femoral pulses, nor could I feel an aortic pulsation in this skinny young teenager. A CT scan of his chest would be incredibly helpful at this point. The nearest scanner was a five- to six-hour drive to Nairobi along rough roads. This would clearly not be a wise course of action, nor could Wesley's parents, who were poor subsistence farmers, afford the costly imaging study. It seemed clear the only viable option would be to surgically explore his left thorax in an attempt to diagnose and treat whatever pathology we found.

As it was now quite late, I elected to keep Wesley intubated and sedated through the night. The blood bank was notified we needed as much blood as possible for Wesley, and we would operate first thing in the morning.

As I was walking home late that evening, I decided to check in on another patient I was caring for at the time. David was an 18-year-old young man of the Maasai tribe who had been an inpatient for many weeks. He was highly intelligent, achieving high marks in his high school work. David intended to pursue medical school training and provide high-quality medical care in the name of Christ to the people in his own Maasai tribe. This would make him one of an extremely small fraternity of Christian Maasai doctors in Kenya. He had been transferred from another hospital after undergoing emergency abdominal surgery for small bowel perforation secondary to a typhoid infection. He had an extremely stormy course requiring multiple additional abdominal operations and intestinal resections and an ileostomy for repeated intestinal perforations. David was suffering from a virulent strain of salmonella typhus, and, despite using multiple IV antibiotics, the disease continued to ravage his GI tract. At that time, total parenteral nutrition (TPN) was not available to us, so David was literally starving to death in front of us. We had decided not to return to the operating room with him any further, as we had already removed more of his intestine than was compatible with life. We continued intensive antibiotic therapy and intensive prayer!

Stopping by the surgical ward late in the evening on that night in 1998, I decided not to wake up David. He was getting some much-needed sleep. I noticed his breathing was more labored than it had been earlier in the week. I stood at the foot of his bed and once again interceded on his behalf before the throne of God.

The next morning, we had an early start on Wesley's surgery. We placed a central line for reliable IV access and began an exploratory left thoracotomy. Upon entering the thorax, I was a bit shocked to encounter a contained ruptured aneurysm of the thoracic aorta, which was approximately 15 centimeters in diameter and was contained only by the thin pleura. The aneurysm had eroded into the left lower lobe of the lung, which explained his massive hemoptysis. "If this aneurysm fully ruptures before we get complete control, we will never be able to stop the enormous hemorrhage, and he will die," I said. "If he does survive the operation, he would be paralyzed with renal failure. If that happens, we will simply put two suckers in the chest and allow him to exsanguinate quickly." I first began work at the distal arch of the aorta to prepare a place to clamp the proximal aorta, while staying well away from the aneurysm itself. I next approached the interlobar pulmonary fissure to isolate the lower lobe bronchus, preparing to clamp and prevent any further bleeding into the airway. I was just completing that dissection when, for the only time in my life, I heard an aneurysm rupture. The "popping" sound was somewhat subtle, but the deluge of blood that filled the chest was incredibly dramatic. I immediately placed the suction devices into our surgical field. "It's all over—we are done here," I told the team. However, our anesthetist was prepared and immediately spiked a bag of whole blood and started squeezing the life-giving fluid into Wesley's superior vena cava. "Daktari, please let us try to save him!"

Despite my misgivings, I proceeded and quickly clamped the proximal aorta and the left lower lobe bronchus and extended to a thoraco-abdominal incision and got control of the aorta at the level of the diaphragm. I remembered that a visiting medical student had brought us an aortic graft recently, so I sent someone running to my house to retrieve it. I ligated nearly all the thoracic intercostal vessels to control the bleeding, thinking I would certainly cause paraplegia from spinal cord ischemia. We eventually completed the anastomoses and closed, and we transferred Wesley to our ICU. He was incredibly sick over the next few days and did experience renal and hepatic dysfunction, but this improved quite quickly. I had to be away for a few days and came back to find Wesley extubated and freely conversing in the ICU. "Has anyone talked to Wesley about permanent paraplegia?" I asked the nurse. "No, no one has," she replied with a bit of a smile. "Wesley, why don't you sit up for the Daktari," she said in the Kipsigis language. I was surprised to see him sit up with no assistance. "Wesley, why don't you stand up and walk for us," she continued. I was completely shocked to see Wesley stand up and walk around the bed. I had no good medical reason to explain how he was walking, but I was seeing the hand of God working before my very eyes.

As it turns out, however, Wesley's recovery was not the biggest miracle of the story. As I reviewed his operative course, I discovered he had been transfused nine units of blood (which was a massive undertaking, given the small size of our hospital blood bank at that time). Wesley had type B negative blood, which is one of the rarest types. I assumed the lab had sent us type O blood to meet this large demand. "No," the lab director told me, "we gave him nine units of B negative blood." "How were you ever able to find such a quantity?" I asked. "We went out for a blood drive to one of the local high schools the day before Wesley's surgery," he explained. "We were quite disappointed because instead of our usual experience of getting 20 to 30 units of blood, we were only able to obtain nine units. After we processed the blood, we were even more disappointed because every single unit was type B negative. We thought we would not find enough patients needing this type before the blood expired, but Wesley came in and we gave them all to him." A bit of calculation told me the probability of this occurring, given the rarity of type B negative blood, is one in 10 trillion! As I write this chapter, the current probability of winning the Powerball lottery in the U.S. is one in 292 million, making it about 30,000 times more probable that any one individual purchaser of a lottery ticket would win than for us to find nine unrelated people in a row with type B negative blood. It is virtually a statistical impossibility!

A few days later we helplessly watched David slip into a coma in our surgical ward and then pass on to be with our Lord. My thoughts were, as you might imagine, "Lord, why did you pull out all the stops and provide a miracle to save Wesley's life, while allowing David to die in the next room? Couldn't you have spared one additional small miracle to allow David to heal and to go on to sharing your love and care to needy people in the Maasai tribe?" From a human, utilitarian perspective, it would have made much more sense to save David, who was headed to medical school, than young Wesley, who had failed eighth grade twice. I am reminded, even though I don't understand, God is good and His ultimate plans for us are for hope and a future. I look forward to the day when we will no longer see through a glass darkly on this side of heaven, but instead we will see Him face to face.

> "For my thoughts are not your thoughts, neither are your ways my ways, declares the Lord. For as the heavens are higher than the earth, so are my ways higher than your ways and my thoughts than your thoughts"
>
> (ISAIAH 55:8-9, ESV).

Dr. Russ White was born in the Belgian Congo to medical missionary parents. He attended Roberts Wesleyan College, the University of Michigan School of Medicine and Harvard University School of Public Health. He completed surgical residency at Brown University and a fellowship in cardiothoracic surgery in Bristol, England. He is a clinical professor of surgery at Brown University School of Medicine. A missionary with World Gospel Mission, he has been the chief of surgery and chief of cardiothoracic surgery since 1997 at Tenwek Mission Hospital in Kenya. He was the program director of Tenwek's general surgery residency from 2008 to 2017, working with other consultant surgeons to train 10 surgical residents in a fully approved five-year surgical residency. In 2018, he initiated the first fellowship-level training in cardiothoracic surgery in the region, graduating its first board-certified cardiothoracic surgeon in 2021. He has served as the Chairman of the Education and Scientific Research Committee for the College of Surgeons of East, Central and Southern Africa, responsible for education and research for surgical residents in 13 countries, as well as the head for cardiothoracic surgery. He has a passion for teaching and mentoring young surgeons in a distinctly Christian setting. He has special interests in rheumatic heart disease and esophageal cancer. Dr. White was awarded the American College of Surgeon's Humanitarian Surgeon of the Year in 2012, the Surgical Society of Kenya's Surgeon of the Year in 2017 and the L'Chaim Prize for Outstanding Christian Medical Mission Service through African Mission Healthcare.

CHAPTER 3

MISSIONS AND MEDICINE

AARON BRANCH, MD

I felt called to missions before I felt called to medicine, and this biased how I understood the purpose of medicine. Since learning in missionary training school about those who have no reasonable opportunity to know what Jesus did for them, I knew I wanted to spend my life to meet the greatest spiritual need on this planet. Medicine was merely the key to unlock the door of these people's hearts, so that they could best understand the gospel. I would follow Jesus' example, healing and preaching, though it did vaguely bother me that the kind of healing I would engage in, with its reliance on pharmaceutical and surgical interventions, seemed quite different from Jesus' miraculous healing.

It was in medical school that I first began to fully appreciate an apparent conflict between faith and modern, science-based medicine, and to question the effectiveness of medicine as a tool for my mission work. As an example, before antibiotics, there was not much that could be done for a patient with pneumonia, so one would be justified in depending primarily on prayer for their healing. From a faith perspective, the benefits of such a dependence on prayer are easily seen. If the patient does not recover, they have had the opportunity to consider their mortality and prepare their soul to meet their Lord; if they did recover, they could thank God for His mercy. Whatever the outcome, the patient is forced to deal directly with God, Who alone has the power to heal.

Antibiotics, however, introduced something that is clearly more effective for healing pneumonia than prayer. True, a patient is still free to attribute the healing to God through the antibiotics, but does the presence of antibiotics help the patient give credit to God? Is there not a temptation to regard antibiotics, and the doctors who give them, as more potent than God? As the atheist may (understandably) say, "When I'm sick, I don't need God; I need a doctor." Antibiotics are just one example of the remarkable technological advance in modern medicine that magnifies this quandary, namely, if it is difficult to discern a spiritual benefit to its existence, but rather presents a clear spiritual danger, can God really be pleased with the use of such medicine?

It was difficult for me to face this dilemma meaningfully while in medical school, when I was occupied with the next round of tests and steadily accumulating hundreds of thousands of dollars in debt. So, I put it away with all my other unresolved questions, and consoled myself with the thought that any healing, whatever the means, must be consistent with God's will. But I learned that the issue would follow me as I brought my training to the mission field in Cambodia. A missionary with our hospital remarked that, before we came, when a villager got sick, the response was straightforward; since there were no other realistic options, the only recourse for the church was simply to appeal to God. With our 'help', however, there were now so many other things to consider – arranging travel, finding funds for tests and treatment, and the difficult decisions surrounding how much families should risk going into poverty for the hope of a cure. Were these young churches better off, at least spiritually, without us?

It could be that my own inability to clearly answer these questions stemmed from a defect in my own faith. In the book *Understanding Folk Religion*, the authors address the pernicious syncretism that develops among many churches with an animist, or folk religious, background, such as exists in Cambodia. They describe how Christianity and other formal religions (e.g. Islam, Buddhism, Hinduism) tend to address "top level" cosmic questions – mankind's ultimate origin, purpose, and destiny. Science deals merely with questions concerning the material world, or the "bottom level".

This leaves a "middle zone," with which folk religions are concerned, that deals with the more practical, everyday spiritual issues, such as why someone dies when they do, how to understand and prevent misfortunes, or what to do when you are sick. Hiebert et al writes, "Modern sciences have systematically sought to answer questions on the "bottom level", and Western Christianity those on the "top level". Both have failed to adequately deal with the "middle zone". The result is a dichotomous worldview in which science explains this world, and religion other worlds."[1] It is because of missionaries' failure to address the "middle zone" that believers with an animist background find it hard to forego their animist beliefs and practices, since they have nothing with which to replace them.

Understanding Folk Religion has helped me see that there is also a kind of syncretism in my own worldview, where materialism oversees the "middle zone." Indeed, the owner of a house rented to missionary friends of mine recently confessed that he could only have rented that house to foreigners, as it had been abandoned for several years because any Cambodian would have considered it haunted. When asked if I was not worried about ghosts or spirits at all, my instinctive answer was "of course not"; but not because I trusted in the power and authority of Christ over all the spirit world. It was just that I did not take ghosts seriously.

The realization of my own syncretism with a basically atheist materialism made me concerned that the gospel I was espousing was actually contaminated with a secularism that would ultimately overpower the faith of many. The fruit of this contamination may not be seen in my lifetime or even for many generations. Still, I grieve at what has happened in Western culture, where the progress of science, including medicine, has convinced many that faith has a diminishing relevance. I fear this secularism, like thorns among the seeds, may grow and, one day, afflict the nascent churches that we desire to see mature "to the measure of the stature of the fullness of Christ" (Ephesians 4:13).

Is it inevitable that modern medicine, along with science, will erode faith and support an increasing secularism? Was I abetting this process in Cambodia even as I wished to spread the gospel? When I turned to the Bible for answers to these questions, I first hoped to establish, if possible, whether modern medicine is part of God's plan for mankind. If we understand medicine as part of the wider phenomenon of technology, and technology as man's exertion of control over the world around him, then perhaps the most important statement from the Bible is found in Genesis:

> And God blessed them. And God said to them, "Be fruitful and multiply and fill the earth and subdue it, and have dominion over the fish of the sea and over the birds of the heavens and over every living thing that moves on the earth. (Genesis 1:28, English Standard Version)

In the garden, before the Fall, it was part of God's original design that man would subdue the earth, and have dominion over every living thing that moves on the earth. Is there anything after the Fall, or in the New Covenant, that suggests this command is superseded in any way? The story of the Tower of Babel is interesting in that God seems to oppose the building of the tower in a way that could apply to technology in general: "'Behold, they are one people, and they have all one language, and this is only the beginning of what they will do. And nothing that they propose to do will now be impossible for them'" (Genesis 11:6). However, the focus of God's opposition appears to be to their stated purpose for the tower, which was to "'make a name for ourselves, lest we be dispersed over the face of the whole earth'" (v. 4). This was willful disobedience to the command to "fill the earth," which was part of the same command to subdue the earth. God confuses their language, dispersing them over the earth by force, and thus it seems God validates this original command and sees it as desirable.

Other mention of technology in the Bible is sparse. There are various references to the Israelites' use of the technology of their time, including in agriculture, architecture, metallurgy, warfare, and engineering, such as Hezekiah's construction of a tunnel to divert water into the city of Jerusalem (2 Chronicles 32:30). Though Psalm 20:7 states, "Some trust in chariots and some in horses, but we trust in the name of the LORD our God," there is no criticism of the use of chariots, as Solomon did (1 Kings 10:26). We get the sense that Israel, though perhaps lagging at times in technological advancement compared to their neighbors, continued to use the technology of their time, something that neither Jesus nor the New Testament writers oppose.

Though the Fall dramatically changed our relationship to God and the world, the command to fill the earth and subdue it appears to still be intact. It seems reasonable that this would include control over the bacteria and viruses that cause infection, and that subduing the earth would also include disease of the physical body, which was formed from the "dust of the ground" (Genesis 2:7). It is worth noting that this biblical command is reflected in our very nature, which seems focused on understanding and controlling this world created by God.

What is the purpose of God in this? The question is not about God wanting to alleviate suffering in the world, but why He chooses to use us and technology, rather than a more direct approach of miraculous intervention. I can only speculate, but when I consider that God created us in His image, to be like Him, it may be that God wants us to experience a small part of what He experiences in having ultimate dominion and sovereignty. God wants to do things *through* us, and wants us to learn how to be active, to accomplish significant, even great things, with Him. I must be careful, because of sin's tendency to deceive and lead me to believe that I alone can do these things, of my own strength and ability. But I should also be careful to not overcorrect in the opposite direction, and deny that God has given us any responsibility or authority over what happens on this earth. If our chief end is to be found in a relationship with God, then this interaction, learning to take on roles like God while ultimately being dependent on Him, results in the kind of relationship that God desires, like that between a father and his child.

So why does it seem like the net effect of modern medicine is to draw people away from dependence and a relationship with God? As I alluded to with my own syncretism, I believe the reason is more cultural than anything intrinsic in science. From the time I was a child, I have been indoctrinated in a strict dualism. Church concerns faith and spirituality; school (in particular, public school) is the domain of science and the natural world. Western philosophy has drawn sharp boundaries between the material and immaterial in an attempt to protect and preserve both from each other, but this has only led to a conflict in which appealing to one may be seen as slighting the other.

This dualism can go both ways. I have encountered patients in my training who refused certain medical treatments in an attempt to be consistent with their faith that God would heal them. They clearly suffered under this dichotomy between faith and science, and the only solution they could find was to reject the "worldly" method of healing. This only further illustrates that our culture has so compartmentalized these two worlds, the natural and spiritual, that at some level many feel that we need to choose one over the other, and so if modern medicine is used, it is a tacit admission that we do not trust God.

Pride also plays a role in technology leading our culture away from God. We tend to believe our technological prowess sets us apart from those before us. While faith may have been more reasonable in the past, we have now seen the steady advance of technology, giving us power that at one time only God could have, and to understand phenomena that, in the past, we could only attribute to the hidden ways of God. I believe this has especially impacted the Western mind, from centuries of enjoying technological dominance over the world. But we forget we are not the first ones to think we rule the world. Nebuchadnezzar could have expressed the modern sentiment well when he asked, "Is not this great Babylon, which I have built by my mighty power as a royal residence and for the glory of my majesty?" (Daniel 4:30).

Fortunately, I don't think it needs to be this way. As the psalmist shows, it is possible to not trust in chariots and horses, even as they are used. Other cultures do not seem to see this stark separation between the physical and spiritual that I do. In *Bruchko*, the Motilone tribe in Colombia are described as making little distinction between healing by prayer and healing by medicine; both were miracles from Jesus.[1] In Cambodia, dependence on prayer seems to come more naturally to the national believers than for myself. Before a long trip, I never forget to make sure the children's car seats are secured and seatbelts buckled; my wife (who is Cambodian) never forgets to pray for safety. Once I was talking to a Christian Cambodian patient about her diagnosis, which was quite complicated and would require careful treatment and monitoring for the rest of her life. After finishing my informative and detailed description, she responded, a little impatiently, "Ok, can we pray now?" It's not that I wouldn't have prayed for her, or that she wasn't going to follow my medical advice. But I got the distinct impression that she was not *trusting* in the medicine like I was. She was trusting in the Lord.

It might be said that it is just from a lack of education, that they simply don't have the knowledge to be able to distinguish between natural and supernatural causes. But even educated, irreligious Cambodians readily admit belief in the spirit world and its impact on everyday events. I have seen this characteristic in Cambodians enough to conclude there is a real cultural difference, which I can only surmise comes from the difference between their animist background, with belief in uninterrupted interaction between the spiritual and physical worlds, and my own background of Western dualism, where any interaction between the two worlds is admitted with difficulty. Again from *Understanding Folk Religion*:

> [T]he Western dualism of spirit and matter, mind, and brain, supernatural and natural [is] a dualism that does not exist in most cultures. Most people see the world as full of beings (spirits, ancestors, humans, unborn, animals, plants, and earth spir-

its) and forces (magic, mana, witchcraft, evil eye, fire, gravity), visible and invisible, that interrelate in everyday life. [Also], from a Christian point of view, this dualism is unbiblical. The distinction in Scripture is between God the Creator and his creation, and creation includes angels (good and evil), humans, animals, and nature. Scripture does not divide reality into supernatural and natural realms – into spiritual and natural concerns.[2]

So, it appears Cambodian and other animist-background believers may have something important to share with Western Christianity. There is something beautiful in this. Western Christianity has done much to bless the world through the gospel and various developmental and social initiatives. But as is often experienced in missions, those we seek to bless bless us in return. Just as each believer plays a different role and contributes to the body of Christ, so every people group and culture will contribute to the worldwide Church and to the glory of God. This reminds me to continue to examine my beliefs, to be able to separate what is biblical and what is just cultural, and let the Cambodian believers teach me to see God's hand throughout the natural world, including modern medicine.

From the beginning of my journey in medicine until now, my concern has been that there would be no obstacle to the gospel bearing fruit among those who desperately need it. While I confess it would seem simpler if we just used prayer and miraculous healing, I believe that God desires us to seek ways of alleviating suffering, using prayer *and* modern medicine, both methods illustrating and pointing to the ultimate healing that Jesus has provided for us. The fact that I could even question whether using modern medicine to heal was pleasing to God probably comes from a culturally unbiblical separation of the physical and spiritual. As the gospel spreads and takes roots in non-Western contexts, my hope is that their theology will avoid the dualism that has needlessly confused and, at times, led many astray. Rather, I pray that they would be able to embrace creation as belonging to and valued by God, and that God has both equipped and commanded us to master it for His purposes. Perhaps then it will be our turn to learn and be blessed by them, as they show a more holistic, biblical way of harmonizing faith and science.

Aaron Branch is a family medicine physician currently serving with In His Image International and partnering with Christian and Missionary Alliance in Stung Treng, Cambodia. He completed missionary training school with Global Frontier Missions in Oaxaca, Mexico, before going to medical school at Loma Linda University Medical School in Loma Linda, California and then family medicine training with In His Image Family Medicine Residency in Tulsa, Oklahoma. Shortly after finishing residency, he left for the mission field in Cambodia, working with Mercy Medical Center in Phnom Penh, a mission training hospital where he was involved with family medicine resident training and discipleship. He is currently working with Stung Treng Provincial Hospital, where he focuses on physician training and church-planting efforts in the province.

Notes

1. Olson B. Bruchko: The Astonishing True Story of a 19-Year-Old American, His Capture by the Motilone Indians and His Adventures in Christianizing the Stone Age Tribe. 30th Anniversary Edition. Orlando, FL: Charisma House; 2006. (Public domain, via Wikimedia Commons)

2. Hiebert PG, Shaw RD, Tienou T. Understanding Folk Religion: A Christian Response to Popular Beliefs and Practices. Grand Rapids, MI: Baker Books; 1999. (Public domain, via Wikimedia Commons).

THE BEDSIDE

CHAPTER 4

RIGHTFULLY AND BEAUTIFULLY NAMED "CHAMP"

TRACY A. BALBONI, MD, MPH

As a small child growing up in rural northern California, I helped raise a brood of chicks from fuzzy, peeping, tiny bodies in a warming cage to full grown hens clucking and scratching in our yard. One chick, however, never fully grew to be a hen. Her body grew to the odd shape of a hybrid between that of a chick and a hen, and, likewise, her plumage was a sort of calico of the fuzzy feathers of a chick and the plumage of an adult. She was picked on by her full grown, healthy, hen sisters, and unlike her sisters who produced eggs prolifically, she never laid a single egg.

Interestingly, as a young child I loved this hen the most. I even named her—though I never named the other hens. Her name was "Champ," short for champion. My older sisters laughed at my naming her Champ. Looking at this misshapen hen, it did seem the most ludicrous of names. I didn't mind their laughter, because I knew without one ounce of doubt that she was rightly named. I loved my misshapen hen Champ and carried her proudly around the yard on my child's hip. I would give her the choicest treats that her sisters would otherwise gobble up since she was weaker and less aggressive. I lavished attention on her, so much so she came to me willingly and rested at peace in the crook of my arm, something her sisters would never allow.

Looking back, I wonder now, why did I love Champ so? I loved Champ because in what she lacked, she emanated something transcendent to me as a young child—life that is not about being whole and productive, but life that is good and beautiful simply because it is. Also, in an inexplicable, visceral sort of way, I saw in her something of myself. In this little hen's biological misfortunes, I saw my own vulnerability and pain. And there was something more, something to a child's recognition of her rightful name. Champ was aptly named because my love for her transformed her to something far greater than herself, something her sisters could not experience in their "hen-ly" perfection. Champ had a tender, meaningful, life-transforming relationship with a young child. Though she never produced a single egg or scratched proudly like her full-plumaged, chubby sisters, she experienced a life of love, protection and belonging that mysteriously stemmed from the suffering she bore in her body through no fault of her own.

Those years, between the ages of five and nine, were those when God spoke to me the most clearly and powerfully, cultivating in me the faith that would carry me into the present. I did not go to church growing up, nor did I have a sense that the God I knew was found there. Here, living a few miles outside a small town in northern California, in a home nestled between a redwood grove and an old Gravenstein apple orchard, was where God was known. His presence was not something I was told or figured out, rather I simply experienced God as I gathered eggs with Champ on my hip, climbed apple trees and wandered through the groves of redwoods. I knew God so distinctly I would talk to Him, mostly not with words but with a calm delight in His presence. On occasion I would pray with actual words. And when I did, I prayed for a horse. It was clear my single mom, who sometimes struggled to make ends meet, was never going to get me a horse. So, I asked God instead.

One afternoon after my sisters and I came home from school, I went outside to play, as was my habit. As I walked out to our dirt driveway, there standing before me was a beautiful, large, dark brown horse. He looked at me patiently as if waiting for me. Without a moment's hesitation, I recognized God had brought me a horse. I quickly went inside and grabbed the dog's leash, returning to clip it to my horse's halter. I then led him out to our field, first walking with him and then running as he trotted beside me. After about 20 minutes, the horse had enough and pulled the leash out of my small hands. He cantered away down our driveway with our leash bouncing and flowing with his beautiful, black mane. I never saw my horse again—presumably, he eventually returned to a paddock down the road from which he must have escaped. I knew God had answered my prayer. He had given me my own horse, though only for about 20 minutes.

My faith, more a knowing than any decision, was ostensibly forgotten in the years to come. I moved on from the pure wonder of childhood to the realities of life as a teenager and young woman. I pursued life like one of Champ's sisters, scratching for whatever I could find and scurrying for the latest scraps to fall. However, by the end of college, those memories of knowing God crept up on me in ways I could not elude: Jesus even came to me in dreams.

By the start of medical school, as my life as a seemingly "full-plumaged hen" fell apart, I began surrendering to the God who held and named me. I reluctantly went to church and started reading a Bible, often writing my disagreements on the margins of the bulletin or in the study Bible a friend gifted to me. I had long arguments with God on bike rides, frustrated by my mind's inability to grasp the budding faith that had been planted in that 5-year-old child. I am not sure entirely how or when, but I gave up my fight at some point, I think out of sheer exhaustion, not out of any new revelation or conceptual clarity. I accepted faith in God, and the direction it was taking me, albeit with fits and starts of fearful resistance of the dangerous path down which it was leading. I met Michael, my husband who was at that time training to be a pastor, when I was a third-year medical student. The idea of being married to a pastor was far too extreme for me, and so I denied his requests for dates. He was persistent, though, and so, eventually, I consented to a date. Soon after the second date, when he had plainly informed me that we would be getting married, I ended our relationship over the phone with a polite-sounding excuse. Three months later, we resumed dating and were engaged and married shortly thereafter.

Internship submerged me into a strange world of exacting medical knowledge coupled with the messy realities of human frailty and suffering. The smells of the inpatient floors captured that complexity—the metallic and sterile pungency enmeshed with the aromas of serosanguinous fluids and human sweat. Late one night, I was called to see Mr. Mason as the night float resident to assist with his worsening respiratory distress. He was clearly dying—even I knew that, now only a few weeks into my internship. He had been "made DNR/DNI"—do not resuscitate/do not intubate—earlier that afternoon. I had ordered an increase in the medication to help with air hunger and stopped by to check on him soon thereafter. The respiratory therapist came moments after I arrived. He ignored me and set to work forcing a suction trocar down Mr. Mason's throat to noisily remove secretions. Mr. Mason protested with a weak cry and flailing arms, but the therapist kept up his suctioning. I stood there helplessly watching until the therapist left, speaking a casual goodbye to Mr. Mason as he walked out of the room.

I slowly came to Mr. Mason's side and put my hand on his shoulder. His matted grey head was stooped down, his chest heaving with each raspy breath through the clear plastic non-rebreather mask over his nose and mouth. I prayed for him quietly. After some silence, he turned and glanced up at me. I asked him if his breathing was better with the increase in his medication, now dripping via IV into his arm, and he nodded. I said I would return and visit him in the morning.

However, I didn't come back. The night was a constant barrage of patient issues, and I blearily left the hospital in the morning forgetting my promised visit. I came back the next evening, recalling my words to him after my daytime fitful sleep, but Mr. Mason was gone. He had died earlier that day. The memory of our interaction at 1:30 a.m. was a sudden weight. Was I the last person to speak with him? Then, my beeper began its incessant beeping. I was off for another night of rushing about the inpatient floors, responding to overnight calls.

Though the patient scenarios were each unique, I regularly found myself in similar, subtly weighty situations—caught between the trocar of modern medicine and the cries of human persons. As often as medicine was a tool to uphold the bodily creation, it also seemed to blindly collide with, and even at times mar, the person's sacred image. Simultaneously and inexorably through my training, I found myself also marred. I was taking on more and more the shape of a plastic, probing suction tube than the fleshly hand of a human person, like the one I had laid on Mr. Mason's shoulder. Would I return to his bedside, or would I continue to reflexively run after the constant, beeping demands of the system that is medicine?

My persistent and growing discomfort found its vent in conversations with Michael, who was knee deep in his theological training. We were both struck by the utter disconnection between our worlds. Both engaged human flourishing and suffering, and yet they might as well be distinct universes. This disconnection led to my request to use my few weeks of elective time late in my internship to shadow chaplains in the hospital. The internal medicine program director paused and looked at me quizzically after I explained my proposal, finally chuckling, "Well, nobody has asked to do that before!" He granted my request but asked I do a presentation at our internal medicine conference at the end of my few weeks. My presentation entitled "Spirituality and Medicine" explored the history of the relationship of spirituality and medical practice and the extant research on the role of spirituality in illness. Though planned for a short three weeks, my "elective" has continued, though in a different form—research and education at the intersection of spirituality and medicine ultimately becoming my primary research area as an academic physician.

Two months before the completion of my medical internship, Ms. Kate, a wiry, white-haired Irish woman, greeted me and Michael at the door of her home in Mission Hill, a traditionally Irish borough of Boston known for its gang activity and nightly gunfire. She led us to her kitchen table, pristinely set with an old China tea set and cookies neatly arranged on a faded, flowered plate. We sat down nervously and the conversation to negotiate the sale of her home began. Her brownstone at the base of Mission Hill was across the street from the medical school and public health campuses at Harvard, and several Harvard teaching hospitals were only a stone's throw away. The row house had sat empty after her husband's stroke that forced them to move in with their daughter six years earlier. Despite his death two years prior, Ms. Kate remained living with her daughter but was unwilling to let go of the home where she had raised her family and been a staunch local community activist.

Unbeknownst to Ms. Kate, our small band of Christian medical students had been praying over her home for about four years now. Long before I met Michael, I attended several of these prayer meetings as a new believer. Our group had no money and scant organization even to coordinate our weekly gatherings, let alone purchase and manage a home. Nevertheless, this was the discernment of the man who led our fellowship, one who knew a calling to ministry in Boston and particularly to those in medicine. God had given him a vision to cultivate Christian community, and, inexplicably to my mind, a number of people in our group shared that vision. I thought this to be amusing and even a bit crazy, but still I joined the prayer team laying hands on the dilapidated door of Ms. Kate's abandoned home asking for it to be miraculously given to our ministry in healthcare.

We finished our tea, and the conversation seemed to be at an impasse. Our offer on the home was not even close to what Ms. Kate had previously been offered by various investors. Finally, we laid out the paperwork we had from our bank—the maximum we would be allowed to borrow. Ms. Kate said she would consider our offer, together with the vision we had for the home to be for family and ministry. Two weeks later she informed us that, after praying, she awakened that Sunday morning knowing she should sell the home to us.

Now more than 20 years later, I have raised my family in this home, a small, 1870s brownstone on Wigglesworth Street in Boston. The home is accompanied by six others, comprising the Longwood Christian Community. The ministry has grown over the years, each home a testimony to God's miraculous provision. Situated at the edge of the Harvard Medical School and Public Health campuses, our shared vocation within academic medicine, in Boston and within the body of Christ, has been mysteriously knit together and carried forward. Just as I had no grasp of how a small band of believers could pray over a home and those prayers come into being, I have had no comprehension of how the God of the universe has deigned to build this community and interweave the callings of the few hundred who have lived here. Though beyond the mind's grasp, unmistakable is the power, beauty and goodness of the shared spiritual life of Christian community.

My walk to work from our home on Wigglesworth Street that morning was like all others— about eight minutes to the radiation oncology department where I work, despite the greying heaps of snow at the roadsides. I was on our palliative radiation oncology service that mid-January week, a service I developed with the help of others in response to the Lord's calling to improve radiation oncology care for those facing advanced cancers. This is a population with numerous needs, often urgent, that can easily go neglected without a structure dedicated to nimbly and thoughtfully meet them. The Supportive and Palliative Radiation Oncology Service started in 2011, four years after I finished my residency training and joined the faculty at Harvard Medical School. Now years later, the service has grown in staff and complexity in response to the growing number of patients and the diverse cancer-related issues they bring.

I dropped my things at my office and went straight down to clinic to visit Mary, prior to her radiation planning session. Her husband was at her side, lovingly stroking her hair. I came to the other side of the bed, their faces turning toward mine as I arrived. Mary was a patient I had gotten to know over two years earlier, when she first presented with metastatic disease at the young age of 27. Her primary tumor was treated with surgery and chemotherapy, and then I treated her with aggressive radiation therapy to a single metastasis in her spine, all with the hope of cure. She had done well for just under two years, but then her disease recurred in multiple locations throughout her body. Despite several systemic therapies, her disease relentlessly progressed. Now she was admitted due to painful metastases in her ribs. I was called to see her urgently for palliative radiation therapy. Mary looked at peace, even if a bit over-medicated. Her husband was silently distraught, continuing to stroke her hair. We discussed the plan for her radiation therapy, which she would receive the following day. Our conversation turned to her next steps, and Mary explained they were considering a phase I clinical trial versus going home with hospice. They were unsure what to do. We had had some prior conversations about her faith; I shared I would be praying for this decision for them.

Mary and her husband were frequently brought to my mind for prayer. After radiation treatment, and shortly before her discharge to home hospice, I visited her once in the hospital, giving her a bracelet I wore which had a portion of Psalm 46 engraved on the inside, "God is within her, she will not fall; God will help her at break of day." After her discharge to home hospice, I did not hear from them for several weeks but continued to intermittently pray for them. One night, while traveling, I had a strong sense of the need to pray for Mary, and I even wondered if I should contact her husband, the urgency felt so great. I decided just to pray and fell asleep praying for her. Early that morning, I awakened after a vivid dream, so vivid it felt powerfully real. In the dream, I was going to visit Mary on the same inpatient floor where I had last seen her and given her the Psalm-engraved bracelet. I walked toward the closed door of her inpatient room. Just as I was about to reach the door, Mary burst out with an energy and vibrancy that astounded me. Beholding Mary, she was arresting in beauty and radiance, even her clothes were sublime. I thought to myself, "She is more alive than I am."

I awakened from the dream. I sat up abruptly in my hotel bed with the sudden realization that Mary must have died. Eventually, I got myself ready for a morning of teaching at the radiation oncology residency program I was visiting. After a busy morning, I headed for the airport and looked at my email. I saw I had a message from Mary's husband. I knew what it would say before opening it. Mary had died that morning. The promise of God's help at break of day, etched in silver encircling her right arm and worn until she died, had been fulfilled.

Despite, and through, my brokenness and smallness of mind, and together with countless faithful saints past and present, I continue to join in God's resounding song sung into the spiritual realities of this fallen world—a song swelling with the redemptive power and unending love of Jesus. And though I grow older, my heart ever stretches and yearns to that little child, the one roaming the orchard fragrant with Gravenstein apples and lying on mossy rocks beside streams, peering up into sunlit redwood crowns. Our calling is to become as little children to our heavenly Father, rightly knowing ourselves as feeble, misshaped hens. Carried in His loving arms, we are miraculously transformed into a vibrant identity far greater than all we could ask or imagine. Champ was indeed rightly and beautifully named.

Dr. Tracy Balboni lives in Boston, Massachusetts with her husband, Michael, three children, mother and father-in-law, two cats and a dog. They live in and help lead the Longwood Christian Community, a community of Christians in healthcare. She serves as Professor of Radiation Oncology at Harvard Medical School and as the Program Director for the Harvard Radiation Oncology Program. She developed the Supportive and Palliative Radiation Oncology Service at the Dana-Farber/Brigham and Women's Cancer Center, a service dedicated to the radiation therapy needs of advanced cancer patients. Dr. Balboni is also the co-Director of the Initiative on Health, Religion, and Spirituality at Harvard University. Her primary research interests are located at the intersection of spirituality and the practice of medicine, including the role of spirituality in illness. Her work also includes forging improved dialogue between academic theology, spiritual communities and the field of medicine.

CHAPTER 5

A Quest for Meaning: Finding Life's Purpose in Christ

Andre Cipta, MD

My faith journey testifies to the Lord's providential work. Through every peak and valley, I perceive God's steadfast hand deepening my faith and shaping me into the likeness of Christ (2 Corinthians 3:18). As my knowledge of Christ grows, so too does my affection and reverence for Him. In Christ, I have found meaning, purpose, and even life itself. As you peruse the brief pages of my life, my hope is that may you gain deeper insight into the One who gives life abundantly (John 10:10).

Existential Musings of a Precocious Kid

I rejected the religion of my upbringing. In junior high school, despite attending Catholic mass on Sundays, participating in catechism classes, serving as an altar boy, and receiving the sacraments from Baptism to Confirmation, I found myself grappling with what I later discovered were significant misconceptions about God.

At the time, I did not know how to study the Bible, so my understanding of God was shaped more by people's opinions than by Scripture. My view of God was muddled and incomplete, as the Bible seemed too complex to grasp. While I acknowledged the existence of a higher power, I viewed God as a distant, impersonal judge to be feared and obeyed rather than someone to trust with my deepest concerns. Consequently, I struggled to grasp His love for me, viewing His role in my life as limited to rewarding obedience and punishing disobedience.

Though raised in a loving home, I wrestled with depression and feelings of emptiness. Existential questions haunted me, and the futility of life seemed undeniable, with death and suffering looming inevitably. I could not shake this overwhelming sense of nihilistic hopelessness.

Additionally, I was baffled by how many people seemed content to ignore these questions, living in denial, sheltered behind falsehoods, and disconnected from life's stark realities. I often felt alone and out of place in my contemplations. People's advice to ignore these concerns and embrace life's pleasures felt irrational and unconvincing. For me, searching for life's purpose seemed fundamentally relevant and deeply rational.

I found that the conventional pursuit of fulfillment through academic achievement, career success, and the ideal family home provided me little solace. Observing the fractured lives of affluent families around me, I grew disillusioned with this traditional path to happiness. Parties and sports served only as temporary distractions, leaving behind an insatiable longing for something more substantial.

As I continued to ponder the fragility of life, these swirling thoughts converged on a simple, fundamental question: Does life inherently possess purpose? If it does not, then everything exists devoid of meaning. Concepts like "good" and "evil" become mere social constructs, based on subjective opinions rather than being rooted in an objective moral framework. Ethical considerations shift with cultural tides, guided by pragmatism rather than by a moral imperative. Within this paradigm, nihilism seemed the most logical conclusion.

Yet, amid this bleak outlook, what remained undeniably clear to me was the ubiquitous and relentless drive within us to seek meaning and purpose, even in the minutiae of daily life. This innate longing propels us out of bed each morning, guides our actions, and shapes our aspirations. It seemed entirely plausible that we were imbued with a predetermined sense of purpose. If our lives possessed purpose, then the following questions naturally arise: What is our purpose, and who has the authority to determine it?

DIVINE REVELATION

This quest for meaning set the stage for a transformative encounter with God and His Word. At the age of thirteen, after our fourth move due to my parents' employment, they enrolled me in a non-denominational Christian school. It was there that I truly understood the Gospel and learned to study the Bible in a way that made sense and resonated with my internal struggles. Each morning, our teacher led Bible study devotionals, sharing openly about her own personal challenges. She often spoke about her husband's battle with cancer and how she drew strength from specific Bible passages.

I found her authentic way of conversing with God, like a child speaking to a loving parent, entirely new and refreshing. It was a revelation to see God depicted as a loving and gracious Father who tenderly cares for His children, as portrayed in the parable of the Prodigal Son in Luke 15:11-32. While the Bible indeed describes God as a righteous judge (Psalm 50:6; 2 Corinthians 5:10; Revelation 20:12-15), emphasizing His holiness and commanding reverence, it also reveals His multifaceted nature. God is not only transcendent but also intimately involved in our daily lives, deeply concerned with our joys and struggles alike.

I was also struck by how the Bible did not discount life's stark realities; it confronts them directly and candidly. In the book of Ecclesiastes, Solomon describes life as fleeting, a mere breath. Despite his wealth and success, Solomon grappled with the inevitability of death and the transient nature of earthly accomplishments. His conclusion was simple: The essence of life is to fear God and keep His commandments (Ecclesiastes 12:13-14).

Similarly, Jesus' teachings directly addressed life's challenges, acknowledging that we will face trials. Yet, His words provided solace and hope. In John 16:33, He said, "In this world, you will have trouble. But take heart; I have overcome the world." Jesus never promised a life free of difficulties; instead, He assured us of His victory over them. Even His call to discipleship was forthright: "If anyone would come after Me, let him deny himself and take up his cross and follow Me" (Matthew 16:24). In John 15, Jesus warned His disciples that their lives would become even more difficult, reminding them if the world hated Him, it would also hate His followers. He prepared them for His departure, yet promised their eventual reunion, likening it to the joy a mother feels after childbirth, when the pain is forgotten in the rejoicing of new life (John 16:21-23). Jesus' words did not feel like a sales pitch but an honest call to a committed relationship and complete submission to God.

Through Scripture, I finally found answers that made sense and addressed my questions. I began to see the beauty in theological concepts and appreciated how they flowed together coherently. The Bible provided answers more satisfying and rational than any advice I had received. I dug deep into concepts which I later discovered had fancy names like "penal substitutionary atonement," "propitiation," and "sanctification." Yet, within this systematic theological framework, it was the Gospel that impacted me most significantly.

THE GOSPEL

As I delved deeper into the Bible, the Gospel's message unfolded, offering answers and a new perspective on both God's character and my own essence. I realized that to truly grasp the Gospel, one must first understand the nature of God and our relationship to Him.

Throughout Scripture, God unveils His nature alongside our own, presenting a striking juxtaposition. He demonstrates His power against our frailty, His omniscience against our finite knowledge, and His righteousness against our sin. Truly, there is none like Him.[1]

A recurring theme emerges in both the Old and New Testaments: When God reveals Himself to people, they are overwhelmed by their unworthiness to stand before Him. When Isaiah saw the pre-incarnate Christ, seated on His throne, he exclaimed, "Woe is me! For I am lost; for I am a man of unclean lips, and I dwell in the midst of a people of unclean lips; for my eyes have seen the King, the Lord of hosts!" (Isaiah 6:5, cf John 12:41). Upon witnessing a miracle by Jesus at the Sea of Galilee, Peter fell to his knees, saying, "Depart from me, for I am a sinful man, O Lord" (Luke 5:8).

Romans 3:23 offers a commentary to this very appropriate response and captures the universal human condition: "For all have sinned and fall short of the glory of God." From Adam's sin, humanity inherited a sinful nature, corrupting our essence and infecting every thought, desire, and action with rebellion against God (Psalm 51:5; Romans 3:10-12; 5:12). We are fundamentally flawed, with sin interwoven into our very being, usurping God's authority by acting as our own gods, defining our purposes and sense of right and wrong.

As I reflected on how fervently I pursued my own honor, desires, and comfort, disregarding God's rule and will this rebellion became evident in my own life. I wanted God to serve me, not the other way around. This defiance was not just in isolated acts; it was the orientation of my heart.

Given this realization, the next question naturally arose: What does a perfectly holy God do with an unholy person like me?

I learned that God's answer was to send His Son. The promised Messiah, revealed to be God's Beloved Son, did not rule from afar. Fully divine, Christ condescended to become fully human, living a perfect life in order to die as a perfect sacrifice (Isaiah 53:6; John 1:29; 1 Peter 1:18-19). Christ died the death I deserved so that, through faith, I can reap the rewards of the perfect life only He lived (2 Corinthians 5:21). He suffered the just wrath of the Father as payment for my sin so I could be forgiven.

Through faith in the death and resurrection of Christ, I am not merely reformed but reborn, as Jesus taught Nicodemus in John 3:1-21. Paul writes in 2 Corinthians 5:17, "Therefore, if anyone is in Christ, the new creation has come: The old has gone, the new is here!" God fulfilled His promise from Ezekiel 36:26, "I will give you a new heart and put a new spirit in you; I will remove from you your heart of stone and give you a heart of flesh." Once dead in sin, through God's grace, I am now made anew, adopted as a co-heir with Christ, and no longer live for myself but for Him Who died for me (Ephesians 2:1-10; Romans 8:17; 2 Corinthians 5:15).

Indeed, God must judge and punish sin, for He would not be a good and just God otherwise. Yet, He provided a way to uphold His justice while offering grace and reconciliation through faith in Christ's redemptive work. Truly, God's justice and love converge perfectly at the cross of Christ.

I was blown away by the Gospel. Why would God send His own Son to die on my behalf? Why would He redeem and adopt a sinner like me? Though I still struggle to fully comprehend why God saved me, the moment I understood the Gospel, I was captured by it, and I believed.

The Gospel offers a solution to our greatest problem and stands in stark contrast to the wisdom of the world. Though our natural inclination leans toward autonomy, true freedom is found not in self-rule but in surrender to the authority of our Creator (Galatians 5:1).

A RATIONAL FOUNDATION FOR FAITH

Understanding the Gospel was just the beginning of a long intellectual journey, marked by rigorous questioning and study, which ultimately led me back to God's Word.

Early in my faith journey, while still in high school, the supremacy and reliability of God's Word became my cornerstone. My school principal was particularly instrumental in instilling a high view of the Bible. He taught me how to study and apply Scripture to my struggles and questions. Grounding my beliefs in something immutable and transcendent made sense, recognizing that only the Creator possessed the authority and wisdom to define truth.

The true test of my faith began in college and persisted through my medical training. I confronted questions surrounding the Bible's reliability, authenticity, and interpretability. Moreover, I grappled with reconciling the existence of evil in a world governed by a loving and omnipotent God.

Over the years, these challenges propelled me into a deep exploration of several disciplines of study, including Christ's fulfillment of Old Testament messianic prophecies, textual criticism of the Biblical manuscripts, Bible hermeneutics and exegesis, and the historicity of Biblical events, particularly the resurrection of Christ. Additionally, philosophical inquiries, especially those involving presuppositional and transcendental arguments for God's existence, offered frameworks that resonated with both my personal experiences and observations of the world.

For instance, I found Immanuel Kant's concept of the "categorical imperative" and his commentary on the moral law to be quite rational, while aligning well with my internal convictions and societal patterns.[2] Furthermore, the presuppositional and transcendental arguments of Drs. Cornelius Van Til and Greg Bahnsen provided a compelling account for the natural, logical, and moral laws that we all appeal to, independent of cultural or societal norms.[3,4] The concepts of the "impossibility of the contrary" and "borrowed capital" from the Christian worldview were logically compelling. I realized that it was not my faith that needed to be rationalized; rather, my belief in the God of Scripture accounts for my ability to rationalize anything.

My theological, historical, and philosophical explorations ultimately strengthened my faith in Christ and the Bible. Yet, it was not through rationalism or empirical evidence that my faith was cemented, but through the grace of God revealing Himself to me. While these studies reinforced my faith, they are not its foundation. The true power of the Gospel lies not in human wisdom, but in God's sovereign grace, opening hearts to His truth (1 Corinthians 1:18-23). The reason I have faith is because He revealed Himself to me, and I believed.

Integrating Faith and Medicine

My faith permeates all aspects of my life, including my work as a hospice and palliative medicine physician. I have the privilege of developing deep connections with my patients as I help them live well across the trajectory of serious illness. My work is a constant reminder of life's fleeting and precious nature. This realization drives me to offer the highest quality of care, ensuring that every moment, especially towards life's end, is imbued with dignity and compassion.

In my roles as a clinician, educator, and researcher, my faith provides both the strength and mental framework to conduct my work effectively. Christ's sacrificial love toward the sick and marginalized exemplify the compassionate and holistic care I strive to provide. I recognize that every individual, created in His image, possesses inherent dignity and value.

Additionally, being made in the image of God means that we, like God, have rational minds capable of observing, testing, and interpreting empirical data. Scientific research itself relies on the uniformity and predictability of God's natural laws, which enable us to test hypotheses and apply findings to clinical practice.

Finally, our spiritual dimension plays a significant role in our overall health. Dr. Tracy Balboni's rigorous and comprehensive systematic review published in JAMA, one of the highest impact journals in medical research, revealed a strong link between spirituality and health outcomes.[5] Another esteemed researcher, Dr. Tyler VanderWeele, Director of the Human Flourishing Program at Harvard University, notes, "Empirical evidence on religion as a powerful social factor associated with population health is now quite strong, and evidence has continued to increase that at least some of this is probably causal."[6] These findings underscore the growing recognition of the importance of spirituality in promoting overall well-being.

A Diagnosis of Neurodiversity

While my faith guided my professional journey, it also helped me navigate personal challenges. At the age of forty-one, my life took an unexpected turn when I was diagnosed with Attention-Deficit/Hyperactivity Disorder (ADHD), an unfortunately misleading term that oversimplifies the condition. I discovered that ADHD encompasses more than inattentiveness; more significantly, it involves emotional dysregulation and executive function impairment.

This revelation not only helped me make sense of what I was experiencing internally but also shed light on a lifetime of feeling different and out of place. I could only guess what "normal" felt like by observing others. I battled anxiety and depression, found simple tasks inexplicably challenging, and struggled to maintain relationships. Academic achievements required Herculean efforts, especially through college and medical training.

Understanding my diagnosis, which affirmed my perceived differences, brought a deep sense of peace. It helped me better understand the unique ways God created me. While it does not excuse my shortcomings, this newfound understanding of my weaknesses, tendencies, and strengths has helped me develop strategies to fortify my vulnerabilities and harness my strengths to serve the Lord and others.

This heightened self-awareness has made me a better physician, enabling me to serve with greater empathy and appreciation for each patient's unique journey. As a leader, I have become even more committed to fostering an inclusive environment where diverse perspectives and problem-solving approaches are valued and nurtured. I now view recognitions and awards with greater humility, seeing them as reflections of God's gracious and sovereign work in my life.

My love and appreciation for God have grown ever deeper, as 1 Corinthians 1:27 strikes a chord within. My humble journey, filled with struggles and failures, illustrates how God uses what the world considers foolish to confound the wise.

HE MUST INCREASE, BUT I MUST DECREASE

Ultimately, my quest for meaning culminates in a deeper, fuller understanding of Christ and my relationship with Him. I have discovered that my deepest needs, greatest questions, and most ardent longings find their satisfaction in the person of Jesus Christ. In Him, I not only find the meaning of life but also the very means to live it fully.

As Paul neared the end of his life, he proclaimed, "To live is Christ; to die is gain" (Philippians 1:21). In Christ, we find life itself, and to die is to gain even more of Him. The true longing for heaven is not for pearly gates or angelic harps, but for Christ Himself, in Whom we find our complete satisfaction and ultimate hope of glory (Colossians 1:27).

Though I continue to struggle with sin, living in the "already but not yet" state, God progressively molds me into the image of His Son, as I grow to hate the sin that I once loved and love the God I once hated (Romans 8:29-30; 2 Corinthians 3:18).

As I journey onward, my heart inclines ever more humbly and affectionately toward Christ my King. John the Baptist's words about Christ speak to me, "He must increase, but I must decrease" (John 3:30). These words reverberate within the deep recesses of my heart, growing louder with each chapter of my life. I have come to realize that our lives are not ultimately about us; our true purpose is to exalt Christ, for He is worthy (Revelation 4:11).

Andre M. Cipta, MD, FAAHPM, is an Assistant Professor of Clinical Science at the Kaiser Permanente Bernard J. Tyson School of Medicine and past program director of the Kaiser Permanente Hospice and Palliative Medicine Fellowship. Dr. Cipta serves as the palliative medicine clerkship director at the Tyson School of Medicine and an associate medical director of the Kaiser Permanente Los Angeles Hospice Agency. Dr. Cipta has received several recognitions for his work, including the Hastings Center Cunniff-Dixon Physician Award for exemplary end-of-life care, the American Academy of Hospice and Palliative Medicine Leadership Scholar Award, and the Christian Academic Physicians and Scientists (CAPS) Faith and Medicine Research Fellowship Award. Dr. Cipta's dedication to compassionate and holistic care is reflected in his diverse educational background. He studied Social Welfare and Molecular and Cell Biology at the University of California, Berkeley, pursued his medical education at Loma Linda University School of Medicine, devoted a year to seminary studies at The Master's Seminary, and completed a Hospice and Palliative Medicine Fellowship at the University of California, Los Angeles.

Notes

1. Feinberg JS. No One Like Him: The Doctrine of God. Wheaton, IL: Crossway; 2006.
2. Immanuel Kant, "Kant's Moral Philosophy," Stanford Encyclopedia of Philosophy, last modified January 21, 2022, *https://plato.stanford.edu/entries/kant-moral/*.
3. Frame J. Cornelius Van Til: An Analysis of His Thought. P&R Publishing; 1995. ISBN 978-0-87552-245-6.
4. Bahnsen, GL. *The Impossibility of the Contrary*. American Vision, 1995.
5. Balboni TA, VanderWeele TJ, Doan-Soares SD, et al. Spirituality in Serious Illness and Health. JAMA. 2022;328(2):184-197. doi:10.1001/jama.2022.11086. Erratum in: JAMA. 2022;328(8):780. PMID: 35819420.
6. Chen Y, VanderWeele TJ. Chen and VanderWeele Respond to "Religion, Spirituality, and Health". Am J Epidemiol. 2020;189(8):759-760. doi:10.1093/aje/kwaa021

CHAPTER 6

AN ENCOUNTER WITH THE GREAT PHYSICIAN

Kristin Collier, MD, FACP

When our son Isaac was born, he had failure to thrive and was losing weight. I desperately needed assistance. At that time, I was postpartum and exhausted. My husband Tim and I had three other little boys at home, David, Samuel and Michael, ages two, four and six. Too tired to travel to a lactation clinic, in desperation, one night I searched the internet for a lactation consultant who would be able to come to our home. Of the 10 or so phone calls I made, one woman called me back. Her name was Brandy. It was the night before Halloween and she had four little boys of her own, but she left her home and came to mine, to help me, another mother in need.

Due to her patient love and concern for both Isaac and me, we made it through a challenging time and Isaac remained out of the hospital, much to everyone's delight, for which I was profoundly grateful. Months later, on Isaac's first birthday, I reached out to Brandy to thank her for helping me and Isaac during that difficult time. She responded with a warm affirmation and then extended an unexpected invitation to me. She said she hadn't told me this before, but she was the wife of a pastor and was hosting her first woman's Bible study on women in the Bible. She asked if I wanted to come. To be honest, I wanted nothing less since, at that time, I was not interested in anything concerning Christianity.

Growing up, I had never attended a Sunday church service or heard Scripture. Materialism, pragmatism and anti-theism were the pillars of my suburban upper-middle class youth. I had been raised to play the game of life. Nothing more. However, it was during my residency training in Ann Arbor, Michigan that I was confronted with the problem of making sense of suffering. During my final year of residency, one of our beloved chief medical residents was diagnosed with a terrible cancer, one which medicine could not cure, and he died rather quickly. Unbeknownst, even to me at that time, I began a wrestling process with God—about who He was and what His purposes were for humanity.

Also, about this time, I became engaged to my husband Tim, whom I had been dating since high school. We officially married in 2002 in a Christian church with traditional vows, at Tim's request. Our first son was born in 2005, and shortly thereafter, Tim became a committed Christian. Throughout 2005 to 2010, our family grew, and Tim would go to church taking our two oldest boys to church by himself. I refused to go. He brought Scripture into the home, prayed with the boys and read Bible stories to them, but I remained indifferent and, at times, even antagonistic. This mindset continued until Isaac's birth, his failure to thrive and then Brandy's invitation to attend a women's Bible study.

Reluctantly, I attended, feeling indebted to her and therefore obligated. During that Bible study, which in itself was ordinary, even unremarkable, I found myself reading Scripture for the first time in my life. The Bible study was about women in Scripture, and one of the first books of Scripture I read was the book of Esther. For the first time, I felt truly moved by what I had read; something in me had changed.

People often ask me what it was in Scripture that especially struck me; it was two things, in particular. The first was the person of Jesus Christ, His promise of redemption, a time when every tear will be wiped away, and that He will accompany us until the end of the age. The second was the realization this current state of the world is not the way things are supposed to be, that someday everything will be restored. As a physician, these promises of God to a dying world moved me, but at the same time they confronted my prideful self, which was bound in my inordinate faith in medicine and being apart from God.

After that season of Bible study, I became motivated and inspired to read more of Scripture, even memorize some verses that captivated me, such as Jeremiah 29:11 and John 16:33. I began to open up about Scripture with my husband and others, to read children's Bible stories with our kids and even, from time-to-time, attend worship or Bible study with my husband at a small local church in Pontiac, Michigan.

God continued to send our way other kind and generous Christians who, much like Brandy, showed me little slivers of Christ. I was not always as receptive as I might have been, but people were kind and patient with me. Every Christian witness was not perfect, but then again, neither was I. Previously, I lacked humility, but in the church, I encountered demonstrated humility, sometimes to my shame. The tough and prideful condition of my sinful heart was being loosened by the humility I experienced in the church of Christ Jesus.

A few years after going to that first Bible study with Brandy, I had a supernatural experience when driving to work listening to Christian talk radio. I felt an overwhelming sense of shame, that everything I had was a gift from God and I had taken it all for granted. I had taken pride in things that were all gifts. For the first time in my life, I confessed my sins to the LORD.

In 2015, I began regularly attending church with my husband and sons, who, up to that time, were still mostly attending without me. Shortly thereafter, in spring 2016, I was baptized into the Christian faith with my sons, who had waited for me. After my baptism, the real work began as I had to confront my biggest fear—that I didn't know much at all beyond the secular world. Though full of information, I was wholly unwise. I knew lots of facts and held lots of medical knowledge, but I lacked a real understanding of the world embedded in spiritual meaning greater than myself. Previously, as a non-Christian, my anti-theism served as a convenient shield for me from all the big existential questions of meaning and purpose, questions my vocation of modern medicine desperately tries to avoid.

What is a human being? What are human beings for? What is health? Why do human beings matter? Why is there sickness and death? Is there meaning beyond the grave? These are basic philosophical questions of meaning and purpose that all human beings must wrestle with, but ones our modern scientific medicine does not address. I came to realize I had been operating solely under a mode of facts and technical knowledge that was absent wisdom, virtue and truth.

Since that time, I have had to learn to read, think and converse differently with others, many of whom are outside of medicine, in ways attuned to the higher realities of life as seen through God's moral and metaphysical perspective. My first concern with this type of thinking was to ask, "How was I going to reconcile my Christian faith with my scientific work as a physician? Is Christianity even compatible with modern science? How would I reasonably bring my Christian faith identity into my profession of medicine?"

Regarding the compatibility of views of medical science with the Christian faith, I have come to learn a valuable lesson: the truth Christianity offers medicine is a real, compelling and morally rich point of view—one which comes from a perspective other than modern science, but a perspective which is a necessary complement to modern medicine, if medicine is to be moral, humane and good. The scriptural narrative, therefore, provides a theistic point of view in which modern secular science can and should participate, if medicine is to be wisely and morally practiced. These two views of seeing the world, the Christian and the scientific, the meta-physical and the physical, are both necessary together if medicine is going to see and treat the whole person: one facing sickness and death not only physically but also spiritually and morally.

I've now come to understand that medicine must strive to hold both the physical and the metaphysical views of health, sickness and death together in one comprehensive view. Therefore, good medicine treats the whole person, not just the body of the person. Without Christianity, or some other metaphysical lens that sees human beings as persons, dignified in the image of God, medicine is unable to become wise and good in its treatment of human beings.

Under the scientific lens, modern medicine is taught and comprehended in only a secular way, which is apart from God and therefore divorced from the scriptural narrative of sin, judgment, repentance, salvation, resurrection and glory. This makes the practice of modern medicine not only reductionistic to the body but a supreme tragedy if medicine only cares for bodies that are dying. Science is helpful and amazing and a gift, but medicine must be more than techno-science for dying bodies. The Christian lens provides medicine a rich, cosmic, contra-narrative to the mundane lens of modern medicine. Without a greater story, a metaphysical narrative in which to participate, our individual lives facing sickness and death have no greater meaning; therefore, sickness and death swallow up all meaning. Christianity integrated into medicine restores hope to medicine, dignifies persons, so death is not the end.

Through the story of Christianity, I now know why human beings matter, what is at stake and what health is for in terms of higher purposes. Bodily health is not the goal of our lives. That is too small of an end, and it is one that fails. Therefore, I have become dedicated to re-framing all the work I do in medicine toward upholding human dignity under the reality of the *imago Dei* and resisting practices that are an affront to human dignity, at both ends of life, and in between. This purpose is bound up in my reflecting upon Jesus as the Great Physician over our lives in health, sickness and death. What am I to learn from Him and the Scriptures about my work as a physician in relation to others? In these reflections, I have come to realize that because of the reality of the *imago Dei*, because of the incarnation of Jesus, the patient-physician encounter is a sacred one and should be holy, because I am treating not just bodies, but bodily-persons made to reflect the Image of God. What type of work matters more than this?

Before my baptism, if you would have asked me if human beings mattered, if bodies mattered, I would have said yes, but I would not have been able to tell you why. Now I know why. I believe the realization I now have about the value of bodily human persons infuses much greater meaning in my clinical work. This has been protective for me against burnout because I genuinely care for patients now, with true meaning and true purpose that is found in God, who is greater than all of us. Second, I now know that matter matters because of the *imago Dei* and the incarnation. We have a special dignity because we are human beings made in the image of God, and this dignity is intensified by God's assuming human flesh in the incarnation and His bodily resurrection and ascension. Bodies matter because Jesus Christ had a body, now has a body, and central to our Christian faith are bodies! We are not going to be resurrected spirits, but resurrected persons in bodies.

My Christian theology of medicine is also based on having a preferential option for the vulnerable and marginalized. I'm reminded of how, in the Gospel of St. Mark, we are told the disciples brought Jesus a blind man and begged Him to just touch the man. And the writer says, "So He took the blind man by the hand and led him out of the town" (Mark 8:23a, NKJV). My entire theology of medicine could be drawn from this one sentence. There was work to do! People to treat! But what did Jesus do? He took him by the hand and walked with him out of town. Why are we told this? What are we to learn from this? First is that Jesus, being divine, most likely could have just healed the man without touching him, getting to know him or even being in the same physical location as the man. But He didn't. He took him by the hand and walked with him out of town. He got to know him personally. Why? Because individual people matter. Medicine takes care of persons. I wonder what they talked about. He probably comforted him and became connected with him—no detached professionalism here! And Jesus associated Himself with someone who was marginalized and disabled, who, as many thought at that time, had a disability because of personal or familial sin. Today, sadly, medicine would likely see this man as "less than" in terms of quality of life because of his dependency on others and his inability to produce. However, none of this happened. Jesus didn't distance himself from the man. He leaned in, got to know him and showed that He recognized and respected his dignity as a blind person.

These simple reflections from Scripture made me realize medicine is wholly a moral and metaphysical practice in relation to the technical and the physical. Medicine, therefore, requires a source of wisdom in its practice of science to make it whole and make it good. It is Christ, as the source of wisdom, who makes the scientific practice of medicine good.

Thus, in practicing medicine as a wholly integrated person, Christ reaches into every part of who I am and the science I practice. Thus, my Christian faith is not something auxiliary, like a hat or jacket I put on or take off depending on the situation. We should not be made to feel like we must empty ourselves of our moral and ethical Christian commitments in order to practice good medicine. If anything, these faith commitments, which inform who we are and inform the way we see our patients within the world, should be re-framed as an asset within the practice of good medicine.

When I think of Christianity in my academic work and patient care, what comes to mind are faith, hope and love. By faith in Christ, through the hope in the resurrection, I am called to love my students, my peers and my patients. This is hard work, and not something science has taught me to do, but loving others is my new calling as a Christian physician. I lament I did not have my Christian faith for most of my life as a physician, but that has all changed now. And, without question, what I learned through the scientific and technical framework of modern medicine is necessary for patient care, provided we use these tools and discoveries wisely.

I continue to work extremely hard to develop and maintain a scientific perspective in patient care, but the scientific work alone is not enough to sustain me or my patients facing sickness and death. I need a greater lens to see through, one that confers greater meaning to science. Now, through Christ, I know I am taking care of bodily persons, made by God, in His very image. I'm grateful to God and others who have shared and continue to share with me this greater perspective of the world I now hold, all made possible by the saving love of God in the world through the bodily person of Jesus Christ.

Dr. Kristin Collier is an associate professor of internal medicine at the University of Michigan in Ann Arbor Michigan, where she serves as the director of the University of Michigan Medical School Program on Health, Spirituality, and Religion. She received her medical degree from the University of Michigan Medical School and completed her internship, residency and chief residency at The University of Michigan Hospitals. Her academic interests are in the overlap of spirituality, religion and medicine, and her peer reviewed work has been published in JAMA Internal Medicine, British Medical Journal, Annals of Internal Medicine, The Journal of General Internal Medicine *and* American Journal of Hospice and Palliative Medicine. *She has also published in Notre Dame's* Church Life Journal, Theopolis, America Magazine *and* Public Discourse. *She is also a wife and a proud mother of four boys.*

CHAPTER 7

SPIRITUAL CARE: ACCOMPANIMENT UNTIL THE END

AMY HAYTON, MD

Towards the end of the pandemic during a virtual video appointment at the Veterans Administration (VA), I said goodbye to a long-term patient of mine with chronic pain. On the video was his devoted daughter who was by his side regularly in the last years of his life dutifully taking care of every medical detail. It was a full-time job, taking him to doctors' appointments and keeping everything in her organized binder. His beloved wife was also on the video call; she had aged significantly since I last saw her, many years ago in the clinic. Finally, Mr. Smith appeared on the screen at the end of the visit to say "hello" (really "goodbye"). What I remember most about that moment was his old smile, attempt at a joke, and the look of peace on his face and his body.

I asked him, "Are you in any pain?"

"No, none at all" he replied.

"Really, no pain?"

I was incredulous. "No pain in your legs? No pain in your armpits?"

"No, doc, I am fine."

I confirmed with his daughter and wife. "Is he not complaining of pain?"

I double checked that he was not on any pain meds. He was off acetaminophen, ibuprofen. He even stopped his gabapentin and duloxetine for neuropathic pain. I could not believe it. This man had suffered with so much pain the whole time I knew him. Now with his mind greatly affected by Alzheimer's, the pain was gone. So sad, yet so interesting in how powerful the mind can be in modulating pain.

I met Mr. Smith ten years earlier when I took over his care from another doctor with whom he was unhappy. His chief complaint was pain in his armpits and enlarged lymph nodes. He relayed to me the lengthy list of doctors and specialists he had seen for this complaint. "What are you most concerned about?" I asked, as I do with all my patients. I find this single question reveals not only their intuition about their body but also their fears that I might be able to relieve with education.

"I am worried it's something bad," he said, "Like an incurable infection or cancer. And this pain is just intolerable doctor." He described the pain as sharp, constant, and radiating from the lumps he felt in both his armpits, extending deep into his thorax. While he felt the swelling bilaterally, the swelling was larger on the left.

I spent that first visit curiously listening, eliciting his main concern, and validating that both the physical pain and his fear was affecting his life. From the beginning, he held a strange mix of optimism and dread. Cracking jokes and shying away from any mention of anxiety or other mood disorder, he declared a great faith in God and commitment to his church. He also expressed certainty that no physician could discover the underlying cause of his serious problem. I examined him thoroughly including a complete lymph node exam in which I did not discern anything abnormal. The nodes he identified under his arms were barely palpable; I had to strain my imagination to feel anything. The rest of the exam was unremarkable, except for some mild neuropathy in his feet. He insisted on his symptoms, and I made a choice to take him at his word, acknowledge his suffering, and would pursue a thorough workup, in hope of finding the source of his complaints that no other doctor had had the patience to discover. At the least, I hoped to gain his trust by taking his problem seriously. Thinking that at the least, if he sees that the tests are normal, he can move on and be less fearful.

So began three years of working up his pain and lumps under his arm. We started with an ultrasound, then a CT scan, then a request for IR biopsy and evaluation. When all was normal, we pursued an infectious disease workup including a consult from a well-respected colleague in that specialty who was also a mentor of mine at the VA. He spent a generous amount of time exploring every possibility, even if remote. When we traced the history back to a visit to his missionary daughter in China we investigated rare travel related infections. Everything came back normal. We even asked a hematologist/oncologist their opinion. They added still more tests which were again normal.

By this time, I felt relieved that we were slowly ruling out anything terrible, but Mr. Smith was not convinced. If anything, his anxiety amped up. He believed he had something truly rare; and we could not find it. He asked for a second opinion, so I arranged a referral to the University hospital. In addition to me, he started seeing another primary doctor. The same workup was again initiated. I knew his other primary doctor well, and we agreed there was possibly a neuropsychiatric aspect to his pain. Neither of us had success in reducing his fear, let alone relieving his pain. All my efforts, more than for most of my patients, yielded minimal results.

The next visit, I resolved to get to the root of the issue. I asked some more spiritually focused questions. With his permission, we prayed together. We prayed that he might look beyond the possibility of a rare and terrible disease and see what God might be offering him regarding any solutions or healing. Afterwards, he shared that he felt a measure of improvement; he felt hope and was grateful that we cared. I thought: now we may have found the underlying cause of this issue.

But medicine is not that simple. Whole person care is not just a checklist. I would later understand that whole person healing for Mr. Smith involved patience, relationship, and accompaniment. Dr. Paul Farmer defines "accompaniment" as *"an elastic term. It has a basic, everyday meaning. To accompany someone is to go somewhere with him or her, to break bread together, to be present on a journey with a beginning and an end. There's an element of mystery, of openness of trust, in accompaniment. The companion, the accompagnateur, says 'I'll go with you and support you on your journey wherever it leads. I'll share your fate for a while'— and by 'a while,' I don't mean a little while. Accompaniment is about sticking with a task until it's deemed completed--not by the accompagnateur, but by the person being accompanied."*[1] I did not know where this journey with Mr. Smith would end, but I knew that I was being invited to stay the course, all the way through.

One visit a few years into our relationship, and well into the very extensive workup, I decided to pursue the diagnosis of fibromyalgia or myofascial pain. I did the appropriate basic history and physical exam which revealed multiple trigger points. Usually, this condition has some correlation to mood symptoms or even physical or emotional trauma. As I tentatively explored these issues, Mr. Smith deflected. He turned earnest questions about trauma, depression, and emotional challenges into empty jokes. Still, I could sense there were some issues. I changed my line of questioning and asked about what gives him meaning and what mattered most in his life. He shared warmly of helping people find their homes as a realtor, being with the people in his congregation, and giving to his family. The most meaningful aspects of his life all related to people. Yet, as his pain progressed, he stopped working, going to church, and visiting with extended family.

I determined that this personal interaction with people was critical to his improvement. While I did prescribe duloxetine, a medication for neuropathic pain and depression, I also encouraged him to visit with several of his longtime friends.

The next visit I asked how the medicine went. He said that he did not take it, "I read about it and it's an antidepressant. I told you doctor; I am not depressed. I am not interested in it." At this time, he began requesting escalation of opioids, which his other primary care doctor had started.

As he continued to press me for opioids, I became frustrated and annoyed that he did not want to listen to me. I was also concerned that his opioids would only make things worse. I wondered if the feeling he got with hydrocodone was treating his desire to escape emotional pain and to numb the fear.

I firmly disagreed with the medication and never gave it to him. In my medical practice, I was learning more about boundaries related to opioid medications and, along with the rest of the medical community, began to understand more about the long- and short-term risks of these meds when used for chronic disease. I felt strong in my resolve, but I also did not see him getting better, despite my best efforts at compassionate, competent care.

As much as I hated to admit it, I began to dread his visits. Mostly, it was because I felt powerless and out of control. Nothing I suggested, no amount of compassion, was making any difference. My best efforts were not yielding results. He still had daily pain; he was still taking daily opioids. We were not making much progress.

I sought the Lord about these struggles. I resolved to show compassion, listen well to his concerns and suggest small changes. I always prayed with him at each visit, not just because I know he appreciated it, but also, I was genuinely inviting God's presence and wisdom into his care. If I could not help, our prayers acknowledged that I believed in One who could. We came to agreement on that one point: prayer. There was power in that agreement and in our relationship.

On visits when he was overwhelmed, I sought to bring a small next step and continued hope. I had faith to believe that things could be better than they were in that moment. As wild as it seemed, I believed that his pain would one day be gone. More than that, I believed that he would find peace, understanding, and acceptance. Prayer invites the power of God into a relationship, and allows the love of Jesus, that is greater than my love, to work in Mr. Smith's life.

Mr. Smith was a fighter; with the help of his children, he continued to pursue answers. But his fight began to wane toward the end of his years. I started to recognize the slowing of his speech and his distant gaze. His daughter began to drive his care. At each visit, I spoke much more to her than him, as he slowly resigned control. He still joked every visit and continued to complain of pain but the list of issues his daughter relayed were related more to activities of daily living- personal hygiene, feeding himself, sleep, and mobility.

Like his journey with pain, the path to accepting the diagnosis of Alzheimer's dementia was filled with denial and difficulty - both for him and his family. They took their cues from him, who was the obvious leader in the home. With great compassion, prodding, and convincing they agreed to have him go to a day program to "give their care-giving a break." My role as his doctor turned from seeking a diagnosis to providing available resources. I completed the paperwork admitting him into a day care program. The few times he attended were a blessing to the family. When the COVID-19 pandemic hit in March 2020, all such programs and any in-person visits ceased.

The last time I saw Mr. Smith in person, he was excited about the day program, but did not really comprehend much of it. We prayed together. I squeezed his hand. I cried with his daughter. We realized the reality of the diagnosis. I "accompanied" him.

We had a few video visits throughout 2020. Most of the talk was with his devoted daughter, refilling of meds, orders for supplies, and referrals for physical support. Each time I asked to see Mr. Smith, he would joke and ask me about my family. We would always pray, but I could see that he was declining. Though they were willing and glad to help him, I could see the toll it was taking on his wife and daughter. His dementia was progressing; and they were tired. We began to talk about hospice, a way to get them support, and how to avoid stressful hospitalizations.

At that that last video visit, I could sense it was time to make the transition to hospice, time to surrender control and accompany him to a stage of peace. I was shocked by how much he had declined. He no longer walked, barely spoke, slept long hours, and required help with all his personal needs.

The family was finally ready. We discussed the details; we discussed their comfort with end-of-life conversations. We discussed who he is and was throughout his life, what he values, his faith, the importance of family. His daughter and wife, guided by my questions and suggestions, made the brave decision that day to transition him into hospice care. We cried together as we said our last prayer where I led them in celebration of his life, I thanked God for what Mr. Smith had taught me, what I came to understand not just about disease management but patient accompaniment. I praised God that he was free from pain, free from worry, free from the search for a diagnosis. I said goodbye to Mr. Smith that day and I closed the chapter on a long journey of learning and caring.

The next summer, I got a message from Mr. Smith's daughter, "My father just passed away last Saturday morning. As a family we wanted to reach out to you and say 'thank you' for your care for him all these years. We appreciate your insight into getting him started with hospice last fall. My dad was able to be home through his Alzheimer's disease. It was quite challenging caring for him, but God provided amazing people through the hospice group and the VA homemaker services. We would love to invite you to his memorial service." I attended the service via live streaming while up in a plane, witnessing from afar the celebration of this life that I had the privilege to accompany.

Mr. Smith was on a journey to healing, to acceptance, and to peace. His pain went away completely, his fear and distress were relieved. As I reflect on what I learned in accompaniment of Mr. Smith, I pay close attention to the ministry of Jesus as he joined his followers on the road to Emmaus.2 Just as those travelers did not recognize, in the moment, the ministry they were receiving from Jesus, until the end of Mr. Smith's life, I did not realize all that I discovered about pain, healing, and hope. I believe healing takes on many forms. My journey of accompaniment with Mr. Smith healed me as well, of the false expectations of myself, of the fear of what happens when I try my best, and when the outcome is less than what I expected. "Then their eyes were opened and they recognized him, and he disappeared from their sight. They asked each other, "Were not our hearts burning within us while he talked with us on the road and opened the Scriptures to us?"[2] May our hearts burn like the men who were with Jesus when we accompany our patients, even until the end.

Amy Hayton MD, MPH was raised as a pastor's kid in the Bay Area, California. She studied biochemistry at Azusa Pacific University then medicine and public health at Loma Linda University School of Medicine. She completed her internal medicine residency at Loma Linda University, and it was during her chief year that she discovered she loved teaching and academic medicine. She practices in primary care within the Veterans Administration, where she honed her practice in whole person care. She served as clerkship director of internal medicine for five years then started the LIFE community mentorship program for medical students that includes a three-year longitudinal course, Christian Physician Formation. This course seeks to equip future physicians in skills of "whole person care, personal spiritual practices, compassionate response to the social determinants of health and principles of lifestyle medicine." She is passionate about equipping medical students to practice Spirit-led, patient-centered care while maintaining their own wholeness. She is married to Andy, a psychiatrist, and has three teenage children.

NOTES

1. Paul Farmer, *To Repair the World: Paul Farmer Speaks to the Next Generation* (Berkeley: University of California Press, 2013), 234.
2. Luke 24:13-35

CHAPTER 8

FAITH SEEKING HEALING: A LIFE INTEGRATING THEOLOGY AND MEDICINE

KIMBELL KORNU, MD, PHD

"All things were created through him and for him. And he is before all things, and in him all things hold together" (Col. 1:16b-17 ESV). In the cosmic Christ, all things hold together, including theology and medicine. In the New Testament, the Greek verb *sōzō* means "to save." But "save" has two senses that are distinct but inseparable: (1) the medical sense of healing as a saving of physical life from acute danger, and (2) the theological sense of saving a whole person from eternal death. In the healing stories in the Synoptic Gospels, *sōzō* is used sixteen times, always referring to the whole person, not a single part of the person's body.1 The use of *sōzō* indicates that the healing power of Jesus as the Great Physician and the saving power of Jesus through faith go beyond the physical life but are not separate from the physical life.

While the Scriptures are clear about the unity of all things in Christ, and that in Christ physical healing and whole-person salvation are unified, my life has been a long journey of integrating theology and medicine. But considering my origins and upbringing, it is a surprise that any kind of integration would be sought or even possible.

I was born and raised in a Texas town near Dallas. My parents were immigrants from Bangkok, Thailand and we were the first Asian family in the entire town. My father went to medical school in Thailand and did his Internal Medicine internship and residency training in the U.S.; he had a solo general internal medicine practice. As Thai immigrants, my parents were nominal Buddhist, but my siblings and I were raised functionally atheist. My parents were not opposed to God, but we just did not think or talk about God. Instead, my core expectation that had the force of a religion was academic success so I could get a good job, provide for my family, and have social prestige. I wanted to be a physician like my father. My older sister and brother became a nurse and physician, respectively.

When I was in high school, I prided myself on academic success. I had what I call *Jeopardy!* epistemology. I learned things like they were pieces of trivia: interesting factoids to know but without an inherent connection between them. I especially enjoyed that I knew more things than other people. But when I went to college, I became a Christian through an Asian American campus ministry and my whole life—and epistemology—changed. Learning that God created everything with the purpose of ultimately glorifying him made me realize that everything is related to everything else, and all within God's economy. The *Jeopardy!* epistemological scales fell from my eyes, and I was able to see the world in nature and in academic studies as inherently connected, thereby revealing a beautiful whole, although, at the time, I wouldn't have articulated it that way. After I became a Christian, the world and learning became infinitely more interesting. My intellectual life began afresh, though now through the lens of Christian faith.

The summer after my sophomore year of college, I went on a mission trip to Guatemala. One evening a campus minister gave a talk on Jonah and the call to missions. After the talk, I had come to realize that my motivations for wanting to become a physician were impure. Sure, I was good at science and wanted to "help people" (which every medical school applicant says), but what I really wanted was the social prestige, high income, nice car, white picket fence, wife, and 2.5 children. I wanted to be a physician, but it had nothing to do with God. If that was the case, then I could not be a physician. So, for a while I thought about attending seminary to become a pastor or going into campus ministry. But two major experiences forced me to begin the journey of integrating theology and medicine: my sister's life and death with cancer, and my own medical training.

During college, my older sister Lillian was diagnosed with chronic lymphocytic leukemia (CLL) during routine prenatal monitoring. It was one of the most formative events in my life, the effects of which are still being realized. CLL is typically found in white men over 60, not Asian women under 30. Since CLL is an indolent cancer, it cannot be treated with chemotherapy. She gave birth to a healthy son and enjoyed her time as a stay-at-home mother. However, 10% of CLL patients have a Richter transformation, by which CLL changes from an indolent leukemia to an aggressive lymphoma. Her son was only ten months old when she received that news. As Lillian prepared to begin chemotherapy, her friends gathered a prayer meeting for her. As her friends prayed, they started crying. In response, Lillian prayed for them, that God would grant them comfort and strength as she traveled down the road of cancer treatment.

Despite monthly chemotherapy and the associated nausea and vomiting, the cancer remained. She underwent a bone marrow transplant and needed to go into isolation (back when that was standard of care). She said goodbye to her twenty-month-old son for the final time. While in isolation, Lillian was not simply "patient" to her disease; rather, she was an active, loving friend. In one hand she held the Dilaudid patient-controlled analgesia button, while in the other hand she held a phone to give counsel to a friend needing relationship advice.

She eventually made it through the weeks-long isolation and was finally discharged home. However, during the post-transplant period she developed intractable nausea and vomiting and was re-admitted. She never left the hospital again. Her liver function tests were elevated, so a liver biopsy was performed to look for graft-versus-host-disease. For reasons that remain unclear, the liver biopsy seemed to be a sentinel event, resulting in Lillian developing acute respiratory distress syndrome (ARDS) requiring mechanical ventilation. ARDS has a 30-40% mortality rate. Lillian was gravely ill.

Since the liver biopsy seemed to be the inciting medical event, my family and I wanted to speak to the hepatologist who performed the biopsy. To our dismay, we were told by a nurse that the doctor was not going to speak with us because he only deals with the liver, not the lungs. We were dumbfounded at his cold response that dissected my sister down to her liver. We weren't looking for an admission of guilt, but rather a comforting presence. I learned then that doctors do not always treat patients as whole persons but rather as medical objects. In this type of medicine that treats patients as an affected organ, healing does not go beyond the physical.

While on mechanical ventilation, Lillian had an extended period of hypoxia. The medical team knew that there would be neurological deficits of uncertain significance. Lillian had already told her husband when she started chemotherapy that if she were profoundly disabled and machine-dependent and could not take care of her son, then she would forego life-sustaining treatment. During the last week of her life, there was a time-limited trial to see if there would be improvement, but to no avail. My family and I had to decide together to withdraw the ventilator as the best way to honor her wishes. We knew it was the right thing to do, but it was one of the most difficult decisions we had ever made.

During that last week of Lillian's life, I had never felt closer to God. Friends and family from around the country descended on the hospital to be at her side. We sang hymns at her bedside, rubbed her hands and feet, and read Scripture over her. We told stories about Lillian, laughing together and weeping together. In the midst of mourning and suffering, God was there, and he was not silent. It was through the pain that God was most present, for Christ himself was made perfect by learning obedience through what he suffered (Heb 5:8-9). Lillian died exactly one month after 9/11.

When Lillian was first diagnosed with cancer, she never asked, "Why me?" So assured of God's love for her, she said boldly, "Why *not* me?" As a general internist, my father had many patients with cancer. Never once did he hear a patient say such a thing. He simply could not comprehend it. But Lillian knew the infinite love and grace of God through her cancer.

During Lillian's memorial service, a close friend of hers shared a story about a note Lillian had written to her during cancer treatment. In the note, she expressed hope and excitement for the future—that her life would be a living testimony of God's love for her. She thanked God that she was given cancer. Why? Because cancer forced her to cast off her idols and rely ever more upon him. Hebrews 11:38 describes heroes of the faith who suffered affliction and persecution "of whom the world was not worthy." Lillian is one of my heroines of the faith. The world was not worthy of her.

The whole experience with Lillian from the time of her cancer diagnosis to the time of her death has shaped me in ways that I could not articulate at the time. It was a transformative experience. I think my life of integrating theology and medicine is still catching up to what I learned through the experience with Lillian. While no death is good, I learned what a good death can look like. I learned that God is present especially in the hardest times, for Jesus sympathizes with our weaknesses (Heb 4:15). I learned that medicine cannot fix everything, but there can still be healing even in the midst of death.

I was slowly growing into the reality that physical treatment is only a fraction of medicine and healing. However, the vision of medicine I had going into medical school was still not integrated enough. I thought that medicine itself was a neutral, technical practice of science applied to human bodies that can be made good if used in the right way. The first semester of medical school was deeply disorienting. Given my experiences with Lillian's cancer and death, I, like many entering medical students, held a high ideal for what medicine should be: caring for the whole person in a humanistic way. But that first year, I was learning the basic sciences of histology, anatomy, biochemistry, etc., which put primacy on matter, molecules, and mechanisms. Was I learning to care for patients as whole persons, or learning to be a glorified auto mechanic that fixes broken cars? The discourses of medicine rang with a mechanistic scientism that reduces patients into objects. I learned early in my medical education that modern medicine has a disturbing metaphysical problem (although I didn't have that language at the time). The medical body is merely matter in motion without inherent meaning, in what Jeffrey Bishop has called medicine's metaphysics of efficient causation.2 So medical practice is all about mastering and manipulating the motion of the body's matter. Meaning is imposed upon bodies at best or made extraneous at worst.

This dominant metaphysics of medicine was so problematic for me that I took time off from medical school to go to seminary for a master's degree, so I could deepen intellectually and theologically in hopes of pushing back against the medical scientism I was facing. I learned that it would not be enough. I then began internal medicine residency training. The mechanistic discourses of medicine that I encountered in medical school then became part of my practice. As a resident, and then as a hospitalist, I felt like a cog in a complex hospital machine. My job was to be efficient, not caring. I could not escape the dominant metaphysics of medicine.

Feeling the need to get more training to push back against this dominant metaphysics of medicine, I pursued doctoral studies in theology. In my studies, I developed the notion that the Western approach to medical epistemology is essentially a logic of dissection, which grows out of systematic anatomical dissection to know the body. To know a thing, a body, a person is to cut it up, into its parts. This is why modern medicine tends to reduce patients into objects to be dissected rather than persons to be known in their wholeness. Parts are much easier to isolate, control, manipulate, and re-fashion into our own image. Instead, what is needed is a logic of incarnation, rooted both in the incarnation of Christ in whom all things hold together and the embodiment of persons, both physicians and patients alike. The logic of incarnation [1] sees no strict dualisms, including between body and soul or medicine and theology (modeled after no strict dualism between the human and divine natures in Christ), [2] embraces the wonder of knowing, and [3] entails embodied knowing.

The difference between the logic of dissection and the logic of incarnation is akin to Wendell Berry's distinction between the world of efficiency and the world of love.3 The modern hospital is the colliding place of these two worlds, where the patient, family, and neighbors come from the world of love and confront the hospital and its world of efficiency. This reduces experience to computation, particularity to abstraction, and mystery to a small comprehensibility, all of which can be standardized according to this logic of dissection.

My whole reason for going into medicine has been animated by this world of love, not the world of efficiency. I learned that through my experience with Lillian. I chose to specialize in Palliative Medicine, getting to practice a humanism at the bedside and whole-person care. I see Palliative Medicine functioning like a counterinsurgency from the world of love into modern medicine's world of efficiency that reduces patients into objects.

Integrating theology and medicine into a life is much more than learning a neutral medicine and sprinkling compassion on top of it. While there is intrinsic value to compassionate care, medicine itself is not neutral. Medicine makes claims on the importance of ensouled bodies in relationships. Christ the Great Physician came to save and heal whole persons, body and soul, by being the divine patient, for "with his wounds we are healed" (Isa 53:5). Indeed, in Christ the world of love holds together.

Kimbell Kornu is Provost's Professor of Bioethics, Theology, and Christian Formation at Belmont University and is a Palliative Care physician. He holds an MD from the University of Texas Southwestern and a PhD in Theology from the University of Nottingham (UK). He is currently helping to start a new medical school at Belmont University that is faith-based and emphasizes whole-person formation for whole-person care. He has taught palliative medicine, bioethics, and theology across the university to undergraduates, medical students, PhD students, medical residents and fellows. His research focuses on the historical, social, philosophical, and theological determinants that shape the metaphysics and practices of modern medicine. He has published widely on the philosophy and theology of medicine.

Notes

1. Foerster W, Fohrer G. *Sōzō, sōtēria, sōtēr, sōtērios*. In: Friedrich G, ed. *Theological Dictionary of the New Testament, Volume VII*. Bromiley GW, trans. Eerdmans; 1971:965-1024.

2. Bishop JP. *The Anticipatory Corpse: Medicine, Power, and the Care of the Dying*. University of Notre Dame Press; 2011.

3. Berry W. Health Is Membership. In: Wirzba N, ed. *The Art of the Commonplace: The Agrarian Essays of Wendell Berry*. Shoemaker & Hoard; 2002:144-159.

CHAPTER

SUFFERING: FOR HIS GLORY

CHRISTINE LIU, MD

THE CALL

God called me to medical missions when I was 18. I had no inkling of going into medicine until I was asked by a missionary, James Hudson Taylor III, if I had asked God what I was supposed to do with my life. The thought had not crossed my mind, but when I got on my knees that night (as it seemed only fitting to do to consider such a question), I seriously heard, "You will be a medical missionary." The call was confirmed many times when I wanted to quit, and the vision of the work He had ahead for me pushed me onward. God would give me His transcendent peace, and doors that seemed closed would open. He fulfilled the call from 2005-2010, when I was so grateful to be mentored at my Christian-based residency and then on the mission field in East Asia. I loved how I got to live out my calling, which I thought would be for a lifetime, when sudden changes in my life led me off the mission field. This led me to struggle fo as to whether the call was real. As I struggled with this, I realized that God himself will fulfill what he says in Proverbs 3:5-6. As we trust in the Lord with all our heart, lean not on our own understanding, and acknowledge him in all we do, he makes our paths straight. As physicians, we plan and follow through with many steps in our career as we carry out our daily work. However, we may get frustrated or anxious when our path may seem to veer and twist, but if we trust the Lord, our paths are made straight in Christ (He is the way, the truth, and the light)! He reminded me in this time of struggle that He fulfills His call His way. If I am willing to walk in His way, He will be the one to fulfill His good purposes. The following is the story of what God is teaching me as I continue to learn to let Him lead.

MICAH: CHANGE IN PLAN

I returned to the United States in 2010 for an obstetrics fellowship with plans to return to mission field to bolster our obstetrics and gynecology work amongst family medicine residents, low-income patients, and trafficking victims in East Asia. During my obstetrics fellowship, I re-met Kenny, an awesome guy who had previously asked me out six years ago, but to whom I said no because then he was not interested in missions. Since he had the nerve to ask me out again and now also wanted to go into missions, we were married that year. As we were raising support for our medical mission work, we discovered we were pregnant with our first child. Our plans and dreams were dashed when we realized Micah had severe hydrocephalus in utero.

The ultrasound technician whispered to me, "I know someone who performs late abortions" and slipped me a number.

I remember mumbling in a daze, "We believe his life is a gift from God."

As my husband and I cried together that night, I fearfully asked him if he could love a seriously handicapped child. And this is why I love my husband so much. "We'll just love him more," Kenny said without hesitation.

As we awaited his birth, Micah's head grew to massive proportions. I was a family medicine obstetrics physician and accustomed to controlling most situations. My pregnancy was the first of many times that God would teach me that *He was* in control, and *I* was not. This was quite unnerving yet good for me; as physicians, we are prone to pride and self-reliance and can easily forget God. During this time, I connected to God more than ever in my life. Newborn head circumferences of 67 cm are rare. My C-section was a peri-umbilical vertical skin cut, a classical fundal uterus filleting cut. Even at 35 weeks, it proved to be a difficult delivery. Prior to delivery, we were told he had a good chance of dying before he was born or shortly thereafter. We were told he may not breathe, drink, or urinate. I remember laying on the C-section table and counting how many people were praying for us---I counted over 400 by the time he was born. The anesthesiologist, hearing me muttering, asked if I was scared, but I said, "Strangely, no!" The peace of God and the love of the people he put in our lives was consistently with us in our most critical moments.

Micah came out screaming and urinating, defying the odds. He weighed 14lb 4oz, a giant-headed preemie with intrauterine growth retardation which meant that I could not eat much the last two months of pregnancy. He looked scarier than Brain from *Pinky and the Brain*. For two months, each day he had about a liter of CSF drained from his brain, and no one could determine why. His head was a severely swollen, shiny globe in the morning but became a deflated, flat planter's box at night after his tap. Everyone was afraid to feed him; he had a nasogastric tube for weeks. One day, a nurse just gave him a syringe of milk, which he guzzled. Then he easily took a bottle, pulled out his nasogastric tube, and fought to live.

We had Micah 6:8 on the wall in the NICU, and a child life specialist gave us the lovely "Praise Baby" song collection, which we listened to daily. Many providers mentioned how peaceful our room was and asked how we could be so joyful. We were not aware we were especially joyful or peaceful, but God's grace upheld us. Because of their questions, we had several opportunities to share about Jesus' love in the NICU.

After two months, a sedated MRI showed a 3x4x5cm choroid plexus papilloma in his posterior fossa. It was strange for this CSF-over-producing brain tumor occurred in a child so young, and in such an odd location. We were offered hospice, but I had seen even more massive hydrocephalus children in Asia; they did not die easily and had much suffering in the process. So, we prayed hard, asked for discernment, and made the difficult decision to have his tumor removed. We were not clinging to his life but wanted what was best for him. We were told Micah may die on the table; his surgery would be treacherous; he would likely be severely handicapped. And yet we experienced God's peace that transcends all understanding again. I do not, by my nature, have a peaceful personality, so I can attest that this was further evidence of God's hand.

Month three brought a VP shunt placement to help drain excessive fluid from his brain. Though the tumor was removed, he had significant brain damage that prevented natural fluid reabsorption, so fluid had to be redirected to his abdomen.

Over the next year, Micah did surprisingly well for a baby with a paper-thin cerebral cortex (we can barely see brain tissue on his MRI to this day). We had no idea what to expect. We transferred him gingerly on a pillow because he was so fragile. He had a plagiocephaly helmet for 2 years, way past the few-month norm, because his head was so misshapen. We met amazing orthotists, therapists, nurses, and physicians who cared for him and encouraged us. We had lots of medical equipment, therapies, appointments. We had so many people visit us. Sometimes we were nervous about Micah, and they probably were too because most babies were cute, and Micah was just plain "scary looking". But our friends put on brave faces and continued to come over to bring us food and just hang out. Their presence was so comforting and taught us the power of presence.

When Micah was 18 months old, our lives took another turn. He developed infantile spasms, a debilitating seizure disorder, which later changed to a chronic encephalopathy, where none of his brainwaves are normal, ever. The milestones he had developed---fine motor movements, double-word phrases, words to songs---began to regress. He would have times of lucidity, then times of "spacing out". He would have innumerable tonic seizures---hands and feet posed like a tiny Karate Kid, stiff for seconds to minutes. We knew then that, short of a miracle, Micah would need full assistance the rest of his life--feeding, bathing, diapering. For seizure control, he went on a restrictive ketogenic diet, which would leave him in a compensated metabolic acidosis. Any upper respiratory infection would lead to a hospital admission. Once he was intubated for two weeks, and we began to discuss if we would ever want a tracheostomy for him. However, after he recovered from that ordeal, we decided he would be a DNI (do-not-intubate) because his suffering had been so great. His seizures improved, but we both had to work part-time to alternate caring for him. When Micah turned five, we began to use a lift machine. When he was eight, Kenny quit work to stay at home with him, aided by a nurse or grandparents, because Micah now needed two people to care for him. Kenny remains my hero for so many reasons, including his immeasurable patience and gentleness with Micah, beyond what I could ever do.

Micah just had a very extensive T 3-pelvis spinal fusion surgery. We are so grateful for excellent care in Dallas. We were worried about many aspects of his care: would his extensive seizure medication list interact with the narcotics? Would he go back into urinary and fecal retention, as he sometimes does with medication changes? Would his pain be controlled? Would he be at high risk for infection because he is diapered? Would he need blood because the bleeding was expected to be extensive? The Lord answered every one of our specific prayer requests, and Micah sailed through it! We were able to call or text about 50 people who reached out to us in the past month with requests, thanks, and praises. Our journey has reminded us of the sovereignty and goodness of God, so we trust him innately to care for Micah, ever more than we can in our strength and wisdom. God continues to work through Micah's life to teach me that He is in control and He loves Micah even more than we do, so that I may continue to relax my tight grip on the situation. God, our ever-gracious teacher, gently reteaches this to me.

We are sometimes asked how we "do it," meaning how do we keep going, seemingly unfazed. We say, first and foremost, at times, we are quite disconcerted; it is God's grace that upholds us. Secondly, we point to the unwavering support of our family and friends. We have never wanted help. Our parents moved down the street to live near us; we know they are a direct gift from God. They have supported our regularly developing second child, Abby, and have helped make her childhood as normal as possible. We were never meant to travel life's journey alone. There is a humility gained in accepting help and admitting we cannot do things on our own. I was not easily humbled but remain eternally grateful for another recurring lesson in humility.

STRUGGLES WITH SUFFERING

We still struggle with coping and suffering. We have had aging parents, one with a stroke, another with metastatic cancer; and we know that as we all live, there is suffering to be had--- physical, emotional, relational, or spiritual. No one is immune to suffering. However, when there is suffering in the young, when there is suffering that seems relentless, it can challenge our understanding of what is good. Specifically, it can challenge our concept of God if we don't ground ourselves in who the Bible says He is. The age-old question: *If He is good, how can He allow suffering?* How did we deal with that? Not just as a question asked in apologetic arguments---but for ourselves?

It was by God's grace alone, not because of any inherent wisdom or fortitude of ours. And that is only because we sensed his goodness every day. If we did not know his goodness, we would have been asking that question. We were struggling with our grief to the point that I *almost* asked, "Why would you allow this to happen, God?" I sensed God answering my 'why' question before I even had to ask. *"For you created my inmost being; you knit me together in my mother's womb. I praise you because I am fearfully and wonderfully made; your works are wonderful; I know that full well. Your eyes saw my unformed body. All the days ordained for me were written in your book before one of them came to be."* Psalm 139:13-16. In times of questioning, God often does not answer in the way I think He should. He often answers me with his Word. He always reminds me of who He is, shows me how He does things, and ultimately, He gives me glimpses of why He does things. He doesn't have to do any of that. We are limited creatures, so we can't understand His master plan because He is infinite, and His plan is tremendous. But we get to see bits of the plan for now, and those bits are glorious, and cause me to praise Him. So, as He answered the unspoken question of 'why' with who He is, I didn't have the need to ask why. He showed His goodness continuously to me, even in my questioning.

We did ask Him with trepidation, "What will this look like? How can we do this?"

He answered with, "I AM" like He did to Moses in the bush. He answered me with who Micah is: His beloved. He loves us. He is good. He is all-powerful. I don't understand it all, but He does. I can trust a God like that. He will show us one step at a time. He always has and always will.

We could have asked, "God, are you truly good?" He is big enough for the question. But, He so graciously spared us the angst. He quickly gave me his presence, and his Word shielded me, and that is the most comforting thing of all, better than any platitude of man.

How will he know God?
There was a time when Kenny and I were changing Micah's diaper, and looking at his helpless state just lying there, I was perplexed by whether Micah would know Jesus. So, I asked Kenny, as he wiped the boy, "How do you know if Micah will know Jesus." Kenny in his uncomplicated way said, "God knows him. That's all that matters." Taped diaper, end of story. It seemed too simple, too trite. I know Kenny was at peace with that answer. Yet, I was not satisfied with such a simple faith-based answer. So, I asked God silently. He was so gracious yet again and instantly gave me two verses before we lifted Micah from the diaper table. I don't think He ever wants to withhold Himself from us when we ask Him:

Jesus said, "Let the little children come to me, and do not hinder them, for the kingdom of heaven belongs to such as these." (Matthew 19:14)

Blessed are the pure in heart, for they will see God. (Matthew 5:8)

The kingdom of God is for the pure-hearted, and Jesus welcomes the pure-hearted little ones. So simple, yet so sweet an answer for me. How is it that He brings to mind verses we have read, meditated on, and even only partially remembered? It is the work of the Holy Spirit, our Counselor. Sometimes, I want to make the Gospel complex. God reminds me that He is the one who purifies our hearts and upholds purity. And He has these little ones close to His heart.

KNOWING THE FATHER IN SUFFERING

Prior to Micah, I always secretly pitied handicapped families. "Poor family. They must have so much to deal with. That person must be suffering, and so must the family." I never knew the blessing, amidst the suffering and hardships, that a handicapped person could be.

Many have said to us that Micah is so blessed to have been born in our family because we both have a medical background. Kenny is an ER nurse. My mother once told me that God found us worthy to have such a child. In one of my lowest moments (I was post-Caesarean from our second child, in pain, tired. Micah was at a low with his seizures and taking four hours to feed per meal), I screamed at her, "Why would God find us worthy? We are not worthy! We don't want to be worthy. We are not able to do this!" I, too, am prone to a pity party. We know we are not worthy of God's goodness, but let me tell you about His goodness in gifting Micah to us.

One of the greatest gifts is knowing God the Father more deeply. I never could grasp the depth of love the Father has for us in giving up his Son to die on the cross for us. It was so personal and yet surreal. Micah is our first-born son, our only son. He is not suffering for anyone. However, seeing him suffer--- three brain surgeries, one gastrostomy feeding tube, a large spinal fusion, a chest tube for a pneumothorax, prolonged intubation for respiratory failure, multiple IV's and intubations for repeated imaging, multiple admissions with deep suctioning for secretions to get over pneumonia or simple URI's, intractable seizures, cortical visual impairment, him trying to say words he used to speak but now can't, reaching for toys he used to play but can no longer hold ---our hearts hurt with each cut, poke, and loss whether big or small. Sometimes our hearts are broken for him. When I look at our son, I feel just a small glimpse of the heart of our Father, who loved US so much he GAVE his ONE and ONLY son to DIE for us that we might live. I want to shield Micah from any pain; I would rather take that pain for him if I could. But, the Father gave up his Son to the worst type of pain, and the Father suffered the worst type of pain...willingly. Wow...

And another profound gift of understanding God's love for us... Micah will never play piano, score a touchdown, learn to read, play with his sister, go to college, or be a doctor. And yet, when we look at him each day, whether he can say Mama or Baba anymore, he fills our heart with joy. I come home and see him just lying there, and my heart melts.

He can do NOTHING, and we still love him---deeply, without reservation, albeit imperfectly. We love him no less than we love Abby, our normally developing daughter. We love him differently with our actions, but we feel just as deeply about him as Abby. God reminded me: *you, Christine, do not have to do anything to earn my love. I love you no matter what you achieve, who knows your name, or how much you have. Your ability or inability to do anything does not change the depth of love I have for you.* The day God hit me with that, I sat in silence before Him for a long time under his overwhelming love. I said, wholeheartedly to the Lord, "May I have the opportunity to share that vision of your love for each person with as many people as I can!"

HIS GLORY IN SUFFERING

Kenny is from New Orleans, the storied city where we met; so, all things NOLA are dear to us. There is the song "When the Saints Go Marching In" that Louis Armstrong made famous. We love that song. Kenny plays it on trombone, and when Abby was little, she loved dancing to it.

Abby was four when she began complaining about how things were "not fair." I hate that phrase. I told her "Not fair" should not be in our vocabulary. When we say "Not fair" we are acknowledging there is intrinsic justice, right and wrong, but "Not fair" is us calling God unjust, because who else calls what is ultimately fair? I wanted her to know that God is just, but how do you explain that to a young child?

"It's not fair Micah can't play with me. Other kids have brothers who can play with them."

What do I say to her? Something should be said. I asked God what to say. He brought to mind the Saints song. Abby, even at four, did understand something about heaven. I told her that even if things seemed unfair now, God is just, meaning he is the "most fair" judge. If He is good, He is always fair. His timing to show us how "fair" things are is up to him. We remembered how we love to march like saints to heaven in the song. I told her we may be doing different things when Jesus comes again. We may be playing... so we'll go play-marching into heaven. Micah may be wheeling...so he may go wheel-marching. She started giggling when I said these things. But then she and I both thought a little more about this. Would Micah still be in his wheelchair? That's not biblical. Revelations 21:4 came to mind: *He will wipe every tear from their eyes. There will be no more death or mourning or crying or pain, for the old order of things has passed away.* So, wait, Abby, let us sing that right. When the saints go marching in... Micah will surely fly-march ahead!

Then, right on cue, like every selfish child who likes to determine what is "fair" in their own favor, she says, "Why does he get to go first?"

Then as if God wanted me to see it, he gave me a vision of Micah, other handicapped children, and those who had suffered more in this life flying ahead of us who had experienced less suffering. But oh, how very fair is our God! As those flying ahead get to praise God for healing, we who suffered less personally---but who suffered watching them suffer and wondered about the fairness of things---get to see those who suffered more flying ahead healed, and we get to thank and praise Him, saying, *"Your righteousness is everlasting, and your law is true." Psalm 139:142.*

For things in the kingdom of God are often the opposite when compared to things of this world. As Luke 13:29 says: *People will come from east and west and north and south and will take their places at the feast in the kingdom of God. Indeed, there are those who are last who will be first, and first who will be last.*

There is a picture Abby drew a little later, unprompted by us. She is sleeping in her nightgown and dreaming of the city of God. She and Micah are walking hand-in-hand into a Disney-like castle. His wheelchair is on the side, and he is walking in with her. (Interestingly, in every picture she has always drawn of him, his wheelchair is there but on the side.) At the side of the picture is an open book entitled "The Lamb's Book of Life." God gave our young child a vision. Of all the pictures she has ever drawn, that is my favorite.

For from him and through him and for him are all things.
To him be the glory forever! Amen. (Romans 11:36)

Christine Liu, MD is an assistant professor in the Department of Family Medicine at University of Texas, Southwestern in Dallas. After learning to love medicine at Tulane University, Christine was accepted into her dream residency at In His Image Family Medicine in Tulsa, Oklahoma, where she was mentored in the beauty of whole-person care. Samaritan's Purse sponsored Christine as a missionary to East Asia, where she helped start a trafficking victims' clinic, served on rural and disaster relief trips, and developed inpatient and obstetric curricula for family medicine residents. She returned to Austin, Texas for an obstetrics fellowship, planning to return to the mission field. Her first child was born severely handicapped, so her family was grounded in the United States. Christine served as faculty at Baylor Family Medicine Residency and then started a community clinic in North Texas. Now she is joyfully back in residency education and avidly supports medical missions.

CHAPTER 10

THE SUCCESSFUL PHYSICIAN

JANET MA, MD

At almost six feet tall and weighing more than 200 pounds, Orson* towered over everyone in the clinic room. After I introduced myself and sat down at the computer, Orson's parents introduced themselves and Orson to me in Spanish. They explained that Orson is a non-verbal young adult with severe autism, and they were there to transition his medical care from pediatric to adult care. As a med-peds physician specializing in healthcare transitions, this is a typical clinic visit for me, but I can still feel my heartbeat quicken slightly before examining him, uncertain how he will react, considering his conditions. Regardless, by maintaining eye contact and using his name to ask permission for each step, we successfully finished the physical exam without incident.

As I got to know Orson and his parents over the years serving as his adult primary care physician, I learned Orson has such a kind and gentle soul. Despite his appearance and the fact that he tends to wander throughout the clinic room during his visits, sometimes actively trying to remove all his clothing, I learned that appearances and stereotypes are deceiving. Orson's parents tell me stories of them visiting local southern California farms that are often staffed by migrant workers. Orson had learned over time that the migrant children have few material things, including clothing and food, and he would insist his parents bring food and clothing to these children when they visit, sometimes even getting upset if they visited without a bag of food. At one routine clinic visit, Orson surprised me with a lovely native plant with red, velvety leaves. Orson's parents proudly told me Orson had himself picked up the plant at the farm the day before and insisted on giving it to me. When I tried to gently decline this beautiful gift, suggesting Orson and his family should keep the plant themselves (knowing Orson and his family do not have much materially), he insisted I keep the precious plant as his gift. My eyes teared knowing that, while Orson may not have a lot financially here on earth, he is more generous in his heart than others who have much more materially.

At first glance, it would be so easy to regard Orson the way the world sees him: neurodiverse, developmentally delayed, non-verbal, perhaps even a little intimidating; he offers no real value to society or the world. Proponents of eugenics would argue this is a person to permanently sterilize, as there is no reason to produce others like him.1 As a Christian physician, though, I am so glad the Bible tells us the opposite and real truth, that God created ALL of us in His image we are equally loved by Him, regardless of appearance, talent, intelligence, health status or any other myriad attributes society promotes as being worthy in this world. Romans 3:23 reminds us we have all fallen short of the glory of God; whether president of the most powerful country in the world or the lowliest servant in another country, we need God's grace equally. The best news in the world is that the God of the universe, who created the heavens and the earth and who loves and cares for each one of us so deeply and who loves Orson and his parents so much, came in the person of Jesus to die on the cross for our sins, thus reconciling all of mankind with the God of the universe. As Pastor Tim Keller once said, "The gospel is this: We are more sinful and flawed in ourselves than we ever dared believe, yet at the very same time we are more loved and accepted in Jesus Christ than we ever dared hope."2 Therefore, Orson and his family can have the blessed assurance that Orson is also equally loved and accepted in Christ just like any other person, thanks to Jesus. Hallelujah!

Working in academic medicine, we are constantly bombarded by the opposite message. To succeed, we are told to constantly climb the academic ladder to the top. The rat race even starts before entering medical school—GPA, MCAT score, letters of recommendation, extracurricular activities, etc. In medical school, the struggle continues—grades, shelf exam scores, rotation evaluations, research, publications and more letters of recommendation to match in that dream residency. Residency and fellowship have their own version of struggles—more standardized exams, evaluations, QI and research projects and more, all to attain our final destination, the attending job. For those of us in academia, however, the ladder continues, as every few years we must prove ourselves worthy for the next step of academic promotion through further evaluations, number of publications, teaching and clinical performance; thus, the race to academic success never seems to end. In direct contrast, Jesus was the King of the Universe who came down from heaven as a humble baby born in a manger to serve, wash our feet and pay the ultimate price we deserved to pay ourselves. He taught us time and again that our worldly accolades don't mean much and cannot be brought to the next world, and that the true definition of success is relationships forged for Him that result in treasures stored in heaven. It can be so challenging to remember these fundamental truths when we are constantly barraged with the busyness of the world, thus I'm so thankful for having a genuine spiritual community of brothers and sisters who regularly remind me of these fundamental gospel truths.

What does it mean to be a successful physician? Is it someone who trains at the best medical school and residency program? Someone who matched into the most competitive and coveted faculty position at a prestigious university or the ultimate private practice position? Someone who has the most publications each year? Someone who gets the best patient satisfaction scores or has the most RVUs every year? Of course, to be an excellent physician, we must be extremely competent and skilled in our field of medicine; however, beyond that we must also view our patients from the "whole person care" perspective. I'm thankful we have the example of the most successful physician of all time as a standard—Jesus. While He might not have had any formal medical training, Jesus knew it was not enough to heal someone physically, but it's more important to address the fundamental issue at hand. He knew for someone to truly be healed, they must be healed both spiritually and physically (Luke 9:10-11).

In a way, Jesus was the Father of whole person care, the idea that true healing involves addressing physical, emotional and spiritual health all at the same time. Medicine, unfortunately, has its limitations, as those of us who have cared for stage 4 cancer patients know. Whole person care takes it a step further, by offering true healing through hope and prayer and offering the love of God for those interested in receiving it. I was blessed to have learned about whole person care as a fourth-year medical student during a summer spiritual care preceptorship program, and it revolutionized the way I practice medicine. I was surprised by the number of patients who were interested in receiving prayer at medical visits, and I sensed the spiritual hunger in countless people who longed for something more than what this world can offer. Some of my patients are so used to prayer at their visits, that if I did not offer prayer, they would ask me for prayer. Some even offer unsolicited prayers for my family and me at the conclusion of our visit. Unfortunately, one of my praying patients developed gastric cancer recently, and she found that her faith and prayer are helping to sustain her through these challenging times.

Prayer and God's Word can offer so much hope for patients. As a med-peds physician, I am blessed to care for patients of all ages, but some of them go through incredibly difficult medical journeys with progressive medical conditions. One of my young adult patients with tuberous sclerosis and seizure disorder, unfortunately, also struggles with chronic pain. I am so impressed as she hangs on to the Lord for strength and hope daily through these constant struggles. She documents her journey by writing numerous physician messages in our electronic medical record system, sometimes even messaging me to ask for prayer for her during her flares. This causes me to wonder what my triage nurses in our secular academic clinic think, but I hope they are also encouraged by what God is doing in our patients' lives.

When I was an intern in residency, I encountered a memorable patient in the MICU. Flynn* was just 21 years old and had developed multiorgan failure from IV drug use. Even as a baby intern, I recognized there was little medicine could do to help him as his body was starting to shut down. I started to visit Flynn each afternoon after rounds, to learn more about his life story and to talk with his sister who was often with him. His sister confided in me that, while she is a Christian, her brother is not…yet. That day, I asked permission to pray with Flynn, and he gratefully accepted. Two days later, while in the process of being transferred to hospice, he asked for a pastor to come visit and baptize him. Two days later, I visited him in our hospice unit, and though he was so weak he could barely speak, he welcomed hearing the good news of the gospel. When I asked if he wanted to pray to accept Christ, he responded with a loud confident, "Yes." There was such a sense of peace in his eyes after the prayer. The next day, he went home to be with the Lord, leaving this physical world of pain in exchange for eternity with his Father. This experience epitomized whole person care for me, and while not every experience is this impactful and dramatic, the Lord has a way to work His healing and love into each person's life for His glory.

Whole person care now looks a little different for me in primary care, as opposed to the ICU setting. Regardless, there is a common theme no matter which medical setting we work in: the need to be open to the Holy Spirit. In medicine, we are often wary of interruptions or unexpected circumstances, as much of our day is tightly scheduled. It is important for us to maintain structure in our day, whether we work in the operating room, the hospital or the clinic, as this allows us to do a tremendous amount of work for our patients in an efficient amount of time. Any interruptions may mean a potential delay for our next patients. I am reminded, however, that Jesus always had time to be interrupted. Even when He was going to heal a little girl who was dying, He had time to pause to heal a woman—both physically and spiritually—who had been bleeding for multiple years (Luke 8:40-48). If the Son of Man had time to be interrupted during His busy days, how much more can we learn from His example of being open to the promptings of the Holy Spirit? This might include praying with a patient, or to offer God's hope and love, or to spend an extra five minutes with someone who recently suffered a devastating loss. The spiritual impact of these connections may be far reaching, and they often bless us even more in return.

For those of us who are Christian physicians, while we are to be in the world, we must remember we are here for a greater purpose—to heal, to serve and to love. True success in God's eyes may look quite different than the world's definition of success, and I can't wait to see the people in heaven again someday whom I have had the privilege of impacting on earth. May we always remember that, while we all deserve the wrath of God, because of Jesus we are more loved and accepted in Christ than we ever could have imagined, and we have the opportunity to share this amazing and good news with those around us. In this broken world, God can use us as His hands and feet to bring a small piece of heaven to earth by actively sharing His love with everyone around us. And this, my friends, is the truly successful physician.

Dr. Janet Ma is an Associate Clinical Professor of Medicine-Pediatrics at UCLA. She also serves as an Associate Program Director of the UCLA Medicine-Pediatrics Residency Program. She is the Director of the Healthcare Transition program, helping adolescents and young adults navigate the challenges of transitioning to adult care. She furthermore serves as the CMDA Faculty Advisor for medical students and residents/fellows at UCLA. She lives in southern California with her husband and two young children.

Notes

1. Pham HH, Lerner BH. In the patient's best interest? Revisiting sexual autonomy and sterilization of the developmentally disabled. West J Med. 2001 Oct;175(4):280-3. doi: 10.1136/ewjm.175.4.280. PMID: 11577067; PMCID: PMC1071584.
2. Keller, T. and Keller, L. The meaning of marriage: facing the complexities of commitment with the wisdom of God. 2011, New York, Dutton.

CHAPTER 11

WITNESSES

JOHN D. MELLINGER, MD

I once had the chance to hear Elizabeth Elliott speak. While referencing the storyline of her husband's death In Ecuador as a missionary in 1956, she developed the theme that the biblical word from which we derive our English term 'martyr' did not have heroic connotations in its initial New Testament usage. It simply meant 'witnesses': individuals who had directly observed the life and ministry of Jesus and were simply called to testify to the reality and veracity of what they had seen.

As I ponder that perspective at the end of a surgical career, it strikes me that one of the greatest privileges of our profession is the chance to be present for—to witness---things of importance regarding both this life and the next. As physicians, we are often observers, bystanders, at moments of transcendence. Birth, death, and the transitions of body and spirit that occur in moments of healing - including the ultimate healing that takes place when someone passes from this life to the next in the context of a trusting relationship with Jesus—these are all moments pregnant with significance. Accordingly, in writing these brief words on the role of faith in the life and practice of the physician and knowing the power of stories in capturing our hearts as well as our heads, I would like to share just a few of the instances I have been able to witness: instances which have buoyed my faith in a personal God who cares intimately and individually for us. These experiences are reminders that our calling as physicians is bathed with meaning and purpose, including the privilege of simply being present to behold some of the often unrecognized, but sacred moments, that mark our lives.

A REDEMPTIVE GOD

My first story began with a tragedy in my life, and highlights the theme of God's redemptive purposes, which often take time to fully reveal themselves. When I was 6 years old, my mother was killed in an automobile accident. As my parents tried to fit in a brief date at the end of our family vacation, the brakes on their car failed on a hill. My mother suffered a ruptured atrial appendage from a blunt steering wheel injury and died in the emergency room as they waited for a surgeon to arrive. Obviously, this event wrought upheaval on our family as my father, a solo pastor of a small church, navigated his way through grief, with three young children—the youngest less than a year old. One doesn't recover from such an experience, but does learn, often in much deeper, redemptive ways than would otherwise have been possible.

Because I lost her at a young age, my mother may have had more influence on my life. As I grew up, stories about her took on a special impact, because of her absence. In fact, I came to see, over time, that her character as a follower of Christ took on heightened proportions in forming my own character. The hallowedness of those memories and stories, made poignant by her physical absence, gave them a gravitas that I would have, no doubt, missed had I had the opportunity to take her for granted as a presence in my remaining developmental years.

One particular account from a family friend stuck with me. They told the story of listening to my mother's response when complimented on her Christ-like character. Her response was, "The things you see in me that you find attractive, those are the things Jesus has produced in my life. The things you see in me that you don't like, that is what I am like apart from Him." The humility and insight of that simple statement regarding what it means to be a jar of clay that is, nevertheless, capable of reflecting His glory, has been a rich resource in my own walk.

Fast forward from that background to my first story of being a witness to His work channeled into our work as physicians. Probably thirty-odd years after losing my mother, I found myself a junior career surgeon with trauma call a prominent part of my duties. One day a young father came in who had fallen off his roof while doing some home maintenance and sustained a severe closed head injury. As is often the case in such circumstances, and without any mass lesion or hematoma to drain or decompress, his brain swelling progressed over the initial days following his injury despite appropriate management measures, and it was clear he would proceed on to brain death. As I counseled his spouse, she expressed that they were believers, and that her greatest fear was not her own loss, but the loss of her husband's presence to influence their two young boys. We discussed the fact that her husband had, in fact, been a godly man, and that His Maker's fingerprints were clearly recognizable in the way he lived his life. As we talked and brought the context of our mutual faith into the conversation, I was able to share my own story of losing a parent at a young age, and the way God had graciously allowed that parent's spiritual and character-forming influence to be magnified, rather than diminished, by her physical absence. Amidst the grief that young woman was experiencing, that story, from my own life, became a piece in the fabric of comfort and hope that God used to clothe her, even in the midst of sorrow and loss. What is more, the opportunity to add meaning to my own story through using the comfort God had granted me a means of comforting someone else in return (as Paul counsels in 2 Corinthians 1:4) became part of His redemption of that personal loss and its lingering impact in my heart and life.

So, my first reflection on medicine becoming a means for us to witness Him at work is this: God's redemptive hand is at work, even when we do not see it, and while it may take decades, or even lifetimes, for that work to reach its full fruition, it is indeed part of the reality of His overcoming love in the broken world in which we live as physicians and healers.

A Small Piece of A Much Larger Tapestry

My second story of being able to witness His handiwork involves the theme of becoming a small piece in a much grander and longitudinal work of the Holy Spirit. During my mid-career years, I took care of a significant number of cancer patients. One of my patients was named Matilda. She presented with an advanced colon cancer and had multiple liver metastases that were unresectable at the time of presentation. In that era, such a diagnosis typically meant a survival measured in months. As I consulted with her about her prognosis, I used a strategy I often used to broach the spiritual dimension in my conversations with patients facing a terminal diagnosis. After first discussing with them the anticipated course of their illness, I would typically say something like, "I am sorry to have to have this discussion with you and wish there was more I could offer you medically. I promise you that whatever comes, we will be here to support and care for you as you navigate this. While it does not soften the blow of hearing such news, I would also offer something that some of my other cancer patients have taught me: it is sometimes possible to truly live more in a period of months or a year than one has lived in decades. Something about being reminded that our time here may be short brings into focus what is important in our lives. For some of my patients it has been relationships they wanted to mend, and finally did. For others it has been things they wanted to do or people they wanted to be with that became more significant in ways they had previously ignored. For others, it has been the opportunity to consider what they think about life after death, God, and what it would look like to feel prepared for that. As you navigate this, my encouragement to you, is this; I am delighted to support you in any way I can on your journey, so you can take as much advantage of the time to live as your diagnosis allows. This is certainly not a silver lining to the hard conversation we are having, but it is an opportunity for you, as it has been for some of my other patients, to make these days their best: days laden with healing and meaning."

Well, when I shared those themes with Matilda, she immediately responded by saying that her whole family were Christians, but she had seen too many fakes, and it just was not for her. I responded that I understood, and that my only added encouragement was that as she considered what she believed, she make her decisions about faith based on looking at Jesus Himself, and not those of us who imperfectly have represented Him on earth.

Over the next few months, I saw Matilda periodically and provided her medical care as her needs arose. It was truly a treasure to be on that journey with her, and to be able to care and, by caring, love her in Jesus' name. I would often end our visits by asking if she had had any further thoughts or insights about her spiritual journey as she prepared for the end of her life. She always responded graciously but clearly as she had stated initially—"faith just wasn't for her", and there were too many examples in her experience of those who professed such, yet showed no evidence of a changed life, that made faith seem to be of little consequence, and which, of course, I understood and accepted.

A few months later, I remember being conscious that Matilda was probably near the end of her journey and was praying that God would comfort her with Himself, allow her to know Him, and not just those of us who, in the past, had represented Him so poorly to her. Shortly after that, one day, I noticed her sister's name on my office appointment ledger; that sister had often accompanied her on her visits to my office, and knew the conversations, including those about faith and death, that Matilda and I had in the course of her care. Over time, I had become aware that this whole family was actively praying for Matilda, knowing her disappointment with those who professed to know God, and the difficulties with faith that followed. I assumed she was perhaps coming to discuss scheduling a screening colonoscopy for herself, given Matilda's diagnosis. To my surprise, when I entered the room to see her that day, she let me know that Matilda had passed away. I voiced my sympathy, but it was clear there was more she wanted to share.

She proceeded to tell me that about a week before Matilda died, at that point bedridden and weakened by her disease, her niece had entered the room to check on her. Matilda said to her niece, "You know, I've been thinking." "What have you been thinking about Aunt Matilda?", the niece replied. Her response still brings tears to my eyes, and I can usually not finish the story verbally without my voice breaking, "I've been thinking it's about time for me to get right with the Lord." The niece proceeded to again review the simple gospel message with her and knelt down and prayed with her to receive God's gift of forgiveness, endless life, and hope through Jesus.

Of course, I was deeply moved to hear this, but the sister was not done. As she became aware of Matilda's decision and discussed It with her, the sister reported that she had asked Matilda if she would like her to let Dr. Mellinger know of her decision. Matilda said yes. Matilda continued that she had a little Precious Moments statue around the house, which showed the baby Jesus in a manger with a sign attached that said, "Just for you." She asked the sister to bring me the statue and offer it as her gift to me, and to tell me that before her passing from this life to the next, she had finally realized Jesus was for her too.

What did I witness in all this? I saw a God who never stops pursuing, a God who hears years of prayer offered by families, even as we falteringly seek to represent Him as

He is, and a God who graciously allows us, as physicians, to play even a minor and supporting cast role in His larger work in the hearts and souls of those for whom we care. What a privilege to be a witness to such a God, and His love for one of His own sheep brought home at last.

VISIONS OF GLORY

My last story is again a somber one, as so many of our stories in medicine can be, but laced with hope of a much weightier kind than the trials in which it was packaged. Bob and Sherry came to my office after Bob was diagnosed with metastatic cancer, which, like Matilda's, had originated in his colon. Bob and Sherry were believers; he was a state trooper, in the prime of his life when that diagnosis interrupted his life path. We wrestled through some months of treatment with them, but, over time, it became clear that the cancer would win the battle over Bob's earthly life. We had many discussions about faith, preparing for death, and navigating the unexpected elements that had intruded on Bob and Sherry s lives. Bob did some amazing things in his last months, including making videos for his younger children so they could hear his advice on key themes when they grew toward maturity or encountered situations in life he couldn't discuss with them at a younger age, but which they would one day hunger to hear. He and Sherry became great examples to me of what I had referenced for Matilda —folks who made the most of a foreshortened lifetime, knowing that it might be brief, even as they prayed for healing and pursued all reasonable medical measures available to them.

As Bob approached the end, he and Sherry made a pact. They agreed, as a way he might offer a final encouragement to Sherry, if God so allowed, that if he saw or experienced anything specific as he was dying, he would share it with her to whatever extent he could. The day came. Sherry was with Bob in his room. As he lay in bed in his closing moments, he uttered these words in succession with pauses between each phrase, "Amazing galaxies...beautiful gardens...Momma!...Jesus is coming!" Those were his last words, and a treasure to his spouse as she walked him to his eternal home.

Sherry shared those words with me in a letter she wrote after Bob went home. She also shared about his funeral and the celebration it was by his colleagues in the State Patrol and the many younger lives he had influenced through his work, his life, and his death. He fought the good fight, he finished the course, he kept the faith.

Being witness to the moment when faith becomes (literally) sight—not every job allows that. What a precious thing to be able to share with a grieving wife and mother. We sorrow, but not as those who have no hope.

CONCLUSION

I began this piece with the premise that as physicians, we have the privilege of having a front row seat on some of life's most meaning-laden moments. We are witnesses. Even for the pastor, there is often a perceived distance between the pulpit and the pew that must be overcome, but that tends to be absent at a bedside. While there are many days we may go home tired and weary from the battle, there is perhaps no other line of work where the veil between the here and the hereafter is so prominently featured in the tapestry of our earthly life. Sometimes, we are privileged to participate in those events in direct and meaningful ways. Sometimes we fail—medically and otherwise. But always, we have the honor of witnessing the sovereign and sacrificial presence of the One who regards as precious the passing of those who are His, and without whose knowledge neither a hair from our head nor sparrow can fall. Witnesses.

John D. Mellinger, MD, FACS, currently serves as Vice President for the American Board of Surgery (ABS) and Professor Emeritus of Surgery and Medical Education at Southern Illinois University School of Medicine. He is a past president of the Society of American Gastrointestinal and Endoscopic Surgeons and the Association of Program Directors in Surgery. Dr. Mellinger has served as a Director and Chair of the Board of Directors for the ABS, and as a Director for the American Board of Family Medicine. Dr. Mellinger's academic interests include surgical education, surgical endoscopy, gastrointestinal surgery, and international surgery. He has received over thirty teaching awards, three national level educator awards including the Educator of the Year Award of the Christian Medical and Dental Association (CMDA), and has served on the CMDA Board of Trustees. He and Elaine, his spouse, are members of Parkside Westside Church and have four children and twelve grandchildren.

CHAPTER 12

THE PATIENTS IN THE POCKET OF MY WHITE COAT

GRACE OEI, MD, MA

I remember when I decided no longer to believe in the goodness of God. It was near the end of the first year of my combined internal medicine-pediatrics residency while on one of the inpatient internal medicine services. I was on call and in the process of admitting a patient in the emergency department when I received a page. I dialed the number and waited for the nurse on the other end to pick up the phone, dread filling my stomach. Our brief conversation confirmed my fears: Mr. Miller's breathing was more labored, and the nurse was concerned that he appeared less lucid than before. Could I come to assess him? I hung up the phone, told my patient lying on the gurney in the emergency department that I would be right back, and hustled up the stairs. Mr. Miller would likely get intubated and transferred into the medical intensive care unit (MICU). I did not see how he would come out of this alive. Of all my patients, why was Mr. Miller the one crumping?

My mind drifted back to when I admitted him three weeks prior. Tall and thin, with piercing blue eyes, he had come to the emergency department because of worsening shortness of breath compounding the hacking cough that he had for months. His chest radiograph showed two nodules and a large pleural effusion in his right lung. His staging CT scan showed a liver mass that was suspicious for metastatic disease. After admission, a biopsy of the mass confirmed the diagnosis of metastatic non-small cell lung cancer. At that point in my short medical career, I had not had much experience in breaking bad news to patients and I was tasked with updating Mr. Miller. I fumbled around, trying to find the right words, eventually delivering the diagnosis amid a great number of "umm"s. Mr. Miller took the news in stride as if my words confirmed a truth he had already accepted. He thanked me for telling him. He was gentle with me, encouraging even, as he cited his devout belief in the goodness of God. After this, our connection deepened.

He stayed in the hospital to receive chemotherapy, and over the next couple of weeks, we got to know more about each other. He was a gifted storyteller and seemed to have a story for just about everything. We talked about politics and books. I learned about his ex-wife and son, both now estranged. I also learned about his conversion to Christianity and why he believed that even now, God is good (all the time). He was open to talking honestly about life and death. He wanted every aggressive treatment modern medicine could offer him. His good humor dimmed considerably as he suffered through the toxic side effects of chemotherapy. Some days, he was too fatigued and nauseous to talk very much. Some days, I was too busy to do much more than spend a few extra minutes at his bedside, or at least that is what I told myself. He developed severe mucositis and lost even more weight. His counts dropped. Then he developed a shortness of breath. The repeat chest x-ray showed bilateral opacities, and we started him on antibiotics. Mr. Miller's breathing worsened, prompting the page from the nurse.

I rushed into his room. Mr. Miller was sitting propped up in bed, clearly struggling. I called my senior resident. We asked him, "Mr. Miller, do you want a breathing tube?" because we were too ignorant to ask a better question. He nodded. My senior resident intubated Mr. Miller, and I wrote orders to transfer him to the MICU. In those days, the MICU was an open unit – we managed our own patients in the MICU with the pulmonologist's consultation. Mr. Miller never made it out of the MICU. He died two days later of septic shock. His organs failed, one after another. I felt like a bystander watching a slow-moving train wreck. He developed an arrhythmia and then pulseless electrical activity. We performed a desultory code before calling his time of death.

It did not seem that there was any goodness. Not only had Mr. Miller died, but his manner of death also seemed to me to be the opposite of goodness. I did not have the wherewithal to unpack Mr. Miller's death at the time. I just remember shaking my head and deciding that it made far more sense to think of God as the casual observer than to believe in God as a giver of goodness. The next day I finished the rotation and started my next inpatient medicine rotation at another hospital. I fell back into the q4 rhythm (call, post-call, post-post-call, pre-call) with a new team. Same old – except with one difference. I now lived in a world of Godly indifference. Perhaps this would bring some congruence to my world.

A few years later, I finally arrived at an emotional place where I could start to unpack some of my residency experience - including the decision to live in a world of Godly indifference. I started the journey by dialoguing with the patients in the pocket of my metaphorical white coat. I am immensely grateful that over the years of my medical practice, patients and their families have granted me access to their lives and have allowed me to be their physician. Through their generosity, they have taught me about God, suffering, love, forgiveness, loss, meaning, and more. The patients who have taught me the most have often been part of my most difficult experiences. Mr. Miller was an early addition to my pocket. He has since been joined by many others - Mr. Portman, my opera singer patient who refused to be intubated because of his fear of vocal cord damage; America, my tiny 28-week preemie who developed necrotizing enterocolitis; Nathan, my 6-year-old ventilator dependent patient with spinal muscular atrophy whose mother was homeless; Jessica, my 15-year-old patient with traumatic brain injury who was making an unexpected neurologic recovery; Jamal, my 14-year-old patient with relapsed leukemia who begged me not to intubate him; Emily, my sweet 6-month-old with medical conditions including spina bifida, hydrocephalus, a large hole in her heart who had been surrendered to the hospital's custody by her mother; Deena, my 17-year-old patient, also with leukemia, whose death, not life, was prolonged by the marvels of modern medicine. Each precious patient is their own masterclass.

I began with Mr. Miller, imagining the questions I would ask him, given what I know now about medicine and life:

Mr. Miller, can you tell me more about your hopes for chemotherapy? You've told me that you don't want to die – can you tell me the things that are important to you for you to live?

Mr. Miller, what does a miracle mean to you? I must confess that I have difficulty understanding the concept of miracles. It seems unfair that some people are chosen for miracles and not others. I think it was really unfair that you died.

Mr. Miller, I know you've been very nauseous today. I'm unsure what else to order for you to help with this. I'm sorry – I feel helpless.

One of Mr. Miller's favorite Bible verses was Psalm 23. I re-read the familiar Psalm.

"Even though I walk through the valley of the shadow of death, I will fear no evil. For you are with me;" (Psalm 23:4)

Mr. Miller, is this what you mean about the goodness of God? That it is his constant presence, regardless of the outcome?

"Your rod and your staff, they comfort me. You prepare a table before me in the presence of my enemies." (Psalm 23:4)

I thought of the complexity inherent in this verse—that safety and comfort are not the absence of suffering—one knows safety and comfort because of pain and suffering. I was struck by the question of how a table should be prepared when one is amid enemies. What is the essence of this type of preparation that allows one to be calm, even to be able to eat in the presence of evil, pain, and suffering?

Slowly, I began to see and then believe that God's goodness is contained in his presence and that his presence is embodied in the actions of those who walk alongside another in "the valley of the shadow of death." Had I been walking alongside Mr. Miller, or had Mr. Miller been walking alongside me?

Mr. Miller, why have you been so kind to me? I'm just an intern. I don't know a lot of stuff.

I started to notice and feel God's goodness in other places in the present day – the nurse who dropped a piece of candy by my computer while I entered in orders ("Just to make sure your blood sugar isn't low," she said); the unit clerk who wordlessly handed me an updated patient list after a long day of multiple admissions and transfers out of the pediatric intensive care unit ("I highlighted the new admissions for you," he said with a smile).

Mr. Miller, I need to tell you that you have with me during my sojourn into "the valley of the shadow of death." You have been my rod and my staff.

I began to see my work as a physician differently – to advocate often and to be present always. In so doing, to become a manifestation of God's goodness.

Mr. Miller, thank you for being the embodiment of God's goodness to me. I wish I could have told you this while you were alive.

After some time, I was able to join in the familiar refrain:

Mr. Miller, God is good...("all the time," he softly said).
All the time...("God is good," he whispered back)

Slowly, surely, the patients in my pocket resuscitated my spirituality. They performed spiritual surgery on my faith and restored my belief in God and in his goodness. My experiences with my patients continue to impact my faith to this day. In fact, they are the medicine I need to keep God centered in my practice and life. Jessica reminds me about humility and the limits of human prognostication; Nathan teaches me about the social obligations of our society to support mothers in how they love and care for their children. And Deena? Well, I'm still dialoguing with Deena, even now trying to find the line between living and dying. I suspect this will be a long conversation.

I owe so much to my patients that I wonder what kind of Christian I would have become had I not gone to medical school. Would my ideas about goodness, mercy, and love be as rich or nuanced? Would my heart be as bruised or as filled to overflowing?

Each day I practice medicine, I hope to continue learning from the sacred space of the patient-physician relationship, even if my patients are no longer physically present on Earth. I do so now from a very different position than when I first started dialoguing with

Mr. Miller. I now know and believe in God's goodness. I look for it in embodied form and pray I can be that for my patients.

Grace Oei is a pediatric critical care physician at Loma Linda University Children's Hospital and a clinical ethicist for Loma Linda University Health. She is also the director of the Center for Christian Bioethics at Loma Linda University.

CHAPTER 13

GOD-SIGHTINGS

BARRY J. WU, MD

GOD-SIGHTINGS

Throughout my life, there are countless times I missed seeing God in everyday events. However, I am thankful to recount my faith journey and, in particular, three patient encounters in which I have witnessed God's presence.

My parents were both born in China near Shanghai in families that held to Confucian and Buddhist beliefs. When my dad was a young boy in China, his older brother, Richard, became extremely sick. The family sought a cure from this unknown illness from Chinese doctors, who employed traditional Chinese and herbal medicines, but nothing helped. One day, a Christian missionary visited their home and prayed with his parents for Richard's healing. Richard remained ill. The Christian missionary visited again and this time, not only Richard's parents, but also his grandparents knelt and prayed. The house they were in shook like an earthquake and Richard was healed. This miraculous healing gave my dad a new faith in Jesus Christ. Shortly afterwards, he left China to pursue education at Massachusetts Institute of Technology (MIT).

My mom too grew up in a family where her father was a nominal Buddhist. Her mother practiced Buddhism by worshiping in temples with many large statues. My mom would accompany her mother and wondered, to herself, "Why do I need to pray to so many different scary statues?" She left Shanghai and received her high school education at a Christian boarding school in Hong Kong. There, she learned about God who sent His only son who died for us and forgives all her sins. She accepted Jesus Christ and journeyed from Hong Kong to Morristown, New Jersey to attend the College of Saint Elizabeth (now Saint Elizabeth University).

My parents met at a Chinese college social event at Lake George in New York. After several months of long-distance dating, they married. Although I grew up in Christian home, I did not personally receive Jesus until I was a high school student and faced the first crossroads in my life.

When I was a 16-year-old, in high school, I was troubled about what college and career to pursue. My dad had my highest respect. He was a MIT alumni and chemical engineer. My life was turned upside down in the Spring of my junior year in high school. Despite being a non-smoker, my dad developed a nonproductive cough over a few weeks and was diagnosed with a malignant pericardial effusion and metastatic lung cancer. I did not know if I should go to engineering school like my dad, medical school because I enjoyed studying biology, or divinity school because I respected his faith. I asked my dad one evening for his advice. He said "Barry, what is your passion? Choose a field you love and not a job that you are working 9am to 5pm to just pay the bills." I did not have any answers for what I should do at the time and struggled during his illness asking the Lord to take my life instead of his.

My dad remained steadfast, faithful, and unafraid. He prayed every evening for us. I remember him reading Psalm 23 from his Bible. He lived for eight months from the time of his diagnosis. Before he died, he made me promise to take care of my mom because she dedicated her life to our family. Following his death, my faith and relationship with Jesus grew. I saw answers to my dad's prayers. My mom, who was a homemaker, found employment as an administrative clerk. As a single parent, she raised my sister, my brother, and me, helping us through college and graduate schools.

I received a college acceptance from MIT, but I chose to go to Rensselaer Polytechnic Institute and, like my dad, majored in Chemical Engineering. I enjoyed engineering, but I still felt a passion for medicine, particularly after enduring the trials of my dad's illness. I was thrilled to be accepted to the University of Rochester School of Medicine and Dentistry. My first year of medical school was very difficult because, unlike engineering where there is a lot of reasoning skills, medical school required endless memorization. Halfway through my first year, I was in a crisis and had to ask myself, if God asked me, whether I should give up medical school or was my pursuit of medicine my god. By the end of my first year of medical school, I could finally answer yes, I can give up being a physician. A burden lifted and I was able to continue onwards. By God's grace, I received my medical degree in 1989 before the next crossroad in my life.

I decided on a residency in internal medicine and matched at Yale-New Haven Hospital. My internship, however, was the most difficult year of my life. I felt completely incompetent, unorganized, mentally, emotionally, and physically exhausted. I was suicidal and swearing underneath my breath before seeing patients. I called my mom for help, but I did not think she or anyone else understood what I was going through. She prayed and even called my residency program director for help. I, however, was too proud to ask or receive help.

Gratefully, I did have two fellow interns who also had a Christian faith, and we began meeting for meals and having short devotionals. Gradually by the end of my internship, I garnered enough strength to go to a local church. At this church, I had an epiphany regarding my faith and vocation. There was a small group led by a retired public-school principal John Knudsen. He shared about looking for God in everyday events what he called God sightings. Instead of calling myself Christian just because I go to church on Sundays, I began to look for God each day and think about my faith at work. I began reading my Bible daily and applying the verse from Proverbs about learning to trust in the Lord and not to lean on my own understanding, to acknowledge God and let Him direct where I should go. I began to practice looking for God in my everyday experiences. Here is what I saw and learned about God from three of my patients Elizabeth, Rebekah, and Joseph.*

ELIZABETH

Elizabeth was a 55-year-old widowed homemaker from Georgia. She had been caring for herself at home and had not seen a physician in years. She had no family members that were active in her life. She came to the hospital with progressive shortness of breath and when I examined her, I found a large fungating breast mass. Her work up, not surprisingly, revealed metastatic disease. She was too weak to receive chemotherapy and her wishes were to be made comfortable and sent to hospice. The last day in the hospital, I went to see her to wish her well. I told her that the people at hospice would take care of her. She had no family members or friends, and I was surprised when she asked me if I would visit her. When I heard the word hospice, it had always meant defeat to me. A place where people died.

I had not been to a hospice and had no real desire to go. It had not been in any part of my formal training. I told her that I would try to visit her, but that I was on call that weekend and may be too busy to come.

Surprisingly, the weekend was not busy at the hospital. I felt guilty and found myself driving in my blue Honda Civic to Branford Hospice. This was the first hospice In the United States. I went to the second floor. There was Elizabeth in a large room with a few other patients. She was laboring to breathe. We exchanged small talk and then I asked her if she was religious. She said of course she believed in God. Her dad was a minister. I asked her what her favorite book in the Bible was. She said Psalm 23. I told her that it was my dad's favorite too. I remembered him reading it daily as he battled cancer. I told her that I had forgotten it by memory, but I would go home and memorize it.

I came back the next day and found her breathing more comfortably. I began to recite the Psalm 23 and I started hearing her reciting along with me. Tears welled up in my eyes reflecting on my dad and Elizabeth. I felt God reminding me that God is in control and the source of all comfort. I wanted to comfort Elizabeth, but God was comforting me through Elizabeth. He was walking with me and Elizabeth through the valley of the shadow of death.

Two days after our visit at hospice, Elizabeth went on to dwell in the house of the Lord forever.

REBEKAH

I met Rebekah on the 4th of July. She was a native of Hemingway, South Carolina, a former custodial worker at Yale, married 65 years, with 12 children, 28 grandchildren and 25 great grandchildren. She retired with her husband and returned to her hometown. While her husband was busy the last week of June, Rebekah flew on her own to visit her son and grand and great grandchildren in New Haven. Her son noted that she was more tired than usual and without her usual voracious appetite. He thought perhaps this was due to the long plane ride. However, she appeared worse over the next several days, so he brought her to the hospital.

Although I did not want to work on Saturday, July 4th, I was on call for this holiday and the first to take Rebekah's history. I asked her the usual questions about her main concern, past history, medications, allergies, family history and social history including her smoking and alcohol use, but also asked about what was most important to her and her support system. She said she loved her family and was active in her church, singing alto in the choir, and serving on the mission board. We finished up the history. I washed my hands, and I began to examine her. She was an ill-appearing older woman sitting up in bed with glistening brown eyes, a cheerful smile, and sunken temples. Her lungs were clear, and heartbeat was regular, without extra heart sounds. I moved to examine her abdomen and observed it was distended. My hands were surprised by feeling a large, irregular, hard mass in her right upper quadrant. I thought to myself, "This is not good." Her knees were stiff, swollen and irregular from wear and tear of many years of physical work. She was cognitively intact and could move all her extremities equally.

After finishing my examination, I looked her in the eyes and said, "Rebekah, I have some bad news." I paused.

"Tell me," she said.

"I found a mass in your liver, and I think you are going to need a liver biopsy."

She did not look surprised.

"You told me you are involved in your church singing in the choir and serving on the mission board," I continued. "Do you believe in God?"

"Yes," she replied.

"Would you like someone to pray with you?" I asked.

She said "Yes". I told her that I would order a consult from our spiritual care team. She said, "No. You pray for me."

Although I had not prayed out loud with patients before, I did not want to abandon her in her time of need. I tried to think but found myself closing my eyes and simply began saying,

"Dear Lord, you are the great physician and one who heals. Thank you that you know what is going on. Please lend your healing hand on Rebekah and grant wisdom to her doctors and nurses. May your kingdom come, and your will be done. Amen."

Rebekah spent the next day in the hospital with several family visitors. On Monday, she had her biopsy and waited several days. I saw her on Wednesday morning to tell her the bad news. The biopsy showed metastatic adenocarcinoma. Her expression did not change. She did not want aggressive treatment and wished to go home with her family. Remarkably by Friday, she was eating better, and I decided to discharge her home with hospice services for the weekend to spend time with her family.

I felt convicted to visit her at her son's home after her discharge. Her son lived in the part of New Haven with which I was not familiar. I found my way to her son's home. Rebekah's husband of 65 years had flown that day from South Carolina to be with her. I noticed a Bible on her bed stand. Her husband and son's family surrounded her bed. I asked if we could pray. We held hands and prayed for comfort, peace, and healing. As we were finishing, her husband low pitched voice cried out "Lord Jesus I am satisfied let her go over the river to you Jesus." I had never prayed with a patient and their family in their home. This was a new learning experience for me. I left their home feeling a sense of peace, witnessing the strength, faith and courage in Rebekah and her family.

A few days later after the home visit, I received a call that Rebekah "went across the river to be with Jesus".

JOSEPH

One of gifts of being a physician is the opportunity to teach and learn from students. I was the teaching attending assigned to the Veterans Administration Hospital in West Haven. It was the first day of the rotation and the student assigned to my team was a third year Yale medical student named Allison who was involved in the Yale Health Professional Christian Fellowship group. We were studying the book of Daniel during her first clerkship in medicine. The clerkship year is a stressful time for medical students. That first day, I reminded Allison of the importance of treating patients as a whole person; addressing not only their physical concerns, but also their emotional and spiritual needs. We reviewed talking with patients, to obtain the patient's present concern, their past medical history, their medications, family history, and social history. This social history often asks about smoking and alcohol use and stops there. It is vital to also learn about where they were born, their level of education, their support system, and faith. So, we also ask if the patient is involved in a church, synagogue, mosque, or other faith-based community and ask if they have a faith to see them through this illness.

Joseph was Allison's first patient. He was a naval radar instructor and had worked on a nuclear submarine. Each year he had to pass an annual physical exam test. This year he was unable to complete the 1 mile run in the designated time. He was sent to the infirmary and had a blood test done which showed an abnormally high white blood cell count. He was referred to the West Haven Veterans Administration Hospital. Allison met him for the first time and noted what peace he had on his face, despite the painful tests that included a bone marrow biopsy. He was married and had one child.

Allison also noted a Bible by his bed during her interview. When she asked about it, Joseph said his mother had left it for him. Allison asked if he believed in Jesus. "Of course," he said. Allison asked if she could pray for him. "Of course," he said. Allison prayed for healing for him and wisdom for those caring for him. As she was closing with an amen, Joseph began to pray that God would be with Allison during this difficult medical school clerkship year. Allison ran to me to share her experience with Joseph; she was so encouraged.

Joseph walked to me the next day and gave me a surprising hug in the hall of the hospital. He had been so encouraged by Allison. Then he shared that he felt like he was like Shadrach, Meshach, and Abednego in the fiery furnace in the book of Daniel. Though he was going through a trial, he would not bow down to any other god. I was amazed by seeing and learning about God through Allison and Joseph.

Reflecting on my over three decades of practicing medicine, I have found the most joy, meaning and satisfaction in my work and life by looking, learning, and experiencing God in everyday events and the surprise this brings. The crossroads and trials in life have made me be a better physician. More importantly, they have helped me to see and know God more. God truly sees everything. God saw my dad when his brother Richard was sick. He saw my mom alone in boarding school in Hong Kong. He saw me as a confused teenager. He saw Elizabeth, Rebekah, and Joseph. God sees you. Where are you seeing God?

Barry J. Wu, MD is a Professor of Medicine at the Yale School of Medicine where he directs the first and last courses which medical students experience at the school: Introduction to the Profession and Capstone. Dr. Wu recruits and trains 200 faculty involved in the clinical skills training and interprofessional education for medical students, nurse practitioners and physician associate students through the Medical Clinical Experience and Interprofessional Longitudinal Clinical Experience courses. He also co-directs the Connecticut Older Adult Collaboration for Health (COACH) 4M to enhance the geriatric workforce in primary care and is Chair of the Health Committee for the Yale China Association. Of note, he collaborated on a model of residency training at the Xiangya Hospitals that has been adopted as the graduate medical education system in China. He is the faculty advisor to the Yale Health Professional Christian Fellowship since 1991 and is a member serving on the mission team at Trinity Baptist Church in New Haven, CT.

CHAPTER 14

LEARNING TO WELCOME GOD'S UNEXPECTED PRESENCE

Scott Morris, MD

Baruch Spinoza, a seventeenth-century Dutch Jewish theologian, wrote, "We are afraid of emptiness. We like to fill up empty time and space." I grew up as an only child and understood what Spinoza meant. I spent much of my time looking for ways to fill up my days. I did it mostly by playing sports, until I went to college. Then I engaged the intellectual life. I sought to learn all I could, but it was still an attempt to fill that emptiness.

As an older teenager, I recognized that a third of the Gospels are about healing the sick, but when I looked to see what my church did in response, there just wasn't much to see. I had felt my heart "strangely warmed" in the Methodist tradition on several occasions, but I was not sure what it might mean for the direction my life would flow. I set out to discover how I might connect faith and health. What would it look like in my world? Could it be the path to displace my emptiness?

After college, I went to seminary. While there, I realized that historically faith and health are closely linked. Hospitals opened as ways to care for the sick who were pilgrims on the way to the Holy Land. Theologians like John Wesley believed that people of faith should always connect faith and health in tangible ways, but philosophers like René Descartes, who stood in the tradition of Plato, convinced us that we can separate a human being into a body and a spirit and these two dimensions of humanity should never connect. Cartesian dualism quickly came to rule the world.

One day in seminary, I was waiting to speak to the chaplain of Yale School of Medicine and saw a pamphlet titled, "How to Start a Church-Based Health Center," written by Rev. Granger Westberg, a Lutheran minister near Chicago.

That was it. A faith-based health clinic. From that point on, it seemed that God said, "This is what you will do with your life." I was called. Or was I just stubborn? I set out to meet Westberg and through him came to realize that there are a lot of people who care about faith and health. It was not just me. And Westberg's vision for caring for the whole person—body and spirit—was just what I needed to take action on my conviction that René Descartes was wrong.

After finishing seminary and becoming ordained in the United Methodist Church, I went on to medical school at Emory and did a residency to be a family medicine practitioner. When I was ready to start my own faith-based health center, I moved to Memphis, Tennessee, the poorest large city in America. I worked for the health department while sharing my vision with anyone who would listen—churches, hospitals, businesses. We would need every level of community support possible.

After a year of groundwork, we opened Church Health on September 1, 1987. Our mission was to provide quality, affordable health care for people who work in low-wage jobs. We would do it without relying on government funding because the government cannot do the healing work of the church, nor should we ask it to. We saw 12 patients the first day—the fewest we have seen since. After that, the floodgates opened.

In 1988, the AIDS epidemic was coming into full bloom. I met Robert, who was a yardman for one of our volunteer doctors. He was 42 years old, soft spoken, with a kind smile and soft hands, despite his job. He also had all the symptoms of AIDS, so I wasn't surprised when his test returned positive. In 1988, the diagnosis was a certain death sentence. There was no treatment except to prescribe antibiotics when pneumonia set in. He took it amazingly well. He even thanked me.

Over the next year, I would see him whenever he got sick and each time he took it so well that I thought something might be wrong. He was too happy—so much so that I sat him down and looked him in the eyes and asked, "Do you understand your problem?"

And he looked at me and said, "I understand, and I know God loves me."

His words sank deep into me and have stayed with me all these years. God's love touches us all, because God loves us all no matter the circumstances. Prior to that moment, most of my understanding of God came from my intellectual perception of who I thought God was. I assumed filling up the emptiness would lead me to God. After getting to know Robert, I came to experience God as a matter of the heart more than the head, and I stopped worrying about Spinoza's way of seeing the world. Robert died a few months later, but I have never forgotten what he helped me to learn.

I care for patients just two miles from where Martin Luther King, Jr. was assassinated. In the early years I was the doctor for sanitation workers as well as people who grew up picking cotton, those for whom King had come to Memphis. I was always taken by the fact that people who truly had no resources in a country that judges people by their financial capital would answer the question "How are you?" in a very similar way: "I'm fine and blessed." I often thought, how can you be fine and blessed when you have *nothing*?

I came to realize that, while they have no capital by the measure of wealth, by which most of America judges others, they have an abundance of "spiritual capital." To this day, when I encounter someone who views the world this way, I spend the first half of the visit making sure I do not compromise my medical exam by asking, "What do I need to be doing to be fine and blessed? What do you know that I need to know?"

My medical practice is built around the belief that being healthy is not about the absence of disease, but, instead, about three critical issues: having more joy in your life, having more love in your life, and being driven closer to God. If those three things aren't happening, then what is the point? And if I am right, experiencing whole-person health does not have as much to do with the doctor as most people think.

This led us at Church Health to create what we call "The Model for Healthy Living." It is a play on the social determinants of health. We believe that there are seven parts that must be in balance to be healthy. No one domain is more important than the next. They are medical care, nutrition, movement, emotions, friends and family, work, and faith life. (See *www.churchhealth.org* to learn more about these.)

My years as a physician for people working in low-income jobs have moved me in many directions on the questions of "How do I know God?" and "How do I show the love of God to those for whom I care?" Refugees make their way to Memphis from every part of the world—Vietnam, Cambodia, Somalia, Ethiopia, Liberia, Syria, Iraq, Guatemala.

"Why did you leave your country?" I ask. "What did you see?"

The answers are bone-chilling. "They killed my children before my eyes." "I was kept in a cage where I could not stand for four years." "I hid in a closet and ate the sponges from the couch."

From all of them I hear, "And now I am in Memphis, and you are my doctor."

I want them to know I do this work because I believe it is what God wants me to do. I have come to love the patients I care for and for whom the reality of God cannot be debated, for whom God is an ever-present reality, for whom amid life's troubles there is always God to carry their burdens; to say otherwise is to be terribly foolish. If you questioned them, they would not debate you; they would just take you by the hand and get you something to eat. I have had many experiences of something greater than myself that I can only attribute to God. Now, my pursuit is to experience this God in a way that brings joy and satisfaction to my life.

Church Health began in a small rehabbed house in Midtown Memphis, but over time we grew into 13 buildings around the neighborhood, and it had become very inefficient. More than 70,000 patients have been on our rolls over the decades. Then on July 8, 2011 a young art historian came to me with the idea that he and his artist friends had of turning a former Sears Distribution Center into an artist colony, a "vertical urban village." This building in square footage is larger than the Empire State Building but had been abandoned since 1992. There were 3,200 windows and every one was broken. It was surrounded by barbed wire. The gangs stopped writing anything on the building, because what more was there to say? All the artists wanted was us to be their doctors once they rehabbed the building. The problem with their idea was that it was not financially viable. No one in their right mind would invest in such a dream.

However, I saw what was possible in God's imagination. Rather than agreeing to just be their doctors, I said, "What if we just move in there with you?" I married one crazy idea with another crazy idea and for the next three years, and together, we became property developers around a vision of health, education, and the arts. In 2017, Church Health moved all our operations to what is now called Crosstown Concourse.

I will not forget my next-to-last patient in our old clinic, a seven-year-old who came to America as an infant from Honduras with his parents. He fell during a soccer game and broke his arm. The surgery he needed was going to cost $52,000. Because they had no health insurance, his mother was told she had to pay upfront. Ironically, with insurance the base cost would have been far less. But the beauty of our work is that through the kindness of orthopedic surgeons and so many others, we could get this done quickly and it would be donated, as well. His mom began to cry tears of joy. It was all I could do to hold back my own. I felt God's presence in that place.

In the process of intentionally trying to live on the right side of justice, I am drawn closer to God. Reading Richard Rohr's writings reminds me that Jesus commands us to love one another. Love is an action. I must *do* love. Since love is the basis on which we know God, doing love takes me where I want to be.

The day before my last day in my office I sat down with a young student from the University of Memphis who was writing a paper on health policy. Before I let her ask her questions I asked, "Why did you choose to interview me for your paper?"

She was forthright. "Because this is the only place in Memphis my family has ever gone to the doctor."

I was taken off guard. "Tell me about your family."

"You helped my father get a new hip. He was having trouble working, and he was able to get back after the surgery. It made such a difference for our family."

I felt pride well up. "So how is he doing now?"

"He died," she said matter-of-factly.

"What happened?" I was taken aback.

"He had a heart attack."

"I am so sorry. Did we do anything to help him with that?" I was afraid we had missed something.

"It had nothing to do with you. He only worked for us. He just didn't look out for himself."

I said, "So that means your mother was left to take care of you. What does she do?"

"She works as a housekeeper for a hotel as one of her jobs and cleans houses for the other."

I kept asking questions. She had a younger sister who was only 12. It turns out this young woman worked 30 to 39 hours a week for Baskin Robbins. Staying under 40 hours prevented them from having to pay her benefits. She made $9.50 an hour.

I gave her time to ask the questions she had come for, and as she did so I did not at first think much of it. She wrote down my answers on notebook paper with a pencil, the same way I would do it if I were asking questions.

My interviewer had planned to go to medical school before her father died, but she realized that to do so would place a financial burden on her mother and she wasn't prepared to do that. She was now planning to be a hospital administrator, since that graduate program is only two years.

"Would you like a mentor to help you make your plans?"

"Of course."

Then it dawned on me. "Are you writing with a pencil because you don't own a laptop?"

"Yes."

I declared, "So today is your lucky day. We are moving from here tomorrow, and we have 70 computers we are replacing. I would like for you to have one of the ones we are getting rid of."

"I couldn't do that."

"Why not?"

"I haven't earned it."

The back of my throat got thick. I had just met this young woman even though I must have seen her father and helped him get a new hip. But I didn't recognize his risk for heart disease. Surely this was one thing I could do for him. It was not that she had not earned it, but that I needed to do this for me, as part of finding my way toward God. It was grace that flowed across me. God's presence connecting us to each other.

I regained my composure. "Come back next week, and I will have the computer ready for you. And if you want, I'll get one of our health coaches who is Latino to start working with you. Would you like that?"

"Yes."

"And maybe—I am not making a promise—we can find a part-time job that will help prepare you to be a health care administrator better than Baskin Robbins can."

And so, my journey continues.

As a United Methodist minister I served a church for 30 years. When we moved to Crosstown Concourse I took what is called an appointment beyond the local church. John Wesley always said, "The world is my parish," and I am trying to live into that same sense of calling. My parish is Church Health, and the work we do is caring for those who come to us who are sick and building a community with those who are part of our vertical urban village.

In many ways Memphis is still Memphis. It's still on the list of the poorest cities. Zip codes divide household economics and access to health care. Yet, the faith that drives my approach to medicine hasn't changed.

Fifty-two entities have signed long-term leases to be in Crosstown. There are 265 apartments, all of which are rented. Along with Church Health we have a charter high school, a radio station, and a variety of other not-for-profit and for-profit ventures. My artist friends have built studio space, a 450-seat auditorium, and a space for innovation makers. There are 13 artists living and working in the building. A Hollywood director works out of the building and a Grammy-winning record producer has his studio here.

There are five restaurants and a variety of retail spaces. There is no telling what might be going on in the building on any given day. It is truly a village enabled by God, far beyond my imagination.

In the end, my spiritual life is intimately intertwined with my experience of caring for patients, building the mission of Church Health, living daily within the vertical urban village of Crosstown with an appointment that sees the world as my parish even as I continue my healing work. Once a month, I am a part of an experience of God's presence that we call The Mystic. Along with a Jewish Rabbi, a world-renowned saxophone player, a singer, a piano player, and two young millennial clergy, I spend an hour in discussion and music. We invite others to join us in a music venue at Crosstown known as The Green Room. We gather on Tuesday night because no one has church on Tuesday night. There is no collection and no sermon, but it fills my soul. I also am part of a Friday group that started as a book discussion around Richard Rohr's book on the second half of life titled *Falling Upward*. We take turns teaching. Our day jobs are all over the board. This all regularly feeds my soul and fills my emptiness.

It has always been my privilege to care for the patients who keep coming day after day for 37 years. I am so often focused on the next task. I want to be productive, to be creative, to have the next great idea when, in truth, God's presence for me has always been unexpected. I now know that I cannot plan for the experience of God in my life. It happens and I just have to be ready to welcome and experience it.

Scott Morris, M.D.; M.Div. is the Founder and CEO of Church Health in Memphis, Tennessee. Church Health is the largest, faith-based primary care clinic in America. He is a graduate of The University of Virginia BA (1976); Yale Divinity School M.Div (1979) and Emory School of Medicine (1983). He completed a residency in Family Medicine at the Medical College of Virginia (1986). He is an ordained United Methodist minister and Board Certified Family Practitioner. He has spoken widely on the connection of faith and health. He was elected to the Tennessee Health Care Hall of Fame in 2022. He received the Yale Jefferson Public Service Award in 2020. He is a Master Entrepreneur in the Society of Entrepreneurs (2011) and the author of 5 books, most recently CARE: How people of faith can respond to our broken health system *(2022); IF Your Heart is Like My Heart (2017) and* Health Care You Can Live With *(2010).*

CHAPTER 15

FROM THE PULPIT TO THE BEDSIDE

Benjamin R. Doolittle, MD MDiv

I met Rosa in 1999 on the day she was diagnosed with HIV. I was to be her doctor. She had just received the news at the public health office, and they sent her over to our practice. She sat in the corner of the room. She clutched her sides and rocked gently back and forth, chanting to herself, "I am going to die. I am going to die. I know I am going to die."

Slowly, ever so gently, we listened - the nurse, the social worker, and me. Rosa shared that she had a young son. The father was in jail. Her employment was spotty. Life was hard before, and now a devastating diagnosis was just too much. "Who will take care of my son?" she asked.

Together, we stumbled through those first weeks, then months. By 1999, there were good HIV medications, and after a few weeks, the HIV virus was under control. Her immune system bounced back. And so did she. She no longer spoke of death. She gained weight. I became the doctor to her young son. She started attending a church – a charismatic, store front congregation. "When I'm at church," she said, "I just feel so good, so alive." She began to play the piano and teach the children. On another visit, she said, "I wanted to give up. I wanted to lose hope. But then God found me and saved me."

Years passed. She took her meds regularly. Our visits were mainly spent catching up about her adventures – her art projects, her church, her friends, her son. We would go over her labs, which had long ago demonstrated an undetectable viral load and a strong immune system. She brought in several of her drawings as gifts.

On one routine visit, she announced, "I stopped taking my pills."

"Why?" I asked, flummoxed, after so many years of good control.

"I believe that God has cured me of my HIV."

In my many years of practicing medicine and serving as a Christian pastor, I had never confronted a moment where the two sides of my life collided in quite that way. What could I say? I could not, in good conscience, affirm her belief that God had cured her of her HIV. But I did not want to quash her optimism, her conviction. I did not want to ostracize her from our practice, from modern medicine, from me.

"I just know that God has cured me?" she affirmed with a joyful smile.

I worried. Was she manic? Naive? Her meds controlled her HIV, but it was her faith that restored her spirit, inspired her art, and gave her that vibrant smile. In a strange way, I wondered if she was too prideful. God had singled *her* out? Who did she think she was?

"Do you ever pray?" I asked.

"Yes, all the time," she said.

"Do you ever pray with other people?" I asked.

"Yes, at church, all the time," she said.

"Would you mind if we prayed together right now?" I asked.

"Of course! I would love that, doc," she said.

And so we did, a simple, brief prayer that God would keep her healthy, keep her safe... and keep her coming back. She agreed to recurrent visits, every three months, to check her viral load and her immune system. I could not, in good conscience, prescribe medications that she would never take. If she took her medications inconsistently, the virus would become resistant, making future regimens more difficult.

She returned every three to six months. We checked labs. We prayed. We talked about her kid, her church, her friends, her art. Amazingly, her viral load remained undetectable for several years (which I really cannot explain). Once, I even clicked the box to recheck her HIV antibody test. Who knows? Maybe she *was* cured? At each visit, we discussed that, at some point, the HIV virus would return, and her immune system would weaken. She would nod in agreement – as if to appease me. We would close our visits in prayer.

Bit by bit, the HIV virus crept back ... 50 copies ... 187 copies ... 1,500 copies. I became more earnest in our conversations. Her t-cells began to drift downwards, an indication that her immune system was weakening... 600 ... 457 ... 378. By then, we had covered a lot of spiritual ground. A life of faith and the way of medicine were not opposed but could intermingle together. You could pray with your doctor.

She decided to resume her medications without fanfare or drama. She decided that these medications were a gift from God to keep her healthy, to keep her in service to God and to her beloved church. Years of connection had laid the groundwork. One day, she simply decided to take the medications again. Today, her viral load is undetectable; and her immune system has rebounded. Her son is now a father himself. I have the joy of caring for all three generations.

My call to ministry came to me when clinging to a ladder in the belly of a church steeple. I had graduated from Yale college with a degree in biology and philosophy and stayed at Yale Divinity School for a Master of Divinity. I had my eye on medical school but had not yet taken the MCATs. I felt a strong pull towards the ministry, and the medical school application process felt like a grind. Divinity school was the right move.

The first sermon I ever preached – November 9th 1991 – was at Pilgrim Congregational Church – just across town in the Fair Haven neighborhood. The Dean of Admissions had sent me over to preach. They were between ministers, contemplating closing, financial problems, on and on.... "Just go over there and preach while they figure out what they are going to do...."

I borrowed a preaching robe, pulled an all-nighter, grabbed hold of the pulpit as hard as I could the next morning, and let it rip. They asked me to preach the next Sunday, and then the Sunday after that.

Around the fifth Sunday, I noticed a rope hanging in the narthex. I knew what this rope was. This was the rope that I was never allowed to touch as a kid, under penalty of eternal damnation. This was the rope that connected to the bell in the steeple. I had preached four, maybe five sermons. Surely I, as their nearest approximation to a clergyman, would have license to ring the bell.

Enter two church guys. The first is Oscar, the lay leader of the church, and Eisten, the other head lay leader of the church. Over time, I would come to call Oscar affectionately the "Big O", and Eisten, "Ace." They both called me "kid."

"Big O, I want to pull that rope," I said.

"Knock yourself out, Kid," said the Big O.

I grab the rope. I heave my weight against the rope. The rope does not budge. The bell does not ring.

"We haven't heard it ring in years," said Ace.

"We just stopped ringing the bell," said the Big O. "I dunno, we just forgot about the durn thing."

It was Ace's idea, maybe the Big O's. I am sure it was not mine. Ace, the Big O, and the Kid meet on a Saturday morning to investigate. We open the door in the balcony and climb the dusty, rickety steps into the steeple. The dark cave smells like a sauna. From cracks in the wall, beams of light catch the dust. At the top of the stairs, there is a step ladder.

Ace looks at the Big O, who then looks at me, "Go ahead kid, this was your idea."

I was pretty sure it was not my idea, but it did not seem the right time or place to discuss the issue.

We climb the step ladder. I am certain that we are the first human beings to stand on the rungs of this ladder in the last 20? 50? 100 years? Since the Civil War? At the top of the step ladder, there is another ladder. This ladder is made of cobwebs and termite spit.

Ace and the Big O look at me. They do not speak. I do not want to wimp out. I do not want to be some geeky, awkward, wimpy seminary guy – even though that was exactly what I was, and everyone knew it.

Ace looks at me and smiles, "I'll go first." He takes to the rungs. Big O is, well, big. "You'd better go."

We climb up the cobweb ladder. We are impossibly high. Breathtakingly high. If this ladder goes, there will be some serious damage to all sorts of body parts (of this I am sure, and I wasn't even in medical school then).

There is a trap door. We push against the trap door. The door does not budge. We lean our shoulders into the trap door. The door does not budge. We heave into the trap door. Nothing.

I have a brilliant idea. I go to my car – a 1986 Chevie Citation. I get the car jack. I climb the stairs. I climb the ladder. I climb up through the cobwebs. I jam the car jack between the top rung of the cobweb ladder and the trap door. I crank the car jack.

There is a loud crack. Something breaks. We are not falling. It is the trap door. But we cannot see. I crank the car jack. Crack. The trap door opens.

No *human* had been up there for 100 years. For the past 100 years, however, the church steeple was the luxury condominium complex for many, many generations of pigeons.

I turn the crank one more time. At that moment, a tidal wave of generations worth of pigeon droppings crashes right into our faces. There is a sting to our eyes, a very unnerving crunch in our teeth, and a sick, sandpaper feeling dribbling down our skin. The pigeons were very pissed off.

But I knew that I had come to the right place. When the good Lord casts down 50 years' worth of pigeon shit right on your head with two other good fellas, your lives become inextricably bound together. I got the message. I was hooked. I loved the place.

Some months later, after several work crews, wearing appropriate apparel to guard against psittacosis, the Big O and Ace looked at me and said, "Go ahead, this was your idea." I was sure it was not my idea, but I was honored to comply. I pulled the rope with all my might. The heave of the bell swept me off my feet. And 100 feet up, the bell rang, and somewhere an angel sang hallelujah. I flew to the sky, holding onto the rope for dear life. And it was very good, very good indeed.

I was the Pastor at Pilgrim throughout medical school. In those days, I often wrote my sermons on hospital progress note paper while on the wards. During my medicine clerkship, my attending saw what I was doing. I showed him my small travel Bible and the scribblings of my Sunday sermon. He cracked a wry smile, "You know, Doolittle, today the real priests are the physicians."

The real priests are physicians? I have thought about his words for decades now. In many ways, he is correct. Patients suffer. They seek healing. Religion does not play such a big role in many peoples' lives any more. And so, patients seek healing from their physicians. More than healing, our patients seek absolution, restoration, hope. This can be baffling for physicians and patients alike. We physicians aced organic chemistry, got into medical, know the work-up for SIADH, and now we need to address our patients' spiritual suffering too? Patients too wonder why their suffering persists, despite comprehensive tests, the cavalcade of referrals, and abundance of potions and pills. I confess that I have not figured this out any better than the rest of us.

Except, I have experienced what real healing looks like. I have experienced the joy of accompanying individuals on their path to restoration – as both a pastor and a physician. I have rung a bell that once was silent, a bell that rings with hope.

The Rev. Dr. Benjamin Doolittle is a Professor of Internal Medicine and Pediatrics at the Yale School of Medicine and Professor of Religion and Health at Yale Divinity School. He directs the Yale Program for Medicine, Spirituality, and Religion. He also serves as the Program Director of the Combined Medicine-Pediatric Residency Program and the Medical Director of the faculty-resident medicine-pediatrics practice. Ordained in the Reformed Church in America, he serves as the Pastor of Pilgrim Congregational Church (UCC) in New Haven, CT. He is married to Christine and together they have two grown daughters.

CHAPTER 16

Whom Am I Called to Serve and Why: A Journey of Self-discovery

Marta Illueca, MD, MDiv, MS, FAAP

Whom am I called to serve and why? These questions provided me clarity as I decided to pursue a master of divinity degree at Yale Divinity School. After a 30-year career as a physician and pharmaceutical medical researcher, I had long fostered a deep personal commitment to the healthcare and service professions. However, a lifelong spiritual calling motivated me to merge my medical expertise with an ordained ministry vocation. Central to that vocational pursuit were my musings about developing new avenues to address the needs of human beings with chronic suffering, the physicians treating them and the clergy supporting them.

Back in 2014, that decision was neither arbitrary nor superficial. My personal commitment to serving others has its roots in my early family environment. Born in New York City, a child of a Latin American statesman and a nursing educator, my youth was invested with profound ethical and human rights values. My father, the late Dr. Jorge E. Illueca, served as President of the Republic of Panama and President of the United Nations General Assembly. My mother, the late Dr. Luzmila Arosemena, was the founder of Panama's first School of Nursing. My parents' professional and academic records, including their Ivy League training, were my source of inspiration and personal challenge. Thus, a commitment to academic excellence and professional leadership was instilled in my early life.

My parents' example played a key role in developing a deep sense of social justice, compassion, empathy and a commitment to excellence, which was not to be limited to national needs but also to a global responsibility. Furthermore, my home environment was greatly enriched by my family's strong Christian and spiritual roots. Besides my family, God was an integral part of my upbringing. The truth is I cannot remember a day of my life when I did not have an inner certitude about the existence of a higher power. Growing up in a Roman Catholic family, God, the Holy Trinity, the Lord Jesus Christ, the Holy Spirit, the Blessed Virgin Mary and the Saints were part and parcel of my daily communing with family and friends.

As I grew up, I was widely exposed to diversity and cross-cultural environments. My personal milieu was not just centered around a family and a country, but rather part of an extensive worldview of several cultural flavors. For me and my family, responsibility and commitment always extended to the world at large, not just to the immediate environment.

My teenage years were a time of spiritual challenge and awakening. Just as I turned 12, my 22-year-old sister Linda suddenly died of an unexpected cardiac event. At that time, a career in medicine became a way of sublimation of my personal loss into an altruistic medical profession. From that time on, I began to discover hitherto unknown abilities in myself that, in my teenage years, made me realize we are more than our physical bodies. A plethora of vivid mystical experiences, including lucid dreams, that faded in my early 20s, only served to convince me there are unsuspected non-physical realities, yet largely unexplored nor explained by science alone. This was a period of intense intuitive development, and, in ensuing years, I spent a significant amount of time reading and studying spiritual gifts, mystical phenomena and treading the sacred path.

Due to my life circumstances and as a woman raised as a Roman Catholic, my interpretation of what could have been an early spiritual calling was skewed until adulthood. Ordained ministry was yet to become a path I could imagine as a realistic vocational choice for me. Hence, I pursued what would become a lifelong personal quest to feed my spiritual hunger with travel, self-guided study and the personal practice of meditation and contemplation.

There is no doubt that life's surprising vicissitudes took hold of my young heart's hope for an otherwise uneventful future. I had been sick with asthma since age five, which had already compromised my early childhood with unwelcome limitations on my playtime and outdoor activities. Then the tragic loss of Linda refocused my life into a whole new vision of reality, which channeled my musings with the idea of a religious life toward a medical career that could save others' lives. Parallel to my emerging spiritual quest, in 1984, I completed medical school in Panama, trained in pediatrics in New York and, for nearly two decades, served in clinical care and graduate medical education at The New York Presbyterian Weill-Cornell Medical Center, the same place I was born.

Throughout my medical practice, as I witnessed countless children's heroic battles for life, I learned that healing comes from more than physical medicine. In particular, my life was deeply touched by one of my patients, Amanda, whose "palliative care" as a newborn was assigned to me as a junior attending. Despite Amanda's incurable bowel disease and life expectancy of less than 12 months, she lived to the age of 18 years. Little did I know she would become my textbook of divine intervention, and her life a true example of Christian faith and the extent of God's mercy.

Amanda and other children helped me realize I had not fully completed my training in the arts of healing. Treating patients with limited therapies did not constitute full use of my potential to contribute to, what I believe, is God's primal will to sustain life and health. Therefore, I made a career move to expand my clinical expertise into the area of developing new treatments to fulfill unmet medical needs for children of all ages. To that effect, I joined the pharmaceutical industry as a clinical researcher for AstraZeneca Pharmaceuticals LP in Delaware in 2003.

For 10 years, I led a pediatric drug development program and was also inspired to help train new teams of researchers. While remaining academically productive through the development of study protocols and the publication of clinical research manuscripts, I continued to pursue what had become a lifelong personal quest to feed my spiritual hunger. I accomplished the latter by traveling and learning about diverse topics including comparative religion, Western spirituality, theosophy and Judeo-Christian mysticism. At this point, the medical and spiritual aspects of my life continued to evolve into what became a crucial period in my journey.

The year 2010 marked the beginning of a major transition in my religious aptitude, as I was led to what would become my spiritual home and formally joined the Episcopal Church. And so, my spiritual calling gradually evolved and was more clearly defined as a path to ordained ministry combined with my work in healthcare. This combination would result in my becoming a "Doctor-Priest" with additional training in Pain Research, Education and Policy (PREP) at Tufts University School of Medicine, Department of Public Health and Professional Degrees in 2019 to complement my theological education.

For me, the church represented a sacred space where my relationship with God came fully alive. Through my early lay work in Bible study, in Eucharistic ministry and as a youth missionary leader, my soul found areas of sacred relationship, dynamic praise and prayerful contemplation, through which I could help build the body of Christ. Most importantly, I found my voice as a female Christian witness. As I progressed through insightful discernment of a call to Holy Orders, I decided to take a pause in my medical career in 2014. This a necessary, but bittersweet, decision to transition and seek formal theological training, according to the statutes of the Episcopal Church, so I may be a vehicle for God's grace in the sacramental work of priesthood.

As a physician, I have been as close as one can be to the extremes of existence: life and death, health and disease, hope and despair. In numerous instances, yearning to act within the fullness of spiritual service, I had felt powerless and longed to operate beyond the realm of physicality. I knew I wanted to step into the space where the lay ministry work inevitably stops and the grace of the Holy Orders begin to operate.

By entering seminary at Yale Divinity School from 2015 to 2018, I fulfilled my goals in a professional, spiritual and personal dimension. Professionally, I was able to build on my past vocation at an institution that afforded me a solid theological foundation to bring sacramental interventions into medical healing. Fully aware that the focus of my work would require the development of educational programs and restructuring of current medical approaches to the chronic care of patients, it was of utmost importance for me to train in an interdisciplinary academic program with access to a major medical center. From a spiritual standpoint, I found a university that provided outstanding formation in the Anglican tradition. From a personal standpoint, my seminary years gave me a deep sense of reassurance about the scholastic expertise and human caliber of the professional circle I was fortunate to become part of.

Soon in my early seminary sojourn, I was inspired to pursue the last piece of my life's vocational puzzle. In our society, by default, we focus our attention on those whose suffering is visible and obvious, the poor, the sick, the imprisoned and the homeless. We forget there are countless others who may appear privileged but also carry deep painful wounds, not necessarily physical but psychological and spiritual wounds. Wounds that are neither obvious nor visible. Many of those afflicted are wealthy, educated people from higher levels of society. These are people who could change the world for the better and help others less fortunate and yet, whose energy is self-centered due to their inner turmoil, who lack a sense of their own spirituality or who are simply unbelievers.

I always felt at the center of my calling was the voice of a higher power, pulling me to serve people who are suffering in silence, from physical, mental or spiritual pain. This group of people may be inadvertently neglected in healing ministries by virtue of their outward appearance, be it wealth, social status or education. I believe there is a higher calling to bring people back from their suffering and, thus, make our society stronger, healthier and spiritually reconnected. Being aware of the reality of pain and its impactful manifestations in our mindset, I believe the medical counterpart to the overall complement of suffering is best exemplified with the medical area of pain medicine.

Whom am I called to serve and why? I venture to answer with three propositions: *to heal, to teach and to reconcile with God*. My vision is an innovative approach to ordained ministry within the Episcopal Church and possibly other Christian denominations.

With my dual training in medicine and theology, I am well-positioned to conduct research at the intersection of religion and medicine, as well as to teach both physicians and clergy about the interplay of the physical, psychological and spiritual dimensions of healing. This plan included my creation of a church and academia research model that brings together healthcare professionals from the academic and theological worlds to work together to advance the healthcare field. Through implementation of this inclusive research model, regardless of a patient's religious background, the world of chronic suffering will gain a deeper understanding of innovative devotional interventions that will support and nurture a healthier and stronger spirit, and, thus, develop a new generation of healers.

Now in my 60s, I am inspired to recognize and highlight the one thing that, for me, is my real and authentic self: the awareness, since my youth, of being enamored by an incredibly intimate sense of God's reality. This journey of self-discovery is shaped by my faith with a spirit of authenticity that bridges my dual character, as physician and ordained minister of the Episcopal Church.

I know this collection of testimonies from and for my colleagues will either raise some eyebrows or draw either an "aha," "ahem" or "uhm" expressions. So, I invite my readers to instead try a reflective "hmm." We all harbor a seed of an inner life, an internal space that is so intimate, nobody, except that mysterious unnamable Creator essence, knows all too well. I am not seeking to convert anyone; I am inviting you to pause for a moment of self-intimacy and bask in your own transcendence. You may be surprised to discover you, too, have faith.

> "Contemplating, Lord, Thy hidden presence,
> grant me what I thirst for and implore,
> in the revelation of Thy essence
> to behold Thy glory evermore. Amen."
> —Translated from "Te adoro devote" hymn

The Rev. Dr. Marta Illueca graduated from the University of Panama School of Medicine in 1984 and specialized in pediatric gastroenterology at Weill-Cornell Medical College in New York, where she joined the faculty until 2003. She worked for the pharmaceutical industry in Delaware until 2014. Marta is a graduate from Berkeley Divinity School and the Episcopal Seminary at Yale University, and she was ordained to the priesthood in 2019. By supplementing her theological training with a master's degree in pain medicine from Tufts Medical School, she develops innovative programs for physicians and clergy on the spiritual dimensions of healing. She is the co-creator of a scientifically validated Pain-Related PRAYER Scale (PPRAYERS) in collaboration with experts from major academic centers. Dr. Illueca is spearheading a novel church and academia research model and publishes widely about spiritual pain.

CHAPTER 17

MEDICINE, MINISTRY, OR BOTH?

CHARLES HODGES, MD

This week I received an email that contained a familiar story and question. "Did you every struggle with going to seminary instead of medical school?" Have you ever been conflicted about whether you might have served God better in the pastorate instead of the clinic? The first word that came to my mind was, "Always."

As you read this, I am finishing my 50th year practicing medicine. At this end of the journey, I believe that I have been where I belong. Starting out, I was not at all certain that I had made the right choice.

I made up my mind to be a doctor at the tender age of eleven, having little idea of what that would mean. The year before I had thought of being an attorney. There was a TV program called "The Defenders" I watched. I had no idea what lawyers did, but mostly I liked the theme music. The next year Richard Chamberlain starred in "Dr Kildare," and I liked that music better. I then decided I would rather be a physician. That choice was constant through the rest of my child and teen-age years. I suppose it became an obsession.

At about the same time another choice was coming to my attention. My parents had started taking us to church, and in the process they and my younger brother had confessed Christ as their Lord and Savior. At the time I was not easily convinced. In the following years, I would do my best to appear as the dutiful obedient son, while striving to get away with as much mischief as possible. As I moved through adolescence, I grew in my quiet rebellion.

Throughout my childhood I attended church three times a week. I heard the sermons and understood the gospel. I just wasn't willing to give up what I thought was my chance to live as I pleased. This rebellion would continue until I completed high school and started college. I had worked hard at being a gold-plated hypocrite, but a choice I could not avoid was coming. The next year would be the most important in my life.

High School was never much of a challenge for me academically. I had to work, but when I applied myself, I could do well. College came as a shock. Suddenly I found that there wasn't a subject that I could coast in and get a decent grade. College required work, and I found that for some subjects like calculus, I was poorly prepared. I knew that getting into medical school required A's and I was struggling to get B's.

For the first time in my life, I was faced with the notion that I could fail. Just because I wanted to be Dr. Kildare, did not seem to make much difference to my professors, or the medical school admissions committees. By the spring of my freshman year, I was desperate. And then two choices in my life began to interact. As I struggled to make grades, I gradually became convinced that my lack of a sincere faith in Christ was responsible for my poor academic performance. I began to make deals with God. Somehow, I decided that if God would bless my grade point average, I would be a better person.

I signed up to teach Sunday School. I still feel sorry for the 4th grade boys I taught. I sang in the choir. I went to men's Bible study and fellowship. I quit habits that I believed were questionable. Finally, my Pastor rescued me from the pursuit of pharisaism. One Sunday morning, he told us that if we really wanted to improve our Christian life, we should read the Bible every year. If we read three chapters a day and four on Sunday, that would get us through in 12 months. Always looking for every legalistic, work-based advantage in my deal making with God, I was all in. But, I had no idea how much it was going to change my life.

I was working hard at reading my Bible every day and going to church three times a week, singing in the choir and teaching Sunday school. I seemed to be making some progress in my self-improvement program. Until, a fateful day in Introduction to Western Civilization, when one of my instructors, Professor Seldon, was teaching and said, "the Bible does not mention the Trinity."

I was eager to answer that statement, so, at the end of class, I made my way to her desk and showed her some verses that I believed substantiated that doctrine. She listened to my explanation and asked a simple question. "Why do you read the Bible?" At that moment, I had no good answer. I stumbled around and finally said something to the effect that I thought it was good for me. I walked away, but her question stuck in my mind. Why was I reading the Bible? Was it just a self-improvement program intended to gain God's blessing on my medical school plan's or was there something more to it? Regardless, I continued in my Bible reading.

Eventually, I made it to the Gospel of John and on the fifth day, I came to chapter 14 and for the first in my life, I saw Jesus Christ for who He was. Reading chapters 14 through 18 that evening was like Jesus speaking directly to me. I eventually saw myself just like Nicodemus in chapter 3, who needed to be born again. I finally understood that I could not work my way into heaven or God's favor. Eventually, that year, I confessed Jesus as my Lord, believed that God raised him from the dead, and for first time in my life, I was a Christian and not a pretender.

It would not be the end of conflicting choices for me. Having now become a Christian, I started to understand that the life I had been given did not belong to me, but to God who loved me and saved me. I began to weigh where I might serve God best. Was I really meant to be a physician, or should I go to seminary? That became the recurrent question that troubled me. By the grace of God, I made it into medical school. Regardless, always in the back of my mind, the question remained.

Having married my dear Helen after college, and finishing most of my graduate medical education, we moved to a small town in Indiana, where I began the practice of medicine. I still struggled with how to serve God best in life and practice medicine. I suspect at times my efforts were awkward, at best. Eventually, my brother finished graduate school to be a pastor and came to our town. Together, with a group of friends, we planted a church.

I found many ways to serve at church, but I still struggled to find how colds and runny noses meshed with sharing the gospel and God's grace. By the time I finished 10 years of small-town medicine and small-town life, I was looking for something more to do. So, I asked my brother/pastor what I might return to school to learn that would be useful to our church. His answer was "counseling".

Within the year, I enrolled in a graduate degree program that led to master's degree in counseling and, eventually, graduation from seminary. I became a part of the counseling and teaching staff for the counseling center at my current church. And there, I believe, I had finally found the purpose for which I was made.

With training in both counseling and medicine, the opportunities came to help counselees who were struggling with effects that medical problems can have on our thinking, emotions, and behavior. While the Bible is not a medical textbook, it gives us the guidance we need to respond to illness in a way that both glorifies God and is for our good. As a dear physician friend would often said, the Bible tells us how to be God's best patients.

At the same time, the training I received helped me as I sought to share the comfort that the gospel offers to patients who came to the office. I found that instead of struggling to find ways to share the gospel, God sent patients who were looking for the answers to life that are found in Scripture. I often have had the privilege of pointing patients to the Savior who says, "Come unto me!"

As time passed, I found that an important part of the work would be helping those with medical diseases that were being mistaken for emotional struggles. Patients who believed they were struggling with worry, sometimes were dealing with diseases such as hyperthyroidism, or episodes of a rapid heartbeat. Receiving an accurate diagnosis and effective treatment would be a relief to them.

Another part of my work is helping patients, counselees, and their loved ones understand the medical and spiritual implications of diagnoses such as schizophrenia, the mania of bipolar disorder, and obsessive-compulsive disorder. These diagnoses often result in real struggles and suffering, so having a good understanding of the diagnosis is vital. Finding the help and hope that the Bible offers for medical struggles gives both me and my patients great comfort.

The longer I practiced medicine and counseled the more I was impressed with the growing number of patients and counselees who were struggling with a prolonged sadness diagnosed as depression. It became an opportunity to help counselees see the difference between normal sadness over an identifiable loss, and that sadness with no ready explanation. Scripture offers great consolation to both groups, but it is important to help those affected to understand the difference.

Another question people often ask is "Would you do it again? Knowing what you know now, would you exchange eleven or more years of your life to have the privilege of practicing medicine?" The answer is "Absolutely yes!" The opportunities to share the good news of the Gospel are present in medicine and in the ministry. The audience may be different in the clinic and the pew at times, but the message they need to hear is the same. I would say to the young man, either profession is a good choice.

I now revel in this profession. I glory to think of Sir William Osler telling his students "Listen to your patient, He is telling you the diagnosis." [1] I have often paraphrased that quote for students and said that if you let a patient talk long enough, they will tell you what is wrong. I am in awe of Howard Kelly, the obstetrician, who would go to street corners on Saturday evenings and share the Gospel with the ladies of the night. His students were known to say, that he cared more for their souls than their education. I smile when I think of my anatomy professor, Dr. Shellhammer, who told me in my application interview to quit breaking bricks in karate because I might have something better to do with my hands. I am glad to have known Dr. John Heubi, who told me that I had chosen well to go into family medicine.

Mostly I am amazed and grateful that God allowed me to be both a counselor and a physician. I enjoy the opportunities He gives me to share the Gospel in both medicine and counseling. My answer to the young man is that "every day medicine offers great opportunities to minister to the spiritual and physical needs of others." After 50 years, it is still a good choice.

Charles D Hodges Jr MD is a family physician in Indianapolis, Indiana. He is a graduate of the Indiana University School of Medicine. He is a graduate of Liberty University with a master of arts in counseling and a graduate of Liberty Seminary with a master of arts in religion. Dr Hodges is a counselor/instructor at Faith Biblical Counseling Ministry in Lafayette, IN. He is the author of Good Mood, Bad Mood: Help and Hope for Depression and Bipolar Disorder. *He is the editor and contributor to the "Christian Counselors Medical Desk Reference" He is a licensed marital family therapist in Indiana. He and wife Helen have four children, 13 grandchildren and 2 great grandchildren.*

Notes

1. Electronically retrieved at goodreads.com. Sir William Osler MD and Howard Kelly MD are two of the founders of modern medical education.

CHAPTER 18

GOD USES EVERYTHING FOR GOOD!

DEBRA A. SCHWINN, MD

In many books, videos, and courses, spiritual leaders emphasize that the Godly life is one of descent. Specifically, one needs to die to self (a.k.a. ego, status, winning, success, judging) to truly find God and begin the journey of sharing love with every person one encounters. In other words, failure is necessary to truly succeed in a Godly sense. While development of the ego and boundaries such as right *versus* wrong are important for the first part of life, compassion and Godly growth is only attained in giving up these very successes over time, however counter-intuitive this seems.

I grew up in a midwestern family steeped in education. Unusual at the time, all four of my grandparents were college educated. While there was never any question of my going to university, the real question was, which one? My father was a perfectionist and expected his children to follow suit. One hot summer day, at the age of nine, my mother gave me a typing textbook for children and suggested I type 30 minutes each day in the basement, which was cool and therefore a reprieve from the summer heat of an un-air-conditioned home in Ohio. Our manual typewriter required precisely equal pressure on all keys to have the same depth of black ink on the page. This meant that one had to learn to smash down the pinkie finger with the exact same force as other fingers to make the printed page look professional. All corrections, at that time, were made with white chalk tape. Because my father often edited my essays, and I typed them from a very early age (age 10), his perfectionism resulted in me retyping each page in its entirely if there were more than 3 corrections. The outcome of this childhood experience was an expectation to be excellent in everything, as well as wanting to honor my mother by being among the first women in my fields of study. Talk about being driven!

Although God used music to bring me to faith in Christ at age 16, and I originally considered being a professional violinist, I pivoted in university to chemistry. I then felt called to be a physician-scientist early in my career. My sense was that this calling was to bring some light to the deep darkness that can sometimes exist in the upper echelons of academia. Outstanding education does not always result in enlightenment or transformation, hence my call, or so I thought.

Along the way I collected a strong pedigree of training institutions including the College of Wooster, Stanford, University of Pennsylvania, Duke, two major state universities (University of Washington, University of Iowa), and the National Institutes of Health (NIH). I trained with some of the best. I studied clinical cardiac anesthesiology alongside David Sabiston's surgeons at Duke; learned about medical education by participating in reforming the Duke medical school curriculum; helped lead the formation of Duke's Singapore medical campus; researched molecular pharmacology and biochemistry for 5 years with the 2012 Nobel laureate Bob Lefkowitz; and enjoyed a sabbatical at the NIH National Human Genome Research Institute during the year 2000, when the first human genome was sequenced. NIH funding is never easy to earn, so I felt fortunate to have been continuously NIH funded for laboratory or clinical investigation from 1989 – 2016. In addition to training numerous clinical and research fellows, residents, faculty, nurses, and technicians, I served on the Board of Trustees for several national and international organizations dedicated to training the next generation of cutting-edge academic physicians and scientists. I was admitted into the National Academy of Medicine in 2002 at the age of 45. These are all markers of success from the world's perspective, and I believed they gave me the "power" to do what God was calling me to do, although I still was not quite sure how I was supposed to shine "light" in academia. So, I did my best to be honest and as ethical as possible, worked hard, and valued my patients, colleagues, and trainees. However, in retrospect I continued to be a hard-driving individual who, to my amazement, my husband, Bob, puts up with me some days!

Along the way God was gracious and protected our faith by helping my husband and me stay associated with local churches, have Godly friends who took integration of work and faith seriously, and the usual humbling challenges of being parents of two daughters. While recognizing life was constantly out of balance with the extremes of academic medicine, I felt there was at least some balance of God, family, and our church community.

When I was called to be Chair of a very large clinical department at the University of Washington in Seattle in 2007, I spent several mornings in our church praying to discern whether this was the right move. After 22 years at Duke, Bob and I answered that call and moved to Seattle. It was energizing, and those five years were some of the most productive and successful of my career, this time putting faculty and department successes ahead of my own personal success. I learned a lot about leadership and change management. I viewed my role as Department Chair similar to being a pastor: I had been given a group of faculty and my job was to love them and to help each person flourish. God also graciously helped me find the Christian Discipleship & Direction Ministries of the Pacific Northwest where I spent two years being challenged in my faith through extra-curricular reading, retreats, spiritual direction, and wonderful Christian colleagues. I also completed Stephen Ministry training and ultimately was privileged to walk alongside a woman in the community for a few years who was struggling with life. Our time in Seattle felt blessed. Bob and I deepened friendships with several wonderful couples through a weekly small group Bible study where we shared our lives quite openly. Despite these blessings, upon deep reflection I felt restless. I increasingly suspected that my nervous system was wired to be like that of a racehorse – winning big stakes races over and over. My passion for our department, research, and academic medicine was deep, positive, and infectious, yet there was a dark underbelly of not being patient with those around me, especially when I was stressed. During these years I began to recognize that God calls us each to be like mares, satisfied with our lives and enjoying the sun, wind, and grass in the barn yard - not continually prancing and training to win the next race. However, I could not figure out how to transform from a racehorse to a mare. I wondered what was up.

Then I was called to be Dean of the Carver College of Medicine at the University of Iowa. What an amazing honor to be asked to lead a NIH-intensive college of medicine in a place that is highly collaborative and known for developing leaders. I have the greatest respect for the leaders and faculty at this unique midwestern academic medical center located within a strong, collaborative Big 10 university. Little did I know I was walking into a journey of descent. God was going to teach me to be a mare through an experience of the dark night of the soul.

I had a hard first several years. God has given me a unique gift of being able to see the potential of a situation. I can see the national and international context and then use the venue I am working in to develop that group to be a model for the future. I did this in my research programs at Duke and in my Department at the University of Washington. Very early I could see the potential at Iowa as well, with its very strong and collaborative medical and scientific faculty ready to be even stronger national leaders. So, I pushed for change to take advantage of that potential. Upon reflection, I now recognize that I did not listen to Chair and faculty responses that they were not quite ready to change (in fact, they were not sure they wanted to change at all, thank you!). I also did not have a clue when I started that the Dean is responsible for the mood of the college. When I discovered that funds I thought were available to jumpstart research had already been pledged to other commitments, I was not pleased. Others could feel that displeasure. Transitions in my office early on also did not deepen confidence or give me the support I needed to get feedback that is so important for a leader, especially Dean of a large academic medical center. In retrospect, I did not develop the deep relationships over my first few years that may have offset these negatives. I found this ironic since I normally work best one-on-one. I had made the mistake of deciding that as a female Dean I must be strong for everyone; I did that to such an extent that it felt as though I was "armored" (i.e., being more cautious, protected, and relationally closed, but out of fear). As I write this, it is almost too painful to read.

Having said this, there were many positives over this timeframe too, including transformation of the physician practice plan from losing millions each year to becoming quite profitable; this success took restructuring of the practice plan and moving our faculty toward working as a truly integrated group practice, rather than individual departments. Over my time as dean, we rolled out a highly innovative and successful new medical school curriculum, opened a new Children's Hospital, and created the cross-campus Iowa neuroscience institute. So, while there was "trouble in River City," it was a complex situation with solid wins and some losses.

With a new university president, the leadership of the healthcare system and medical school were merged, so I transitioned to become Associate Vice President for Medical Affairs which was not the original academic role I loved. This was devastating to me. Indeed, it was a very painful experience for someone who had been highly successful in the world's eyes. Yet, several years later I came to understand that perhaps I had been brought to Iowa for precisely this reason, to be put through a purifying fire that helped get rid of lots of extra dross (pride, impatience, armoring) that was covering what God recognized as my true self. For someone who had unwittingly tried to earn love all her life, it was also somewhat freeing to fail, since, oddly, this allowed me to drop the armor and begin to open myself to God at a deeper level, with the unexpected result of being able to be more compassionate in my dealings with people. In retrospect, I now understand that the key to being a great leader is to have the right combination of strength and vulnerability. I also shared my struggles with my husband (who was incredibly supportive), children, key Christian friends, a few people at work who were able to help, and, to a lesser extent, thought leaders on campus and across the country. I wanted to learn to lead with a combination of openness and strength. God provided amazing situations where such vulnerability was honored, which in turn has strengthened my leadership. There is also nothing like failure and humility to reset one's nervous system to be more like a mare than a racehorse. I found myself appreciating those who entered my path each day more deeply and heard amazing stories of sorrow from random individuals during that time that loaded my soul with empathy to the point that it was hard to get home at night due to all the weight. Through the process, I clung to my trusting that God was transforming me into one who has deeper Godly wisdom. This transformative experience (my dark night of the soul) led me ever closer to God.

The Bible speaks of a contrite heart and rejoicing in our suffering. Psalm 51:15-17 states, "O Lord, open my lips, and my mouth will declare your praise. For you will not delight in sacrifice, or I would give it; you will not be pleased with a burnt offering. *The sacrifices of God are a broken spirit; a broken and contrite heart, O God, you will not despise.*" In addition, Romans 5: 3-5 states: ...*we rejoice in our sufferings,* knowing that suffering produces endurance, and endurance produces character, and character produces hope, and hope does not put us to shame, *because God's love has been poured into our hearts through the Holy Spirit who has been given to us.* (Italics mine)

I have never been more radically open to God's will in my life than during this period. My husband and I had already moved out of our beloved home into an apartment because we sensed God was nudging us to move on. I developed a morning practice that was transformational. Over a period of 3 years, after reading scripture, I sat in silence with a candle burning in the early morning darkness for at least 30 minutes every day, simply meditating on Him, and imagining I was floating in God's love. For two years I heard nothing but silence, but then, one day, realized that I was different. God's unconditional love had gradually moved from my head to my heart and soul; His love for me had become embodied. Another year of sitting in silence each morning then ensued while I searched for a new job, until one day I was startled by distinctly hearing God say, "Am I not enough?" Wow. My response was, "Yes you are enough, Lord. I have had a wonderful career, so will stop my job search right away and be content knowing this is your path for me". What I heard next was equally startling, "No, your job search is your job for now; however, *practice* moving aside your ego and let me shine through you during every interview interaction this fall." By this time, I had no more vacation time due to my job search, so I needed to start working part-time to continue interviewing. Of note, during interviews (often in non-Christian settings) I would see people looking around the room searching for a reason that they felt different suddenly as if they felt touched somehow. This was so confirming that it led me to wonder if to "practice moving myself, my ago aside" meant I was being prepared for a skill that would be needed in the future. Toward the end of this period, I was asked to be President of a wonderful non-denominational Christian University on the intercoastal waterway in West Palm Beach, Florida, named Palm Beach Atlantic University (PBA). God had led me to my calling.

Moving from my position as Dean of an academic medical center to President of a Christian higher education institution was a fairly smooth transition because so many aspects of the jobs overlap. I love how faith and academics (with excellence) are beautifully intertwined in everything we do at our university. PBA's mission is to equip our students to *grow in wisdom, lead with conviction, and serve God boldly;* in other words, whole person education. Starting two weeks into the COVID pandemic, having both a clinical and science background was quite useful in keeping PBA open (through both prayer and science) for in-person education with lower COVID rates than our surrounding county. My spiritual journey has also been helpful. Indeed, the first pillar of our strategic plan is being mission-driven as a Christ-first university with excellence, and the 17 Fulbright awardees since 2018 attest to the quality of PBA's programs. Families and students are responding, with applications soaring. Given my personal experience from the difficult time described above, I recognize that recruiting leaders who can articulate their own crucible experiences results in more mature, spiritually deep, and compassionate members of the President's cabinet. I could not ask for a better preparation to be a university president in today's unique environment.

In summary, I recognize that *God uses everything for good!* As physicians, we are accustomed to success along the way (best in class in high school, university, medical school, residency, even career), because that is what it takes to succeed in medicine, especially academic medicine. It is a hard fall once we reach our limits (and we all will at some point) and "fail" at something. Yet God loves each of us so deeply, and it is in our being humbled that He finally gets our attention. Leaning into Him during such times allows us to be more radically open to His will. I am deeply grateful for the unique journey God has led me through. Thank you, Lord!

Debra Schwinn, MD has been President of Palm Beach Atlantic University (PBA; West Palm Beach, Florida) since May 2020. An accomplished innovator, physician scientist (MD, Stanford; clinical anesthesiology, University Pennsylvania; academic career, Duke University), and leader (department chair, University of Washington; medical school dean, University of Iowa), she has published more than 200 scientific manuscripts and is a member of the National Academy of Medicine. Tracing her spiritual journey from accepting Christ as a teenager through a successful academic career, Debra is quick to point out how life's most humbling moments (including times of suffering) are crucible moments with the potential to deepen faith, which can result in being more radically open to God and His call. Her key lesson is to note that, in the end, God uses everything for good!

CHAPTER 19

REAL RELATIONSHIPS

JEANNETTE E. SOUTH-PAUL, MD

When corporations are being launched and want to build their identity, they choose a motto to promote themselves and/or develop a mission statement. If I were launching myself as a corporate entity 40+ years ago, I would have selected a verse as my mission statement or motto – "I can do all things through Christ who strengthens me," Philippians 4:13. I embraced this spiritual assurance because I dreamed of joining a profession to which I had had very little exposure – no one in my family had ever earned a doctoral degree. I was part of the first generation to go to college but was so proud when my mother went to night school for nine years and walked down the aisle with me when we both graduated from the University of Pennsylvania. I had never had my own doctor or a medical home – if one of my siblings or I became ill, mom would look it up in the nurses' manual she bought to get suggestions regarding treatment. If one of my athletic brothers broke something and the limb was obviously displaced, then we went to the emergency department and prayed we could pay the bill. But we never knew anyone's name or felt at home in any medical environment

When choosing a career in medicine one can usually identify a person or event that motivated them to pursue the long and often arduous path that would lead them to become a physician. It has been interesting to see how those motivating people or events have changed during the more than four decades I have been privileged to serve since graduating from medical school. I was raised hearing many stories - usually recounted by my Jamaican immigrant father and mother - regarding the importance of tenacity to be successful, their determination for their children to have opportunities they did not have, their strongly held convictions, and their commitment to serving Jesus Christ.

The foundation of our lives, priorities, and dreams are developed very early and then retained, reshaped, and disseminated to all with whom we come in contact. My earliest memories were of beginning the day around the kitchen table before sunrise reading the Bible and having breakfast as a family of eight. Each of my five siblings and I learned to read by my mother holding our index finger and moving it from word to word in a Bible verse while repeating each word. She impressed upon us the importance of beginning the day in the Word. Such memories have anchored my day throughout my life and helped me focus on where I would find my strength for the day.

While we lived in an apartment above the Helping Hand Rescue Mission in Philadelphia, where my father was the superintendent as I began high school, I came face to face with a population that was struggling. All my assigned activities revolved around service – brewing coffee, making sandwiches, cooking hot meals on weekends to serve the (mostly) men who attended our gospel services, sorting clothes while running the thrift shop, or accompanying my father to pick up day-old pastries at the local grocery store to give to the gospel service attendees. I would talk to the men and hear their requests for medical care and how their feet or backs or legs hurt, but they would still walk from center city Philadelphia up town, across the Schuylkill River, and through the campuses of Drexel University and the University of Pennsylvania to get to Philadelphia General Hospital – the city hospital – seeking free medical care. I also heard the despondency and frustration when, at the end of the day, they might still not have been seen and would then walk back downtown to one of the handful of missions there, since that was where the only beds to accommodate the homeless could be found.

So, when I completed my undergraduate degree at Penn and received my acceptance to Pitt for medical school, I was laser focused on primary care in general, and family medicine, in particular because I wanted the broadest training possible to have the skills to care for any and every condition. As I look back on a myriad of clinical experiences, the most memorable are those rooted in building personal relationships. Through the busy years of medical school and residency, through sleepless nights on call in the days before duty hours requirements, and well before technology facilitated the gathering of patient data, I moved from one location to another, trying to balance the demands of life as a wife, a mother, a physician, an educator, a military officer, a daughter, and a sister, the thing that sustained and energized me was my belief in the power of the Lord to guide my daily walk and the reminders of this focus through patient's stories that I heard daily.

As one of only two females among the 36 residents of our military residency program and coming from a family who had never had access to medical care growing up, I wanted to demonstrate caring to my patients. I recall that eight of our twelve rotations as an intern were on either the internal medicine or family medicine inpatient services with chronically ill patients or those who were unlikely to survive. One night, I was on call (each intern usually carried 12 to 15 patients), and called to see a woman with metastatic breast cancer who was still struggling after 2 weeks of hospitalization. We got to know each other because she was assigned to me, having been in the hospital before I came on service. When I was on call, I found myself checking on her more than once during the night. On a particularly busy evening one of the housekeeping staff pulled me aside and asked if he could mention something to me privately. I stepped into a corner with him, and he said, "I know how important your patients are to you. Please step into room 10 – I think that patient needs you." I felt compelled because a member of the housekeeping staff was so concerned about a patient that he sought assistance and the fact that it was my patient in room 10. When I walked into her room, she said how much she appreciated seeing me and asked if I would spend a few minutes with her. In my frequent visits to her room, I realized I had never seen any family members, so I would sit next to her bed to talk. Though I had very little to offer her therapeutically, she seemed so comforted by our regular 10 minutes of conversation and my efforts to make her feel special. She passed away a day later but seemed so at peace. I don't actually remember speaking with her of spiritual things, but I wanted her to know she was more than a room number to me.

Some of my most treasured experiences were caring for women throughout their pregnancies, delivering their children, and then caring for the entire family– something I have always appreciated about my training in family medicine. One particular woman came to me for care at the beginning of her second trimester. I was convinced she disliked me intensely but could not determine why. I would walk into the exam room and greet her, ask how she was doing, and she said very little other than "Ok." Invariably, my next question would be, "You're still smoking, aren't you?" She'd look at the wall and that would end the conversation. I would go through the rest of my exam, provide my assessment of how she seemed to be doing, and ask her to schedule her next visit. I couldn't get her to open up until she went into labor. I always tried to arrive on the Labor & Delivery unit shortly after the nurses notified me of an admission so I could support my mothers during their labor. I saw a man sitting in the corner of the labor room whom I did not recognize. My patient said he was her husband. For the next 30 minutes he said nothing and did not come near his wife, although she was becoming increasingly uncomfortable. We could not offer epidurals at my military facility at that time. Not being shy, I turned to him and instructed him to come stand at his wife's bedside, wipe her forehead, give her ice chips, rub her back - do something to show you appreciate how much pain she is experiencing! Fortunately, she did well and delivered a healthy baby girl. My patient continued to see me for a few more months, until she was transferred out of the area. She returned 3 years later, having divorced her husband, and asked if she could return to my practice. I told her I was shocked because I thought she did not like me. She said the only thing she did not like was my constantly referring to her smoking. Her husband had been physically abusive to her, regularly stole her cigarettes, and would then taunt her about it, making her guess where they were. She subsequently remarried and had triplets, one of whom she named after me. When I retired from the Army, she asked if we could stay in touch, and I said of course. Twenty-eight years after we first met, she continues to send multiple texts weekly, we share Bible verses, and she asks me to pray for her as she struggles with parenting issues. I have helped her in dealing with the death of one of her children, aided her as she served as a caregiver for her mother with dementia, and walked with her in other challenges in her life. Again, I don't remember when we first started speaking of spiritual things, but it was years after we first met and through those rocky moments in between.

A colleague and I helped create the first Federally Qualified Health Center (FQHC) based at an academic health center (AHC) in Pittsburgh at a time when the federal government was piloting a model of allowing AHCs to be the primary sponsor, rather than a community entity serving as a sponsor. After more than 15 years, a small team of family physicians, social workers, nutritionists, clinical pharmacists, and dentists were able to provide what we now call a "whole health" model of care. I was able to provide personalized continuity of care for 15 to 18 pregnant women annually, many of whom were adolescents. When I saw the struggles of these teen mothers, I started a mentoring program for these adolescents and identified older female mentors (we called them "Maikurus," meaning the wise women of the village in the southern African Shona language). We met weekly one night each week, served dinner in our department conference room, provided baby sitters, and had discussions, over dinner, on such varied topics as self-esteem, spirituality, parenting, contraception, job interviewing, intimate partner violence, and money management. Our team of volunteer Maikurus, graduate and medical students, ran this program for more than 11 years and spent many hours listening to these young women reveal life's challenges and learn to be responsible parents to their children. When I announced my retirement from the University of Pittsburgh, the clinical team who had worked with me for almost two decades organized a luncheon at our health center, especially for my senior citizens. Their rationale was that these seniors were unlikely to have such a long and personal relationship with a physician again and should have some dedicated time with me in honor of my retirement. Two hours before the luncheon was scheduled our front desk manager called me and said one of my younger patients was up front and wanted to speak to me, since she needed to go to work and could not come back later. She had heard about the luncheon for the seniors but wanted to come since I had cared for her for so much of her life. When I came out to the desk she was standing there with a bright gift bag, balloons, and wearing her professional scrub uniform and carrying an envelope with a letter she had handwritten to me. She wanted me to read her letter while she was there and after reading the first three lines we were both crying and hugging each other. What did she write – "you took care of me when I got pregnant at 17, you encouraged me through the pregnancy, you sat by me when I was in labor by myself, you listened when I said I didn't know how to raise a child, and you saw me again and again or we spoke on the phone, you encouraged me to go back to school so I could take care of myself and the baby, and you helped me grow from being a girl to becoming a self-sufficient woman. I knew you cared about me just as I was!"

In addition to cherishing my time caring for my patients, I was a department chair, served on committees, helped create and then co-chaired a physician diversity and inclusion council for the health system, served on a community research advisory board, but felt like I was working all the time. When you are that busy you rarely have time to reflect on what you have been doing, or to determine a vision of who you want to be next. Your goal is to maintain the highest quality in everything you do. So, you can imagine my surprise when one of the health system leaders called to say that the local seminary had reached out to the health system CEO to ask whether he could send a faculty member to represent the academic health center at a pastoral counseling conference they were sponsoring to spotlight the value of embracing spirituality in the care of those in need. The health system leadership team had determined I was the person who should represent the health system in this discussion of spiritual matters. I could not remember having any particularly momentous spiritual conversations with the leadership but realized the Lord had provided me an opportunity to speak of Him to the community. The additional incentive was that the visiting speaker was Dr. Tony Campolo, a sociologist and minister whom I remember being a visiting faculty at the University of Pennsylvania when I was an undergraduate student. To this day, I remember the hundreds of students who had flocked to his introduction to sociology course and exclaiming what a dynamic speaker he was and how he shaped their thinking about people and society. So, as I saw him sitting in the front row of the seminary the day of the conference to listen to me present my talk, I said I wanted to thank him publicly for showing me, as an undergraduate student, how important it is to live your faith every day in your professional life. You might not know who is watching, but must rest in knowing the Lord will be pleased to see you model Him to others! Forty-two years after completing my residency, whether I know their faith beliefs or not, I still try to encourage those around me to remember they are not alone, and that part of their mission as health care professionals should be to assure those for whom they care of the divine presence amidst their struggles, and to represent the Lord in their lives.

> [3] *For though we live in the world, we do not wage war as the world does.* [4] *The weapons we fight with are not the weapons of the world. On the contrary, they have divine power to demolish strongholds.* [5] *We demolish arguments and every pretension that sets itself up against the knowledge of God, and we take captive every thought to make it obedient to Christ.*
>
> 2 CORINTHIANS 10:3-5 (NEW INTERNATIONAL VERSION)

Dr. Jeannette E. South-Paul joined Meharry Medical College as the Executive Vice President and Provost in December 2021. Prior to this appointment, she was the Andrew W. Mathieson UPMC Professor and Chair of the Department of Family Medicine at the University of Pittsburgh School of Medicine from 2001 – 2020, retiring from Pitt in 2020. Prior to joining the Pitt faculty, she served as a Medical Corps officer in the U.S. Army, retiring in 2001, while serving as Chair of Family Medicine at the Uniformed Services University of the Health Sciences and previously as Vice President for Minority Affairs at the same institution Dr. South-Paul has served in leadership positions in the Society of Teachers of Family Medicine (STFM), the American Academy of Family Physicians (AAFP), the Association of American Medical Colleges (AAMC), and the Association of Departments of Family Medicine (ADFM) to include serving as President of the Uniformed Services Academy of Family Physicians (USAFP) and the STFM. After more than 10 years of service as a member of the Meharry Medical College Board of Trustees, Dr. South-Paul stepped off the Board to begin her new leadership role. She is excited to collaborate with the academic leaders of the five Meharry schools: Medicine, Dentistry, Graduate Studies, Applied Computational Sciences, and Global Health. She is a member of the National Academy of Medicine, the Gold Humanism Society, and the Alpha Omega Alpha Medical Honorary Society

CHAPTER 20

ON THE POWER OF STAYING

WARREN KINGHORN, MD, ThD

When I was a first-year medical student, our CMDA campus minister was expelled from my medical school's campus. It was a rough start to my life as a Christian in academic medicine. But it taught me a great deal about what Christian faith is really about.

I arrived at Harvard Medical School in fall 1997 as a Southern Baptist who had never lived for more than a few weeks outside of upstate South Carolina. Filled with stereotypes about the godlessness of both the North in general and of the Ivy League in particular, I was not sure whether I would find any other Christians in my medical school class.

I was wrong to be worried. The Christian Medical and Dental Associations (CMDA) group at Harvard was a small but vibrant, diverse, and thriving community. At my undergraduate college in South Carolina, the Christian student group in which I participated was comprised of mostly white and, mostly southern, evangelical protestants. The CMDA group at Harvard, in contrast, was my first close encounter with the global church. The students who participated regularly were Protestant, Catholic, and Orthodox; Black, Asian, and White; international and American; children of immigrants from Nigeria, Egypt, China, Greece, and many other places. Holding the group together was Bill Pearson, a warm-hearted, white evangelical who attended medical school in Georgia for a year before hearing a call from the Holy Spirit to focus his life less on doctoring and more on mentoring and encouraging other Christians in medicine. Bill worked as an instructor in the gross anatomy lab, regularly met students for lunch and coffee conversations, led our weekly Bible studies, and invited us to share in the life of his home and family.

Like me, Bill was a southern evangelical—but he was not like some of the Christian physicians I had met in South Carolina. Like them, Bill encouraged us to develop regular rhythms of prayer and Bible study and to think as Christians about hot-button ethical issues like abortion and physician-assisted suicide. But he also encouraged us to ask deeper, more structural questions. He would observe that we were in the middle of one of the world's pre-eminent academic medical communities: Boston's Longwood Medical Area, where Harvard Medical School and several of its affiliated teaching hospitals are located. The Longwood Medical Area is a dense urban cluster of gleaming research and clinical towers that was larger than the entire downtown of the South Carolina city in which I had lived. Look around you, Bill would say. There is immense power, privilege, and prestige here. But what is it all for? Modern medicine is immensely powerful. But is its power being exercised for the good? Could it be that medicine functions as a power in the New Testament sense (1 Cor 15:20-28, Eph. 6:12), as a good, but fallen, structure that might serve sinful ends? What would it mean, Bill asked, for medicine to be redeemed and oriented toward the kingdom of God?

I was enthralled. I had spent my undergraduate years immersed in debates between conservative evangelicals and protestant liberals, secretly wondering if Christian faith was strong and deep enough to withstand the challenges of modern science and medicine. But now, as a student at one of modern medicine's most celebrated institutions, I found myself surrounded by witnesses who were sounding the Gospel's depths. Some of my CMDA classmates began working closely with the Catholic liberationist physician Paul Farmer, who would teach and practice at Harvard when he was not in Haiti, Rwanda, Peru, or other parts of the world. Others desired to contribute to the empirical religion-and-health research literature. Still others focused on becoming excellent clinicians and classmates. At the center of all this activity was Bill, unapologetically encouraging us to center our lives and careers on the kingdom of God. Harvard was not the godless place I had feared. It was where I was learning what it meant to be a Christian.

All of that, however, would soon be challenged.

In February of my first year of medical school, our CMDA group invited, to speak on campus, Dr. Carolyn Klaus, a physician who founded and ran a Christian health center in an underserved area of Philadelphia. Bill and several physicians who were connected to our CMDA group knew and respected Dr. Klaus. At any rate, we reasoned, if the Gospel mattered for the work of medicine, it involved caring for people on the margins and who often fell through the cracks of market-driven American health care. We invited our medical school's Black and Latino student organizations to co-sponsor the event, and titled the event "Challenges in Caring for the Urban Underserved: Lessons Learned in Latino North Philadelphia." It was a neutral title, we thought, that would draw a large crowd—and hopefully those who came would learn something about Christian faith as well as about health care.

The sizable crowd who attended Dr. Klaus' talk heard her speak at length of the challenges of providing medical care in an urban neighborhood with high rates of poverty, violence, chronic illness, and lack of health insurance. She shared compelling stories and clinical wisdom. She also paused around the midpoint of her talk to say (as I remember), "A lot of people ask why we continue to do this work, when it is so hard. We do it because we believe that every human being is made in the image of God and deserving of love and care, and we do it because we believe that the Holy Spirit has told us to do it. That is why we are still doing this." She then resumed her talk.

A few days later, a senior administrator at the medical school called Bill into his office. There had been some complaints about Dr. Klaus' lecture. Some students—Bill never learned who—had felt blindsided by the introduction of theology into a talk about community health care. Their discomfort with the talk, moreover, reflected their discomfort with Bill himself—his open talk of Jesus, his frequent presence on campus for conversation with students, his evangelistic spirit. For this administrator, it was too much. Bill would no longer be welcome as an anatomy instructor. Moreover, the administrator asked Bill not to set foot on the campus of the medical school again. Bill's openly Christian commitments, he was told, had no place in a multicultural environment like Harvard.

I was a student, and rightly or wrongly I avoided any personal adverse consequences from the talk, which I had helped to plan and advertise. But I was horrified by what had happened to Bill. For Bill, it was a potentially devastating blow. He had moved with his young family from Georgia to Massachusetts less than two years previously, following God's call, and now was barred from the very institution that he felt called to serve. It was bad enough that he was fired from his lab instructor role, which provided some needed income. But to be banned from campus threatened his ability to connect with the students who were at the center of his work. How could Bill minister to students if he was persona non grata at the medical school? With other students, I appealed to the administrator on Bill's behalf, but to no avail. The decision was made. I worried that Bill and his family would leave Boston. I also worried that perhaps Harvard was not a hospitable place to be a Christian after all.

But Bill didn't leave. God had called him to Boston, he reckoned, and that call had not changed just because he had run afoul of the medical school administration. So, he continued the work he had been called to do. He didn't come to campus to meet students for lunch and coffee, but he did continue to invite us to his home and to meet off-campus. We resumed our weekly Bible studies. Things were hard, but our small CMDA group was surviving. And so was Bill.

About a year later, as I was finishing my second year of medical school, the same administrator who had banned Bill called me into his office. The administrator told me that he had reconsidered. He now believed that his previous response had been too severe. He apologized to me, and told me that he had spoken with Bill, had invited him to teach again in the anatomy lab, and had invited him to return to campus without any restrictions. The immediate crisis was over, but I had learned lessons that have formed my life and career since that time.

It has now been more than 25 years since Bill was banned from Harvard Medical School. Both of our lives have moved on since then. Now, Bill is also a medical school professor, leading innovative educational work at a different medical school. I am now a psychiatrist and theological ethicist who understands those events of 1997-1998 as an important inflection point in my spiritual life. Given the tensions in our culture both then and now, it would have been easy for Bill's story at Harvard to have ended with his expulsion from campus. He could have packed up and returned with his family to the South. If he had wanted to do so, I'm sure that he could have become an evangelical culture-war hero. I can imagine the headlines: Christians Not Welcome at Harvard Medical School. No Free Speech at Harvard. Those headlines could be written today.

But that is not what happened. Bill stayed. And in his staying, I learned four powerful lessons.

First, I learned about the power of faithful witness. To be clear, as he would say then and now, Bill is not Jesus. He makes mistakes and is a flawed human being, as am I. But at a pivotal time in my life, when I was a first-year medical student wondering if and how the gospel mattered, Bill showed me what it meant to lean so strongly on the truth of Jesus that he was willing to lay his career and financial security on the line. I realized, as never before, that Christianity is not a set of moral values or spiritual principles for living. Either Jesus has been raised in the flesh, or he has not. Either death rules, or it does not. Either the kingdom of God is worth everything, or it is not (Matt. 13:44-45). By staying and focusing on his call, Bill was a witness to me. He was Barnabas—a son of encouragement—to me (Acts 4:36). I began to want more and more for my own faith to be at the center of not just my personal life, but of my clinical and academic lives, as well. In my third year of medical school, when I began to consider a small act of courage of my own—leaving medical school for two years to pursue seminary training—Bill again encouraged me. It is worth it, he said. The kingdom of God is worth every part of your life.

Second, I learned the power and necessity of truthfulness and transparency. I do not believe that the Harvard administrator's reaction toward Bill was just or appropriate. Bill had done nothing wrong. Eventually, even the administrator realized that. But I do regret my own complicity in the decision not to clearly and transparently advertise Dr. Klaus' lecture as a talk by a Christian physician that would include a description of her Christian faith. If the Gospel is powerful and healing and true, it does not need to be hidden under a bushel (Matt. 5:14-16). There is no need to use stealth or deception to lure people into a position where they will encounter it. If some non-Christian students felt blindsided by Dr. Klaus' talk of her Christian faith, that was not Dr. Klaus' responsibility, but it was partly mine. To this day, I regret that for these objecting students, the talk may have functioned not as a gateway to faith but as a skandalon, a stumbling-block, to it (Rom. 14:13). I learned from that experience, as Paul exhorted the Thessalonians, to be "children of light and children of the day" (1 Thess. 5:5). If your Christian commitments affect the way you approach work in medicine, then say it! Be transparent and truthful. People may hear your words and reject them. But they will not feel deceived.

Third, I learned the power of loving a place and its people over a prolonged period of time. Bill did not stop loving Boston, Harvard, or our student community when he was dismissed from campus. Instead, he took seriously the call to "seek the welfare of the city where I have sent you into exile, and pray to the Lord on its behalf, for in its welfare you will find your welfare" (Jer. 29:7). And out of the roots of that commitment, out of his decision to stay, incredible shoots of faith in action grew. Before long, our CMDA student group had adopted a new name, the "Longwood Christian Community." In the years after I graduated from Harvard, and thanks to the hard work and leadership of Michael and Tracy Balboni and others, the Longwood Christian Community grew from a student group to a residential intentional Christian community dedicated to "ministering to healthcare trainees and professionals who strive to integrate their faith and the practice of medicine and health sciences."[1] It continues to exist a quarter-century later, and has now nurtured generations of Christian clinicians, researchers, and scholars. Some of the most distinguished Christian scholars and leaders in academic medicine today—scholars who are now speaking at CMDA national meetings, leading major health agencies, writing articles in peer-reviewed medical and public health journals, and shaping entire fields—were formed within the Longwood Christian Community. The younger Theology, Medicine, and Culture Initiative at Duke Divinity School, which I co-direct, has been deeply shaped and formed in important ways by the Longwood Christian Community. Of course, there are challenges today to being Christian at Harvard or Duke. But there are also incredible, faithful Christian scholars and practitioners who have chosen to stay and seek the good of these cities and institutions.

Fourth, and finally, I learned about the power and presence of the Holy Spirit. It has taken me a long time, but I now understand that when as a Christian I enter complex, mostly-secular institutions like Harvard or Duke, I am not alone. The Holy Spirit is already there, working. The Spirit is working in the hearts of students and faculty who long for wholeness and healing but do not know where to find it, or seek to find it in the idol of modern biomedicine. The Spirit was working in the heart of the administrator who banned Bill and who then repented of his decision. The Spirit is working in the colleagues with whom we work and in the patients for whom we care. As pastoral theologian Andrew Purves has put it, Christians are not little Jesuses who bear the responsibility for saving and redeeming the world on our own. Rather, through baptism and sanctification, Christians are invited to participate in the saving and redeeming work of God in Christ that did not start with us, will not end with us, and ultimately does not depend on us. It is God's work, not ours. We are only part of the story, and there is great joy and freedom in that.[2]

Bill and his wife recently visited North Carolina, where I now live. We stood together in the warm late-afternoon sunlight of Duke Gardens in the late spring, speaking about all of the remarkable people whom we knew in common during my four years at Harvard. I thought later about the apostle Paul's comment to the Corinthian Christians that he did not need a physical letter of recommendation for his ministry because "you yourselves are our letter, written on our hearts, known and read by everyone. You show that you are a letter from Christ, the result of our ministry, written not with ink but with the Spirit of the living God, not on tablets of stone but on tablets of human hearts" (1 Cor 3:2-3).

Bill would be too modest to say this, but those remarkable people, at least in part, are Christ's letter of recommendation for his ministry. I too am his letter. I am glad that he stayed.

Editor's Note: Because it adds to the impact of the chapter, the author has asked, and received, permission from everyone named to use their names. This is the only chapter in this book in which the exception has been granted.

Warren Kinghorn is Associate Professor of Psychiatry at Duke University Medical Center, Esther Colliflower Associate Professor of the Practice of Pastoral and Moral Theology at Duke Divinity School; Co-director of the Theology, Medicine, and Culture Initiative at Duke Divinity School, and a staff psychiatrist at the Durham VA Medical Center. He is author of Wayfaring: A Christian Approach to Mental Health Care (Eerdmans, 2024).

Notes

1. Longwood Christian Community, *https://lccboston.org*.
2. Andrew Purves, Reconstructing Pastoral Theology: A Christological Foundation (Louisville, KY: Westminster John Knox Press, 2004).

CHAPTER 21

Trusting God as a Good and Loving Father

Richard M. Allman, MD

The Gospel Changes the Course of My Life

This is a story of how Jesus Christ called a boy whose father died before his second birthday into a relationship with God, the Heavenly Father. As the boy became a man and he grew in this relationship, the Lord continued to guide and make it possible for him to become a husband, a father, an academic physician, a senior executive for Veterans Affairs (VA), and then, in retirement, serve as a coach for healthcare leaders nationwide. This is a testimony of how God has been a good and loving Father to that man. This is my story. I pray it will inspire your trust in the Lord.

A neighbor invited me to attend church services when I was in 7th grade. I then attended weekly worship and youth services regularly. As I came to believe the truth of the gospel, I was increasingly burdened with the sense of my sinfulness and my need for a Savior. I told God that it would be hard to be a follower of Christ since my mom and stepdad were not believers. However, at the end of a worship service in March 1968, I accepted Jesus Christ as my Savior and Lord, praying for the Lord to forgive my sin. I became a new person, committed to following Christ, and being a witness before my family, and doing whatever was required of a Christian. Everything was different after that.

Calling as a Physician and Husband

When I was in ninth grade, I began praying for guidance about what I should do with my life. I felt that the best way for me to serve the Lord and help others would be to become a physician. Subsequently, I studied hard and excelled academically. After graduating high school, I pursued a biology degree at West Virginia University (WVU). I was accepted into medical school after completing courses required for a biology degree. My first year of medical school classes then counted as the elective courses needed to get a bachelor's degree in May 1977. I was married a month later.

Four years earlier, I had met my wife, Connie, at a church worship service the first Sunday I was on the WVU campus. We became best friends, both serving in the music and youth ministries of the church. We studied together and spent most of our free time together. Connie and the Lord worked together to make it clear that I needed her to be my wife!

Calling to an Academic Career as a Physician Researcher

After graduating medical school, I stayed at WVU Hospital for a residency in internal medicine. I began praying and asking the Lord to guide my next career steps. Supervising faculty members inspired my desire to pursue an academic career, leading me to accept a research fellowship at Johns Hopkins Hospital.

During the fellowship, I once again prayed for the Lord to guide the search for a job. During this time, I had a crisis of identity. I learned that if I wanted a research career in medicine, I would need to focus most of my effort doing research. However, I had initially thought that my career would primarily involve direct, hands-on, patient care.

As I explored job opportunities, I realized that by conducting patient-oriented research and serving as an academic physician educator, I could potentially have a greater impact than if I focused exclusively on patient care. I accepted an offer to join the faculty of the University of Alabama at Birmingham (UAB) School of Medicine, with eighty-percent protected time to develop a research program.

On a house-hunting visit to Birmingham, my wife and I worshiped at a small, but growing church, and, after the services, went to lunch with a private-practice Christian physician and his family. These interactions further confirmed that the Lord was leading us on an academic career journey.

Pursuing an Academic Career

I started my faculty position at UAB in July 1986 as a generalist, expressing an interest in geriatric medicine. Both the chair of medicine and the President of the University had made the development of programs in geriatrics a priority. Since my interests aligned with the institutional priorities at that time, I am confident God was guiding my career decisions.

The expectation was that I would receive grant funding to support my research within three years of my faculty appointment. During my first year on the faculty, I applied for several grant awards that were not funded. I also applied to be the principal investigator for a four-site study of cardiovascular disease in older adults. The application scored well and UAB was selected for a site visit.

We subsequently were asked for "just-in-time" information from the NIH program office. Such information is generally not requested unless a study is going to be funded. Months later, I got a telephone call from the program officer who had been responsible for coordinating study reviews. She told me that UAB was ranked fourth among grant applicants and should be funded; however, senior leadership at NIH had said the recruitment of minority older adults we had proposed would be impossible, and therefore, another site would be funded.

The program officer indicated that she was resigning her position from NIH because of this decision by her supervisors, and that UAB should protest the decision. Senior leaders from UAB sent a letter protesting the decision but informed me that funding from NIH was too important for them to pursue any other actions that might alienate NIH leadership. I finally did obtain a five-year NIH grant in 1988, early in my third year of a faculty appointment. These early experiences in seeking research funding made it clear that peer-review processes and leadership decisions in academic medicine were not always going to be objective, fair, or based on my perceptions of right and wrong.

ACCEPTING LEADERSHIP ROLES

About the same time that I received grant funding, I was appointed to search committees for a director of a new division of Geriatrics and for a university-wide Center for Aging. After two failed nationwide searches, I was appointed as the division director in October 1990 and as the center director in April 1992. Initially, the Division only consisted of nine faculty that included seven members in a research group focusing on the basic understanding of lipid structure and function. The need for faculty members to support the development of patient care, education, and research programs in geriatrics prompted me to pray for help from the Lord. Each faculty recruitment involved multiple phone calls, hosting visits with candidates, obtaining feedback about the candidates, and then follow-up as needed.

I found that developing and leading a highly functional division within an academic medical center can be quite challenging. Individual faculty members often have personal priorities that do not support a well-balanced and integrated program of patient care, education, and research. Faculty members who focus on clinical care or education can feel like they are not as appreciated as research-focused faculty; while those who are dependent on grants for funding feel like their jobs are not secure. Administrative support staff often do not understand how critical their roles are in supporting the overall mission of the Division. Resource limitations and changes in leadership at higher levels can make program development and maintenance difficult. Despite these challenges, recruitment efforts were successful resulting in a division of more than fifty faculty members with four sections: Geriatric Medicine, Palliative Care, Social-Behavioral Science, and Basic Science.

SPIRITUAL RENEWAL IN THE CONTEXT OF DIFFICULTY

Thankfully, the Lord provided friends and resources during these times of professional difficulty to seek Him more fervently. In the early 1990's Promise Keepers, the Christian men's movement, began stadium events that were attended by thousands of men. After participating in the large worship events, Promise Keepers emphasized the importance of men meeting regularly in small groups to encourage and support each other to grow spiritually.

After returning home from one of the Promise Keeper meetings, a physician friend called me asking if I would be willing to meet weekly with him and one other Christian faculty member as part of an accountability group. I eagerly agreed. Such small group meetings became a key component of my spiritual development. The members and the size of the groups have changed over time, but the focus has remained on the application of Scriptural truth to real life situations.

In 1995, my small group studied a book entitled, *Point Man – How a Man Can Lead His Family*. (1) Steve Farrar argued that most people remain immature in their faith because they suffer from spiritual anorexia – they are not regularly meditating on the Word of God – the Bread of Life. Moreover, others who may do some Bible reading, suffer from a spiritual bulimia; such people know the commands of Scripture but ignore them. Farrar also introduced the concept of describing prayer as "aerobic kneeling." He argued that prayer is to the soul what exercise it to the body. He stated, "The man who studies the Bible without praying will develop a good mind with a cold heart. The man who prays without knowing Scripture will consistently pray outside the will of God, for that is where His will is revealed." Today, as in the past, the primary way God speaks is through the Bible.

The Holy Spirit used these concepts to convict me of my self-righteousness and prompted me to pray and study the Bible daily. I began the practice of reading through the entire Bible annually, a practice I have continued most of the last thirty years. I realized that I had previously studied the Bible so I could appear intelligent before others. Getting to know God better became the motivation for my study of Scripture and for praying.

My spiritual growth was also fostered by changing membership to a large church that focused on Bible-based teaching and preaching, evangelism, and missions. During the first year of attendance at this church, I regularly experienced a sense of conviction about my sins of pride and self-righteousness at almost every worship service. This led to repentance and a deepening commitment to the Lord.

The Lord also led me to start going on short-term mission trips. My first such mission was in 2004, when my wife and two sons (ages 22 and 19 at the time) participated in a choir mission trip to Northern Ireland. I have subsequently gone on mission trips to Mexico, China, Romania, Jordan, and North Macedonia. Most of these have included a medical component as well as support of evangelism and church planting efforts. These mission trips have inspired me by providing the opportunity to meet brothers and sisters in Christ who have been true to the Lord, despite their many difficulties that include persecution by government and religious authorities. The believers in the host countries have given testimonies of miraculous answers to prayer. By returning to the same area multiple times over several years, I have seen the impact of the gospel on individuals, families, and whole communities.

In 2008, Jack Parker, who had been serving in Eastern Europe as a Cru (formerly Campus Crusade for Christ) member, moved to the Birmingham area to start a ministry focusing on supporting Christian faculty members at secular universities, like UAB. Jack became my mentor, and we worked with several other faculty members to support the development of a Christian Faculty Society. We met monthly for lectures by faculty that focused on how one integrates Christian faith into research, teaching, or service activities. Ultimately, these meetings attracted 20-30 participants, and gave us all the opportunity to identify fellow believers within the University with whom we could pray and thereby support each other to serve as ambassadors for Christ in an increasingly difficult mission field.

BLESSINGS, LIFE-TRANSITIONS, AND CHALLENGES

Blessings, life transitions, and challenges increased as my wife and I assumed caregiving responsibilities for aging family members and our two sons grew beyond their teenage years. In 2000, my mother, at the age of 77, was diagnosed with Alzheimer's Disease and had to move from West Virginia to Birmingham, Alabama, so Connie and I could care for her until her death, three years later. Connie's father died in 2009, at which time my 86-year-old mother-in-law also moved from West Virginia and lived with us.

My older son, Justin, graduated from high school in 2001 and finished an undergraduate degree in physics from George Tech University in 2004. While in Atlanta, GA, he met Kate, a student at Emory University, who became our daughter-in-law when they married in 2005. They subsequently blessed us with a granddaughter in 2011 and a grandson in 2015.

Our younger son, Philip, began abusing alcohol during his freshman year of high school. In the middle of his junior year, he stopped drinking and began leading Bible studies in the basement of our home. He said that "God had changed his life." Sadly, he began drinking heavily again and demonstrating aberrant behaviors when he started college. He responded well to a one-month substance abuse rehabilitation program and finished an undergraduate degree in philosophy in 2010 and a master's degree in philosophy three years later.

In 2013, the Lord led me to accept a position in the headquarters of the Veterans Affairs in Washington, DC as the head of policy and planning for Geriatrics and Palliative Care. Two weeks before the move to the DC Metro Area in January 2014, I fell down a set of stairs and broke my right ankle. My mother-in-law fell the morning of the move and broke her right shoulder. Thus, Connie was the only fully functional adult at the time of our move. These experiences reinforced our understanding that even when following the Lord's guidance, we can experience difficulties. He will never leave or forsake us and will provide the strength to persevere through the challenges.

We gradually settled into our new home and the DC area; we transferred our church membership to a wonderful congregation there. Connie's mother and I recovered from our broken bones, and I started my daily 45-minute Metro commute into Washington, DC.

Connie's mother became increasingly frail and fell and fractured her hip in February 2015. Despite responding well to rehabilitation, my mother-in-law began developing symptoms of heart failure. She died in her sleep five months later.

Four months later, Connie and I faced a new crisis. Philip experienced a psychotic episode that was diagnosed as bipolar disorder. After a one-week hospitalization and some improvement, Philip was discharged to live with Connie and me. However, his mental status deteriorated, and a week later he physically attacked us, prompting his arrest and served two months in jail.

Over the subsequent five-years, Philip's mental health symptoms resolved for periods of time that ranged from weeks to months, giving him opportunities to get jobs in the DC Metro area in a law firm and even as a government contract employee. However, he ultimately succumbed to severe depression and death due to suicide by hanging in the basement of our home in June 2021. Despite previous deaths of my mother and my wife's parents, I never experienced grief like that I have experienced by the death of my son. Finding my son hanging by a belt from his closet door and getting him down on the floor brought to my mind the scene at the cross of Christ when his body was removed from the cross. My sorrow prompted me to realize how much God, the Father, grieved over the suffering and death of Jesus on the cross.

The prayers and comforting presence and support of Christian brothers and sisters have strengthened Connie and me in the grieving process. We have participated in support groups and a Bible-based curriculum called Grief Share. These supports have helped us put Philip's death in the context of our Christian faith, giving us confidence of God's presence in our loss. I pray the Lord will continue to use this experience to make us "better and not bitter."

Finding Meaning and Purpose in a New Phase of Life

I retired from the VA in June 2018. Retirement provided an opportunity for me to take a "sabbatical" from professional responsibilities and to ask the Lord for guidance for my next steps. During this time, the Lord helped me realize the importance of my roles as a husband, father, and grandfather.

In February 2019, I pursued coach training offered by the Christian Medical and Dental Associations (CMDA). I completed additional training, provided the required over 100 hours of coaching to clients to be credentialed as a coach by the International Coaching Federation (ICF) and, in 2020, started a part-time life and leadership coaching practice via Zoom.

My part-time coaching practice now provides the flexibility to love and serve my family and volunteer in Christian ministries. I can also commit to daily personal times of prayer and Bible study, weekly small groups meetings, and worship services. For years my mission has been to bring people and ideas together to improve programs and people's lives – to serve as a connector. Now, my desire is to be more focused on personally connecting with the Lord and inspiring others to trust in Him through caring, coaching, teaching, and consulting.

I do not know how my story will end, but I will continue to trust in Jesus. We all trust in something or someone. Our trust is only as good as the object of our faith. Jesus has proven faithful to me and worthy of my trust. He is "the image of the invisible God, the firstborn over all creation. For in him all things were created: things in heaven and on earth, visible and invisible, whether thrones or powers or rulers or authorities; all things have been created through him and for him." (1 Corinthians 1:15-16-NIV). I pray that my story will inspire you to trust Him as well.

Richard M. Allman, MD attended West Virginia University in Morgantown, WV for college, medical school, and a residency in internal medicine (1973-1983). He then completed a three-year research fellowship at Johns Hopkins Hospital (1983-1986). Subsequently, he served on faculty at the University of Alabama at Birmingham (UAB) School of Medicine (1986-2013) and on staff at the Birmingham Veterans Affairs (VA) Medical Center (1988-2014). At UAB he served as the Director, Division of Gerontology, Geriatrics, and Palliative Care (1990-2013); Director, Center for Aging (1992-2013); and Director, Birmingham/Atlanta VA Geriatric Research, Education, and Clinical Center (GRECC)(2001-2014). He was the national leader for policy and planning for VA Geriatrics and Extended Care in Washington, DC (2014-2018). Currently, he holds academic appointments as Professor Emeritus, Department of Medicine, UAB, Clinical Professor of Medicine, George Washington University, and Adjunct Professor, Wake Forest School of Medicine, and serves as a coach for healthcare leaders nationwide.

Notes

1. Farrar S. *Point Man: How a Man Can Lead His Family.* Page 138. Multnomah Books. 1990.
2. *The NIV Study Bible: 10th Anniversary Edition.* The Zondervan Corporation. 1995

CHAPTER 22

ONWARD!

ANDRE VAN MOL, MD

We all get to where we are through the efforts and lives of others, and so it is with the team endeavor that is Christian life in the family of God. I was born in Montreal of my mechanic, welder, and pastor Belgian father – orphaned during World War I -- and my very Italian seamstress mother, who both came to Quebec from southern Belgium for pastoral ministry. Ten years later, after Dad lost the terminal phalanges of his middle three right fingers in a work accident, we were led to warmer climate in the USA to prevent the phantom pains he experienced in the Montreal winters. Mom, Dad, my eleven-year-old sister (the only English speaker in the car), and me, a toddler, drove across the border with $300 to our name. Welcome to America! We joined my recently married older brother in Miami in the early 1960's. My parents prayerfully considered the advice of some dear Cuban friends, and moved across the country to rural Redding, California, sight unseen. Could anything good come out of Nazareth or Redding? We came and saw.

Nestled at the northern tip of the Sacramento Valley with mountain ranges on three sides, the Sacramento River winding through it, and surrounded by lakes, Redding is an outdoorsperson's dream. Urban centers lie a few hours south, available and yet conveniently out of the way. My formal education was entirely secular, a product of local public education through junior college, then on to private colleges and medical school before the US Navy "took the reins" for 8 years. Redding's most profound and lasting contribution to me came through my home congregation.

Bethel Church is now a megachurch, but then had only about 500 members, and was then only the second largest of many churches of orthodox faith in an area considered among the Bible belts of California. I recall committing my life to the Lord there at seven years of age in response to a visiting evangelist from the Billy Graham Crusade. I also recall recommitting my life a few hundred times, not unusual for insecure Christian kids who missed a few theological details concerning salvation. However, one Sunday morning -- December 29, 1974, at about 11:30 am to be precise – fourteen-year-old Andre was met by the Holy Spirit during a sermon I do not recall anything about, save for the Lord telling me my childlike faith had become just that--childish, and asking what I planned to do about it. I fully surrendered to the Lord and found myself full of a joy and a lovely desire to share Jesus with my family, friends, and others. Also, I was gifted with a fire in my gut for Christian apologetics (the reasoned defense of the faith) and bioethics that would last a lifetime and for which I would become known.

Bethel has remained my home church to this day, despite my 14-year absence for higher education and repayment of my Navy service obligation. The pastoral staff, along with my family, imparted in me a deeply rooted worldview and life path. Pentecostalism is sometimes known for being emotionally heavy and academically soft, but that was not my experience. Pastor Earl Johnson, a series of youth ministers, and other pastoral staff demonstrated and facilitated growth in a faith that was intellectually encouraging and spiritually grounding. A lifestyle of continuous growth and education in the Lord was the expectation. I don't recall even one anti-intellectual conversation with my pastors. They instilled in me an anticipation and expectation of co-laboring with Christ toward a bright future.

In the 1970's, apologetics was a topic of great discussion in California during my adolescence. CS Lewis, Francis Schaeffer, and Josh McDowell were recognized for their ability to translate Christian orthodoxy to a modern era, and C. Everett Koop was noted for his views on bioethics. The "fire in my gut" was becoming well stoked. One of my shortfalls was that intimidation, fear of man, and fear of possibly losing an argument, contributed to my unconsciously being defensive and reflexively retaliatory when patience would have been more appropriate. Thanks be to God for His patience and ongoing work of sanctification to smooth out my rough edges, grant an awareness of how I come across to others, and to develop in me a fatherlier and patient interaction style.

Nothing is wasted in the Kingdom of God, in which our weakness is made strong through God's power and provision. My weaknesses are many, some glaring. There was the impressive Tourette's syndrome, obsessive-compulsive disorder (OCD), and attention deficit hyperactivity disorder (ADHD) which combined to make me highly noticeable in my youth, and not in a good way. Now in my 60's, I am humbled and amazed at the kindness and patience of so many of the people around me in church, schools, and public, particularly my own family, during my youth. The Tourette's was largely corrected through the neurodevelopment of maturing to adulthood and divine intervention after years of prayer. Still, a bit remains as minor tics that manifest when I'm too tired, over caffeinated, or stressed. The OCD mellowed to a much more professionally useful trait (OCT), which I've learned to recognize and control. The ADHD and obsessive-compulsive traits contributed to study avoidance, difficulty with academic task completion, and sometimes had me in tears in elementary school, as I found long reading assignments and English composition painfully challenging. Ironically, my nickname among the CMDA leadership, as well as various other organizations and task forces I work with, is "The Energizer Bunny". I'm known for my writing, speaking, advising, and the ability to whip out projects in rapid fashion. Just know that all of that is a testament to God's redemptive power, giftings (remember that God's gifts reflect His character and not our merit), and co-laboring with Him. That's not modesty, but a simple matter of fact.

As a final note on the Tourette's, my economically poor parents took me to a series of specialists n elementary school. Those that impressed me most inadvertently taught me how doctors and mental health specialists should not be with patients. A sensitive kid like me did not benefit from shaming, blaming, or being embarrassed from often ill-equipped professionals, when what I needed were insights and other tools. Today, it brings me joy and puts a smile on the faces of young patients dealing with similar problems to be able to reassure them with a "Dude, you should have seen me! There is hope for you!" and "My wife, I, and three of my four kids have ADHD. In my home, you're kind of nothing without it."

Another of my shortcomings was my mistaken expectation of what I believed to be common knowledge of others. Paul told the Church in Rome, "And how shall they believe in Him of whom they have not heard?" (Romans 10:14, NKJV.) But I expected what I heard in sermons and read in publications was more widely known among the general public. It wasn't, and I reacted poorly. Paul's second letter to Timothy instructed, "in humility correcting those who are in opposition, if God perhaps will grant them repentance, so that they may know the truth." (2 Timothy 2:25) but I had other ideas that would need repentance. Bill Johnson, my senior pastor, asserts that they are as close to heaven as some people will ever be, so we should be patient with them.

Fast forward to the Medical College of Wisconsin on a Navy Armed Forces Health Professionals Scholarship. We had an active Christian club which, in years to come, would become a CMDA chapter. With believers being rare in medical school, denominational barriers fell quickly in favor of the strength of unity in Christ. Expectations determine a lot, and if one realizes that disappointment, failure, and even betrayal are a usual and customary part of Christian living, and not necessarily reflective of personal failure, persevering becomes easier. Pastor Bill Johnson calls rejection "a stepping-stone to spiritual growth and advancement".

Our med school bioethics instructor, a former Jesuit priest married to a former nun, was not pro-life. Against the advice of friends, I met with him and voiced my concerns, provided him 3 books, each authored by CS Lewis, Francis Schaeffer, and CE Koop that I thought conveyed errors in his position. To my surprise, he read all three, and immediately changed tone in class. He announced that the heretical and brief chapter on Christianity in our bioethics book was non-sense, and he began pushing back against some (but not all) of what he had taught. God was at work.

Courage is what you do despite your fear and intimidation. I have had several memorable examples of such personal interactions in medical training and beyond. My public writing on apologetics and bioethics, which started in university, would expand over the decades, often in direct conflict with proponents of secular bioethical and anti-Christian zeitgeist. It fosters a better attitude and Kingdom-of-God focus to remember your opponents are also created in the image of God, therefore worthy of love and respect, and they are the Lord's harvest field He came for (thanks to Gene Rudd for that last point). Avoid discounting or resenting the lost; it doesn't help anyone.

The various facets of my cultural engagement efforts as a physician received their greatest promotion following completion of the CMDA media training course, at the recommendation of CMDA master-level life coach, Pastor Ken Jones. From that time on, every interview, lecture, article, blog, amicus brief, legislative testimony, and request to advise came by invitation. All of them. What was left for me to determine was the "God things" from the simply good things, or worse. My senior pastor, Bill Johnson, offered this thought: both the "God things" and the good things take effort; but completing the good things only leaves you fatigued, while accomplishing the God things makes you feel alive! Akin to this was guidance from pastor Kris Vallotton: the world already has a Savior, and He is not me; there is always time and grace for what the Lord wants you to do; and be present for your family. Also, in keeping with the final of those three recommendations, I give my wife and children veto power over my invitations to speak, since that time comes out of their lives.

Four continents were traveled during my eight years in the Navy as a family medicine physician, including a tour as a carrier airwing flight surgeon. My past 29 years of practice have been back in in my hometown in California, 23 in private practice and the past six in corporate medicine. With over 50 letters to the editor published in our local paper and several appearances on the various local media outlets, my positions related to Christianity and culture-of-life bioethics are well known. The CMDA strongly asserts that competence is your first evangelistic priority as a physician, and I have found that to be true, particularly with those who disagree with you. How can one know what to say to them? A pastor and multifaceted business consultant friend once told me he had a two-part prayer when faced with a potentially contentious interaction: "Lord, is this person teachable, and what would you have me say." That can be prayed rather quickly and silently, and I often do so.

Among many memorable encounters with patients was one with a member of a lesbian-identified couple, in my practice, who stated "Dr. Van Mol, before we go on, I have to tell you something." I assumed a "constructive criticism" was coming. She continued with a smile, "You are outspoken and well known in the community for your opposition to my lifestyle. I want you to know that I love you. You and your whole staff always treat me like a woman, and never a [air quotes] lesbian. I tell my activist friends who say I shouldn't see you that they should also be your patients. Even if I move from this area, I'd want to travel back to still have you as my doctor." CMDA CEO Mike Chupp told us years ago that CMDA members from around the country report having gay-identified patients tell them they preferred Christian doctors to others they have had. And so, it should be. We're the ones who believe each patient is created in the image of God, and that the proper practice of medicine is an act of worship to God.

My prior 23 years of private practice gave me many opportunities to tailor my practice. The office website informs patients of our pro-faith practice, our values and priorities, our availability to pray with them, and offer health tips in office handouts. It also informs them of what is not provided: unethical medicine, elective abortions, euthanasia, or referrals for the same. My transition six years ago to corporate medicine left me wondering how much would change in my new employment. Interestingly, though some margin was removed and an increased caution necessary, some things were gained. As an employee, not as a private practitioner, I had paid time off and cross-covering colleagues to allow me to testify in legislatures, speak at conferences, and advise government and private organizations.

My first year of testifying in legislatures and meeting with elected officials and their staffs was 2018. I was speaking in opposition to a bill that would fast-track gender transition procedures (euphemistically called gender affirming health care) in foster children (my wife and I are 9-time foster parents) in Sacramento, my own state capitol. Our team lobbied in the most pro-transition legislative offices to make our case. Over the course of that very challenging year, I learned and applied four key guidelines that I call my battle benchmarks that have now been proven in the trenches. 1. Rest in the Lord and let your adversaries exhaust themselves. Understand that rest in the Lord is not passivity, but a posture of mind and heart. 2. Co-labor with Christ. The New Testament mentions this many times; it is empowering and reassuring. 3. Just get the message out. That's the priority, regardless of the outcome. Finally, 4. Our goal in Christian engagement in culture is conviction in the truth of your statements that are delivered with courage, compassion, and civility. I call these the 4 Cs.

I am conflict averse and know well what fear and intimidation feel like. I find motivation in these challenging quotes. Titus Brandsma, a 1942 Dachau martyr, urged, "Those who want to win the world for Christ must have the courage to come into conflict with it." AW Tozer instructed, "A scared world needs a fearless church." Pastor Bill Johnson teaches, "The Church needs a baptism in courage." And from a practicality perspective, I like to end most of my lectures with these quotes:

> "The future belongs to those who show up
>
> – MARK STEYN

> "We succeed by outlasting the crowd"
>
> – MY CHURCHMATE HAVILAH CUNNINGTON

"To stand is to win"

– Pastor Ade Omooba, MBE.

Onward!

André Van Mol, MD is a board-certified family physician in full-time practice in California. He co-chairs the Christian Medical & Dental Associations Sexual & Gender Identity Task Force and is the transgenderism scholar for both the CMDA and the American Academy of Medical Ethics. Dr. Van Mol writes and speaks for the CMDA on issues of bioethical and Christian concern and is extensively published in professional and general literature on these topics. He works with Alliance Defending Freedom in a coalition of professionals advising on policy matters addressing sexual orientation and gender identity, including serving as amicus curiae/friend of court in federal appellate and SCOTUS cases. He advises legislators, government agencies, and advocacy organizations internationally regarding sexuality and gender identity. Dr. Van Mol serves as elder at Bethel Church of Redding. He and his wife Evelyn —both former U.S. Naval officers—have two sons and two daughters, the latter of whom are among their nine foster children.

CHAPTER 23

GOD PROVIDED A LIFE I COULD NOT HAVE IMAGINED

SHARON A. FALKENHEIMER, MD, MPH, MA (BIOETHICS), PHD

It was my first trip to Kyrgyzstan, a country in central Asia, where I was to teach in a new family medicine residency. Since Kyrgyzstan had no international air service, I landed near midnight in Almaty, Kazakhstan, where I was supposed to take an airline bus to Bishkek, Kyrgyzstan's capital. However, I could not find it, no one spoke English, and I was unsure what to do. Long ago I had learned to trust God. I began to pray and knew many others were praying for me and my trip. I had no local money, no information on how to use the local phone, and no way to contact my hosts. I used my limited knowledge of Russian to ask about the bus and was told it was several days before the next one. Two taxi drivers used sign language to offer to take me to my destination. I saw no other choice. They could have done anything to me, but they took me across the steppes of Central Asia in the middle of the night, through multiple checkpoints, and even passed the airline bus enroute to my destination, where my hosts met me. God had answered and provided for me again. This was one of many trips I've made alone to remote places as a single woman.

As a young child, I wanted to be a doctor, learn to fly, and serve in the US Air Force. I believe the Lord put this in my heart, as I have no other explanation. It did not work out as I planned, but, with God's guidance, my life has been even more amazing than I had dreamed! As a teenager, I became a private pilot through scholarships from the Air Force Association and Civil Air Patrol. It was embarrassing to be approved to fly airplanes alone, but had to have a licensed driver with me when I drove to the airport. It took me three times to pass my driving test; and I still cannot parallel park to save my life! Receiving my private pilot's license made my desire to learn to fly a reality!

The Lord provided a generous scholarship that enabled me to attend Union College in Schenectady, NY. I could not have otherwise afforded it, but God's timing was perfect.

The fact that Union had been all male since 1795 but was recruiting its first female undergrads helped. I did not believe I could become a doctor due to the stringent admission requirements, so initially I planned to get a PhD in science.

For some reason, I thought I would only live into my twenties, so, as a teenager, I wondered how I could be certain of going to heaven. I attended church all my life, but thought I had to earn my way to heaven and knew that if this were true, I was in trouble! Through a campus college group, I first came to understand the amazing transaction available to me through Jesus' death. He had suffered for all my sins on the cross, and if I would accept his free gift of forgiveness, I could become His child, have His Spirit in me, know that I had eternal life, and would go to heaven after my earthly death. This knowledge transformed my life. A couple years later, I attended a student missions conference and committed to serve God cross culturally, if He would permit.

Since I did well in my first year in college, I realigned my thinking and decided to apply for medical school. I was accepted and prayed for a way to afford it, not wanting my parents to support my post graduate education, since they had already helped pay for college. I applied for several scholarships and accepted one from the United States Air Force. This fully funded my medical education and even allowed me to pay off my college loans during my first year, since I received a salary equal to half of the pay of a second lieutenant.

However, my medical school experience did not have an auspicious beginning. During the "an evening with a physician," orientation event, I found myself with several classmates whose parents were physicians. Though I tried, I could not find a way to join the conversation. Being the first college graduate in my family, I felt like an outsider, and, being shy, I did not say anything. Soon the physician looked at me and asked, "Don't you talk?" That made me feel even less worthy to be there! Despite this experience, I persevered, though the going was rough. I struggled with gross anatomy and experienced my greatest fear: I failed a test. To my surprise, I was not expelled but was able to continue to study ... and struggle. I was often on my knees praying and crying to the Lord to help me pass. He answered my prayers and always helped me through the many struggles of those years. I found encouragement through our campus Christian Medical & Dental Society group, our times of Bible study together, weekly meetings with my prayer partner, and my church. I graduated and found that overnight I was transformed from a medical student into a doctor! I had realized my second childhood aspiration.

I had also wanted to become an Air Force pilot, but women were accepted when I was halfway through medical school, so I did not apply. However, my desire to fly in the Air Force was not dashed. I went on active duty and entered the Air Force internal medicine residency at its 1,000 bed, tertiary care hospital in San Antonio, Texas. This was a lonely and stressful time. Apart from a classmate from medical school, I knew no one in San Antonio. Days were long and on-call nights largely sleepless. Often the aeromedical evacuation aircraft ("air evac" or as we often called it the "air attack") would land around midnight, keeping me up most of the night evaluating several new patients who were arriving from all over the world. Many were young and many had already received all known treatments and died soon after their arrival. I became increasingly tired and depressed. I knew I had to complete a clinical internship to obtain my medical license, so I persevered. I prayed nearly constantly. The support of my family by phone and of fellow Christian residents sustained me, along with my times of devotion and worship (although I often found myself nodding or even falling asleep in church).

Since I couldn't see myself practicing internal medicine for a career, I resigned from my residency. Because of my four year education commitment to the Air Force , I had three choices:. another residency, be a general medical officer, or become a flight surgeon. I wasn't sure what a flight surgeon was, but it sounded a lot more fun than being a general medical officer!

After basic flight surgeon and hyperbaric medicine training, I was assigned to a fighter squadron in Okinawa, Japan. I was the first woman on flying status at this base of over 10,000 active-duty personnel. This was an adjustment for me, as well as the many airmen! One day walking in my flight suit, two young airmen saluted me and said, "Good morning, Sir." As they passed, I heard one say, "I don't think that was a Sir!" I was assigned to an F-15 fighter squadron as its brand-new planes were just arriving on base. At a time when female pilots were not allowed to fly military fighters because they were combat aircraft, I flew with them on air-to-air training missions and deployments. In this way, God enabled me to experience flight in one of the newest, high-performance fighters with an air-to-air mission that included aerobatics. So, in a much different way than I expected, God had fulfilled my three desires: to become a doctor, fly, and serve in the Air Force!

I was then assigned to an arctic base more than 20 miles from Fairbanks, Alaska – then a town of 60,000. The northern lights were amazing, the winters extremely cold and dry, and sunlight ranged from 3 to 21 hours, depending on the season. Our wing flew its real-time missions out of the island of Shemya, the second westernmost Aleutian Island. It was inhabited by only a few hundred Department of Defense personnel, arctic foxes, and birds. It is so remote that we had T-shirts that read, "It's not the end of the world, but you can see it from here!"

After my next assignment, I entered the Air Force residency in aerospace medicine. It was only the second class that included female Air Force physicians. In addition to aerospace academics and visits to aeromedical facilities of the Army, Navy, NASA, FAA, Water and Arctic Survival School, helicopter dunker training, and Aircraft Accident Investigation School, we received formal jet training with instructors in the T–38 and T– 39 Air Force training aircraft. So, I did get to fly jets myself in the Air Force. To complete the required minimum flight time of 4 hours per month for flight pay, I had the opportunity to fly in about 40 different aircraft and helicopters during my 27-year USAF career.

Aerospace medicine was an amazing specialty for me. I like variety and was able to serve as a clinical flight surgeon, medical planner, researcher in aircrew protective equipment, squadron commander, associate residency director for the Aerospace Medicine program, and Director of International Medical Training for students from other countries, including those who received training in a 6 month mini-residency in Advanced Aerospace Medicine for International Medical Officers, for which I was the course director. I About 30% of my Air Force career was spent on deployments, participating in conferences, teaching NATO allies and colleagues from the newly liberated countries of Eastern Europe after the fall of the Berlin wall, and consulting with allied colleagues on aeromedical equipment and joint plans.

To my amazement, I received a call one day from an Air Force General! He asked me to become the physician for the Air Force Combat Operations Center at the Pentagon. When we were not involved in conflicts or exercises, I served in the medical readiness division of the Air Force Surgeon General's office. During operations Desert Storm and Desert Shield, I often found myself in briefings with the Chief of Staff of the US Air Force.

After those conflicts, I was asked to meet with the Assistant Secretary of Defense for Health Affairs and was offered a position in medical readiness to follow-up on action items from the Gulf War. While there during the Balkans conflict in the early 1990s, I spent time each day in the Secretary of Defense's command center reviewing updates from medical units in the field and updating the Assistant Secretary of Defense for Health Affairs on medical events in the combat theater. At times, I was part of interagency virtual meetings (a new concept then) with representatives from the National Security Council, other cabinet departments, the military services, and the International Organization for Migration which helped arrange care in other countries for injured civilians in hospitals that were able to provide the necessary treatment. To be able to serve in these capacities was beyond my wildest dreams. God's plans for me were so much more than I could have imagined! I am amazed how God moved me so many places and carried me through the continually increasing responsibilities for which I had initially felt unprepared. But I have learned to pray and rely on him and found the Scripture true that says, "His power is made strong in weakness." (2 Corinthians 12:9)

After five years in Washington, I became a squadron commander, at a time when Air Force hospitals became medical groups that were comprised of several squadrons. I had never desired to be a commander, but, after accepting a position as Chief of Aerospace Medicine at a major air command, I found myself being urged to command an aerospace medicine squadron by the command surgeon and a medical group commander, a colleague with whom I had served with in Japan. This became my greatest struggle in accepting God's will in my career. For several days I struggled. I told God this was not in my skill set, and that I would probably be a failure. Regardless, I eventually accepted this leadership role, knowing that if I stepped outside of God's will for me, my relationship with Him would be compromised. I had faith that He would equip me for something that was His will.

To say two years as a squadron commander were very stressful is an understatement. Although I learned a lot about leadership and encouraging the airmen in my squadron, it took a toll on my health, required me to strenuously exercise after work to relax, and made me more dependent than ever on God for strength and wisdom, not only day-by-day, but minute-by-minute. In the end, He provided and got me through that tour of duty.

We typically don't know why God calls us to difficult and undesired things, but occasional, He reveals it to us. This was one of those times. I was appointed the Associate Residency Director for Aerospace Medicine at the USAF School of Aerospace Medicine (USAFSAM). After he interviewed me for the position, the school commander confided in me that I would have never been considered for this, my dream position, if I had not recently been a commander at base level! Needless to say, I was thankful I had accepted that command, rather than choose my own way.

Many physicians assigned to USAFSAM were able to stay there for many years. That was my hope, too. But it was not to be. After four years, colleagues began to tell me that my position was being cut and added to the job responsibilities of another faculty member as the Air Force drew down its forces around 2000. By the time I confirmed this was true, most assignments for my rank and specialty had already been made, so I felt I should retire. Interestingly, in a kind of poetic justice, a few months after my position was cut, it was reinstated, when they realized there was more to the job than they anticipated!

Sudden retirement presented another difficult time in my life. I didn't know what to do. I remained active in my church and my position there. I even assumed additional volunteer responsibilities, making my church work more full-time. Sometime later, I was surprised to be offered several unexpected positions. This included an appointment to represent the Air Force at a review of Department of Defense medical research, an appointment by the Secretary of Health and Human Services to the Centers for Disease Control Advisory Committee on Environmental Health, and, most surprising of all, a Presidential appointment to the Board of Regents of the Uniformed Services University of the Health Sciences. Being selected for these responsibilities did encourage me but did not prevent me from becoming clinically depressed. I was lonely, sad, and disappointed. The antidepressant treatment was successful and put me back on a "more even keel". But I still was unsure of my future and how to apply the skills I had gained during my career.

Several years, later I heard that there was a need within CMDA for someone to help organize teaching teams in response to requests from low- and middle-income countries for additional training for their healthcare professionals. This was something I had a passion for, believing that most short-term clinical teams did not provide a lasting impact where they served. Teaching healthcare professionals new skills could provide that. I have taught in 30 countries and have found great joy and satisfaction in it. I've enjoyed working with other volunteers in settings in many countries, some of which were more remote and less known than places I had served with the Air Force. I hope to continue to do this for several more years as my age and health permit. Now that my parents are with the Lord and no longer need me to care for them, I would love to work long term overseas if an appropriate position becomes available. I'm thankful my pension and Social Security enable me to do this, even as a volunteer, if necessary.

So that is my story. God has done amazing things through me, which I could have never done on my own. I was "pathologically" shy in high school. I was my family's first college graduate. I felt unqualified to become a doctor. I did not have the money to attend medical school but received an Air Force scholarship. I felt unsuited for the residency I chose, but discovered and entered a field I loved. When I joined the military, I was afraid of colonels and then I became one! I felt inadequate to brief senior officers and found myself briefing generals and senior Department of Defense leaders, including at one point the Assistant Secretary of Defense. I retired sooner than expected, but eventually found a role for which I had a passion in a second career with CMDA. None of this would have been possible without the Lord and what I believe was and is His plan for my life. What a joy! What a privilege to know and serve Him, help colleagues advance their skills as healthcare professionals, and serve alongside others with the same passion! I don't know how others make it through life in their own strength but can never be thankful enough to have come to know Jesus, His forgiveness, love, care, guidance and empowerment!

Sharon A. ("Shari") Falkenheimer has over 45 years of experience in teaching, applied research, clinical medicine, medical leadership and planning, and has taught in 30 nations. She earned a B.S. in Biology from Union College; an M.D. from State University of New York Upstate Medical College, a Masters in Public Health from the Harvard School of Public Health, an M.A. in Bioethics, and a PhD in Educational Studies from Trinity International University. She is board certified in Aerospace Medicine and is a retired USAF colonel. In 2002, she was appointed by the Secretary of Health and Human Services to the Advisory Committee to the National Center for Environmental Health and by President George W. Bush to the Board of Regents of Uniformed Services University (USU) of the Health Sciences. She has held academic appointments at USU, the University of Toronto, the University of Texas Health Science Center at San Antonio, University of Texas Medical Branch in Galveston, the USAF School of Aerospace Medicine, and Trinity International University. She serves on the boards of the Christian Journal for Global Health and the Christian Academy of African Physicians and is a lifetime member of the Christian Medical & Dental Associations (CMDA). In 2024, she was appointed as North American Regional Secretary for the International CMDA.

CHAPTER 24

EPISODES OF GRACE

John Patrick, MD

Nothing moves me more than the eruption of life changing grace into a life; the gift of eyes to see the reality of sin and a heart to repent. Unless the Spirit comes, that cannot happen. I have no dramatic story. The stories of the Bible were, from the beginning, my stories, my way of understanding everything. It never occurred to me there was any other way of understanding how we ought to live until I reached high school.

When we look back from an eternal vantage point, I suppose we will be even more aware than we are now of how easily our lives might never have been redeemed. In my case, there was steadfast daily prayer for me from known conception until I was 30 years old. Three requests prayed daily, unknown to me, in the middle of Africa, that I would be redeemed, that I would become a doctor and that I would go to the Congo. Only when we went to the erstwhile Congo in my late 40s was the third request answered, and I learned the story. Such prayer is amazing in its persistence, and I believe it contributed to the strange fact that I rarely worry at all.

God designed a world in which death and mourning are essential ingredients. I am reminded of George Herbert's poem "The Pulley," where he portrays God giving us all His wonderful gifts, but reaching the bottom of the box, only rest remains, and God says no.

> "For if I should," said he,
> "Bestow this jewel also on my creature,
> He would adore my gifts instead of me,
> And rest in Nature, not the God of Nature;
> So both should losers be.
>
> "Yet let him keep the rest,
> But keep them with repining restlessness;
> Let him be rich and weary, that at least,
> If goodness lead him not, yet weariness
> May toss him to my breast."[1]

Repining restlessness! What a description of the modern world.

All my extended family were mainly skilled working class. My maternal grandfather was an intimidating figure, a militant vegetarian who ate the eggshells with the eggs (for the calcium). He had a huge thick moustache, which caught the froth from his beer on occasion. He was a socialist who had read Karl Marx, and he was militant trade unionist who always referred to Winston Churchill as "Brimstone." It was his response to one of the worst decisions Churchill made—to send troops into Wales to shut down a miner's strike demanding a living wage! He could quote Marx, Friedrich Engels, George Bernard Shaw and William Shakespeare. I never met my maternal grandmother who had borne eight children, all of whom survived to adult life. Only my mother became Christian.

My paternal grandparents sent their children to a Plymouth Brethren Sunday school, and half of the eight became lifelong Christians. I never met this grandfather, who died before I was born.

The grace that brought my mother to faith as a teenager also led to the 30 years of prayer for me. My grandfather was scornful of "academics." None of his children were allowed to go beyond the minimum level of education decreed by the state, so my mother found herself working as a seamstress in a sweat shop for her teenage years. Again, by grace, she found herself working next to a Christian woman who wisely simply loved her. When her genuineness touched my mother, she was able, easily and naturally, to invite my mother to listen to some missionaries who had been in the Belgium Congo for several years with no guaranteed salary. Missionaries without a salary pray a lot and learn to trust their Father in Heaven, who never lets them down. As a bored teenager, my mother agreed to the invitation, and, shortly, she was born again. The contrast between a materialist Marxism and the call of Christ exhibited in the life of those two missionaries was night and day to her. The only real effect my grandfather had was to turn his daughter into a pietist who wanted nothing to do with politics, but who did pray for just government every day.

These good folk, Herbert and Annie English, felt called to the Congo for life. They did not have children, so young people like my mother who were converted on their infrequent trips to England became their children in the faith, and letters went back and forth. They knew when my mother and father were married and when I was conceived. From that point on, they prayed for me daily. To our great joy, they came to our wedding, having been evacuated from the Congo during the Simba horrors.

My parents lived from wage packet to wage packet but never went into debt, living on six pounds ($20 in those days) per week during my early years. Nevertheless, they tithed faithfully. I had no sense we were poor, because I was loved, fed, clothed and sheltered. The Scriptures were read twice a day during the week and numerous times on Sunday. What a gift that was, because it gave me a foundation for living well. I knew every story in the Bible, and because they are all morally consequential, I knew what to do when problems arose, as did the men of Issachar.

There was another wonderful element to my early life—freedom within remarkably wide boundaries. There were no "helicopter" parents. From dawn to dusk we played in the streets and wandered from dawn to dusk when not in school, returning for meals. Because married women only had part-time jobs outside the home and the population was stable, we were all known indirectly through multiple relationships. If we misbehaved, other women would rebuke us, and our parents would know. Interestingly, we were also morally rooted. I believe it had much to do with the education system. The working class was dismissive of intellectual activity (only a few percent of the entire population went to university) and read little beyond the local paper, but they inhabited a tacit world that went back centuries. They learned to read, write and do arithmetic in school, but they were also formed, largely unknowingly, by the Bible, because the Bible was read every day in school. The 10 commandments were written on their hearts, and the Bible stories gave almost unconscious moral structure to their lives. The consequences were that there was very little crime, doors were not locked and neighbors cared for one another. For example, a woman with severe multiple sclerosis who lived three doors from us was not lonely because neighbors dropped by. The postman, the baker, the rentman all came into her house and knew the money was in the teapot. At school, we had no lockers. In six years, there was one episode of theft solved by assembling the entire school until the thief owned up and was duly caned on the spot.

Working class arguments about right and wrong would be settled by, "The Bible says...." I did not, of course, think about this phenomenon for almost 40 years when I was given a copy of Lesslie Newbigin's *Foolishness to the Greeks*, which I have since read numerous times. That led to Polanyi, Wright and MacIntyre. The key idea is set out by Polanyi thus:

> "The adherents of a great tradition are largely unaware of their own premises, which lie deeply embedded in the unconscious foundations of Practice... if the citizens are dedicated to certain transcendent obligations and particularly to such general ideals as truth, justice, charity and these are embedded in the tradition of the community to which allegiance is maintained, a great many issues between citizens and all to some extent can be left – and are necessarily left – for individual consciences to decide. The moment, however, a community ceases to be dedicated through its members to transcendent ideas, it can continue to exist undisrupted only by submission to a single centre of unlimited secular power."[2]

Newbigin refers to this sort of knowledge as tacit knowledge—things we know with certainty but cannot usually describe how that happened. Conversion is a good example. We are certain of it, but it is better to say, "I can't tell you how it happens, but if you seek you will find," than it is to set out a list of propositions to be accepted. The devil knows all those propositions to be true.

The COVID lockdowns were a relatively innocent example of how easily a liberal elite bureaucracy, largely without such a tacit moral inner life and therefore unable to see that people can make sensible decisions, can rationalize their love of power and become authoritarian without discussion and no tolerance for dissent. Thus, wiser people understood there were going to be serious psychological and educational problems from draconian lockdown policies, which were not considered at all except in Sweden.

The next episode of grace was due to Shakespeare. My grandfather's love of Shakespeare was passed to my mother who, despite being sent to work around 12 years of age, went to night school for a course on Shakespeare. The teacher was a wonderful eccentric lady who had always wanted clothes made from fabrics she found, but she could never find anyone to make them to her design. Then she discovered my mother could sew and didn't need a pattern—a sketch was enough! So, over the ensuing years, Mrs. Horsley got the clothes she wanted, and when my mother married, she would visit our home for fittings. That's how she met me. She had lost her only son in World War II, and maybe that led to her interest in me. She realized I was somewhat unusual and decided I ought to go to the school her son attended. King Edward's school had a 400-year history and was ranked academically as one of the top schools in England. The competition to get in was fierce, and only the children of the elite families, who could afford coaching, could get in because the entrance exam included French and Latin, and only private schools provided those languages at the elementary level. However, Mrs. Horsley knew the school had agreed after the war to take two boys per year from the working class, and that opened the door for me. I was so amazed to see what real learning looked like. My first homeroom master spoke five languages, and I was told I was going to function in three! Classes were alive with vigorous interactions. Debating was a major activity. Chess was as important as cricket. I did not understand how much my life had changed when I entered that school, but it had. Everyone in that school went on to university, unless they joined the officer training programs for the armed forces.

About the same time, I started to travel on my bike during vacation time, and not just locally. My mother wanted to say, "No," but my father said, "Yes." I had to stay at youth hostels and send a postcard every day. I traveled all over England, Wales and Scotland, and then I crossed the English Channel and rode all over Europe before I went to university. My father knew I was careful and would not get into trouble, but I also matured through that travel. My wife Sally also loved to travel as a teenager, and all my children have traveled extensively to exotic, and sometimes dangerous, places.

Medical school was less demanding than King Edward's, but another act of grace occurred on my first Sunday in London. A student asked me to go to church with him on Sunday evening, and we went to hear Dr. Martyn Lloyd Jones. I had never heard preaching of such depth and passion. Thereafter, I was in his church frequently with occasional visits to All Souls to hear John Stott and his curates. In the late 1950s, London was awash with great preachers. They gave my unconsidered faith deep foundations which have endured. Anselm's "Credo ut intelligam" (I believe, in order to understand) has been a central concept for me. C.S. Lewis says the same thing slightly differently, "I believe in Christianity as I believe that the sun has risen; not only because I see it but because by it, I see everything else."[3]

Most importantly, I met Sally in those student years. She maintains we met at a Bible study, but I do not remember the Bible study, only her! Initially we went to church and to the opera, but it was an intermittent relationship for about seven years because we are both always right. I had recently started my second year of residency when I was about to make some bad mistakes spiritually. There was no space for the nurturing of the soul in residency, and I had not been to church for a long while when grace brought us back together, and we were shortly married thereafter. I was not much engaged with the arrangements for the wedding, so I was unprepared for a sermon. The text was: No man setting out to build...does not first work out whether he can complete the project. The sermon was directed at me. The implication was crystal clear—the preacher did not think I had the resources for a successful marriage. I knew he was right, so we began marriage by finding a church, which led us to a wonderful small house group. That church also took us to the Keswick family week in the Lake district, where we camped in a field. The children loved it. We were fed spiritually every morning, and the children were cared for by a wonderful Christian organization, Scripture Union. In the afternoons, we walked a lot and stowed away many happy memories. One year we stumbled into our own Narnia, not through a wardrobe but through a hole in the dry-stone wall where no one else went, and it was stunningly beautiful.

We hadn't talked about children when we married, but God gave us four in a row. I was a busy physician and not seeing enough of my children when Sally told me I needed to change my work habits. So, I did a doctorate in cell physiology and was regularly home for supper and stories, for which I shall be eternally grateful. My academic work was successful, but that story is for another time and place. One episode of grace wrote itself on my heart during that time.

About a year into my lab career, nothing was working, and I got viral meningitis and was off work for the summer. We were living in an apartment block of six, surrounded by a walled garden. Our neighbor, a Reuters journalist, went off to the Middle East for a year and a young family moved in. The father was doing a year at the Greenwich Naval College on the topic of nuclear engineering. We got to know one another because we began to play chess in the garden in the afternoons. Both of us came from blue-collar backgrounds, but David's dad had made him leave school at 15. He started as an apprentice electrician with Rolls Royce in Derby. Being a good company, they soon realized he was extremely talented. He did an external degree in mathematics at London University in quick time, so Rolls moved him into the research section of the nuclear engines group. By his early 30s, he was running the heat flux analysis section. Rolls wanted him to get a PhD, but he refused, saying he had to teach folks with a PhD to do their work. Rolls just wanted him to have some more letters after his name. In the end, he agreed to do an MSc in Greenwich, which he could do in one year. He really came so his children could see the sights in London. He could have taught the course himself; hence, he came home in the afternoons, and we played chess. One afternoon I got a bad headache and had to go and lie down. The next afternoon David greeted me with a question: "Do you have any more books like the one you were reading yesterday?" "Oh, that's where it went," was my reply. "Yes," said David, "I read from cover-to-cover last night; I have never read anything like it before. Do you have any more like it?" The book was Martyn Lloyd Jones' *From Fear to Faith*, a commentary on the book of Habakkuk! Habakkuk cannot believe what God is going to do with the children of Israel. "Why," he says to God, "do you make me look upon injustice?" He ends up writing one of the most amazing discussions of justice and God's inscrutable ways, and he ends by writing one of the most moving poems in the Bible. I didn't know it, but despite all his successes, David was deeply discontented. He needed a deeper meaning for his life. That little book was the beginning of his conversion. I gave him *Mere Christianity* by C.S. Lewis next, and he read it in a few days and asked to come with us to church on Sunday. I had witnessed teenage conversions, but I'd never seen anything like this. He later told me that when he got back to Derbyshire, it was as though he had new eyes and saw needs everywhere that he had not previously noticed, which he could meet. Ultimately, he ended up in charge of human resources for the entire Rolls Royce organization. I had to come to terms with what I had seen, but it was going to take some time.

My doctoral work went well, and when it was complete, Sally did not want me to go back to the treadmill of internal medicine. Find an application for your work in a nice place, preferably warm, was her undemanding request. One of my colleagues had spent a little time studying malnourished children in Jamaica, and I realized there was an application for me. I talked to the Wellcome Trust, they gave me a personal fellowship and off we went to Jamaica for a couple of years, which turned into six. This was a wonderful experience for my family. No TV, a good little Catholic school and home for lunch. Living on the university campus with the beautiful Blue Mountain as a backdrop and lovely beaches at the weekend was like paradise. There was also a little Brethren Chapel, which attracted some university students. Here was another episode of grace. Christian students coming from conservative churches were unprepared for the onslaught of militant communists. It was the heyday of Fidel Castro and utopian dreams of Jamaica as a socialist paradise.

I had considerable sympathy for the idea that more needed to be done for the poor. After all, I would not have become a doctor without the post-war demands that class barriers should not keep all but the wealthy out of the professions. As a student, I was involved with left-leaning groups campaigning for political independence and more education in the colonies, but I also knew politicians would manipulate this process for their own ends. I had been horrified by the brutality of the communists in Czechoslovakia and Hungary. At some point, I stumbled upon a letter from Vladimir Lenin to another communist which said, "When we have got rid of God, it will be necessary to legalize terror." Lenin was realistic, and he knew his own capacity for evil was not unique to him. So, he had no illusions about people, and control would require a brutal disregard for human rights. Then, I went climbing in the Tatra Mountains when the Iron Curtain opened up a little, and I was on a rockface climbing with a Hungarian when Marxism died. He had been sent by his government to get photographs showing the destitution of the poor in Paris, and I had listened to him in the climbing hut the previous evening spinning the party line for the other students about the terrible plight of the poor in Paris, France. We sat on a ledge, and he said, "You didn't believe a word of what I said last night, did you?" "Of course not," I replied, "It was lies," "Yes," he said, "but I could not know whether there was an agent provocateur in that group." I was stunned to realize how terrible that was. The destruction of freedom of speech. I have used that experience numerous times to teach students that the Christian doctrine of intrinsic human sinfulness is brutally honest. It is also the start for the formation of a better society by building a basic commitment to truth telling and freedom of speech. For the students in Jamaica, we spent several Sunday afternoons looking at how Jesus engaged with the elite by using parables and skillful argument like, "Let him who is without sin among you be the first to throw a stone..." (John 8:7b, ESV). Peter Kreeft's last chapter of *The Best Things in Life* is a master class in how to do this in our world.

Those Sunday afternoons, talking about life with intelligent but naïve students, were more important than I knew. We have a number of friends in Jamaica that resulted from those conversations. Until COVID came along, I visited Jamaica annually to teach in several different settings, but all were the result of Mona Chapel, where I was always welcomed. However, I was still far from a public Christian.

Eventually, the time in Jamaica came to an end rather abruptly. One evening I developed chest pain but said nothing to Sally and went to bed early. The tightness in my chest continued the next morning. I was due to do my much-loved weekly internal medicine clinic, but instead of going to the clinic, I went to the ECG dept. The technician wouldn't let me see the recording but went for the cardiologist. I had inverted t waves all across my chest, which was not good news. There was no interventional coronary program in Jamaica in 1979. Florida was too expensive, and London was a long flight away. Finally, it was decided I would rest for a couple of weeks and then fly to London. I was 39 years old with four children and inadequate insurance. I was incredibly anxious for my family. One morning I had a unique experience: I was praying and telling the Lord that I was not coping well and was very anxious. At that moment, it was as though a hand was laid on my shoulder, and I was told it was not my problem, and I was to trust. The anxiety lifted immediately and did not return, and even when I watched the contrast injection in my coronary arteries, my pulse did not flicker and the arteries were clean. Then we discovered I had a Coxsackie viral infection with presumed myocarditis. A floppy mitral valve was also diagnosed, and slowly I recovered.

The next act of grace took a while to recognize because, after Jamaica, I was supposed to come to a position in London, but Margaret Thatcher had come to power and canceled the program. However, I received two invitations to visit, with a view to join the faculty at Harvard and Ottawa. The Harvard invitation was because they had a new dean of the medical school whom I knew because of shared research interests. This was 1980, and he was ahead of the curve in realizing that nutrition in medicine had no academic standing and, consequently, most doctor's nutritional knowledge could be written on a postcard. The idea of an academic nutrition program in the medical school was novel. The only problem after I had met the faculty, whose co-operation I would need, was that there was no serious interest in collegiality, because they all had their own little empires. When I explained to the dean why I didn't think the project would work in the Harvard ethos, he understood and regretted my decision, but he said I would have a much better life and better hope of success in Ottawa. He was right. A good friend did accept a position in nephrology at the same time, and I said to him, "Be careful, the only thing that seems to be guaranteed at our career level in Harvard is a divorce." He laughed, and he was divorced in a couple of years!

Fortunately for us, Ottawa was 25 years behind the times socially. It still had what amounted to a grammar school, there was little crime and drugs were behind most of the crime that did occur. My daughters could walk home in the late evening quite safely, and I had a perfect setting in which to work. What I was not prepared for was the undergraduate culture. I had not taught undergraduates for 20 years, when students were supposed to take notes and read original material. I was brought up intellectually by teachers who wanted to challenge us, rather than spoon-feed information for subsequent regurgitation. After my first lecture to medical students in Canada, half the students wanted more, and half wanted me fired. A compromise was achieved, but too many students were simply good at regurgitating handouts and objected to anything being required that was not on the handout. This was hardly training for problem solvers.

The next development occurred at a church social event at which I got into a discussion with another Brit, who got his degree at Oxford and joined Intervarsity Christian Fellowship. He was the regional organizer for Ontario. I said I had gone to some of their meetings as a student, but I am allergic to evangelical smiles, so I only went when there was a good speaker like Lloyd Jones or John Stott. I did take part in a Bible study for medical students, but most of them lost any active faith during their training. He asked me if I had any ideas why that happened. My response was, "Not enough teaching about the issues they face during medical training and life." Sometime later, he asked me to be the speaker at his annual fundraising dinner. My response was that I was unlikely to be a great success. He was not concerned about that: "They need to hear what you have to say, but try and be a little less cynical." I gave the talk, and early in the next academic year a medical student came to my office to ask me to help the Evangelical Christian group. He had been at the talk discussing the long-term failure rate for faith in students with only the shallow training in apologetics available in most churches. I was reluctant but agreed to do a few weeks of small group study at my home. That somewhat grudging commitment grew into a 10-year gift to me and my family.

It also started me thinking about the need for better Christian education, because the university, although invented by Christians, was clearly losing its way, primarily because of scientism (the idea that science could solve all our problems by substituting measurement and experiment for deductive and teleological thought), although I could not have argued the case very well in the 1980s. I did have a somewhat jaundiced view of academic life and avoided scientific conferences as much as I could, because I knew only a small percentage of the material presented would survive the peer-review process, and only if you thoroughly understood the methods used could you claim to be an expert and be rational (i.e. a very limited claim for any of us).

When the nostrums of the faculty of education invaded medicine, I was appalled by the naiveté of my colleagues. Students were to be assessed on the basis of knowledge, skills and attitudes! Character was just a disguise for oppressive power. Knowledge was to be measured using multiple choice questions where complex questions were avoided, and no analytical skill was tested. Skills were verbal—no testing by experienced physicians watching and working with the student. As for attitudes, a method actor would ace the test, but a humble caring student, who would be loved by patients and obsessively thorough, would fail for not acting and displaying hypocritical empathy of the "I feel your pain" variety. A good physician would rarely if ever use such a trite phrase. I was once spontaneously hugged by a female patient whose husband had died during the night while she was in hospital. When I got to her bed on my morning rounds, I said, "I don't know what to say, I cannot begin to comprehend how you feel." She reached out and hugged me saying, "Everybody says they understand, but they don't, you are the first to be honest." Read the first chapter of Wendell Berry's *Life Is a Miracle* to see how a great writer opens up these issues. The faculty of education does not understand that teaching is not something that can be taught like tying your shoelaces, but it the conjunction of two loves, the love of a subject and the love of a pupil.

The next act of grace was humbling. Churches in Ottawa were not satisfying, so we went to the nearest one that believed the Scriptures and that the gospel is true. They were warm, loving and accepting folk, but they were untaught. One Sunday, missionaries from Zaire were speaking and Sally brought them home to lunch. They rapidly learned that I knew more about the treatment of severe childhood malnutrition than all but a handful of physicians. The effective treatment of malnutrition had been worked out in Jamaica, and I was there for the final years of the program where the mortality rate was reduced to zero. They said, "We need your help." I was not keen, because I followed literature and our work had not changed the prevalence in Africa, and I didn't know why. I was due a sabbatical, and the family decided it was going to be in Africa!

I put an array of barriers in the way, and they were systematically removed. The last one was the cost of staying in Nairobi for a few days waiting for the best connection. We had a party of eight by this stage, but after I gave a lecture on the treatment of severe childhood malnutrition, a gentleman, who was the head of pediatrics in Nairobi, asked if I would give that lecture in the medical school if I ever went through Nairobi. I told him I was probably going through Nairobi, but I had a problem with hotel costs. He smiled and told me that if I would lecture, the university would provide accommodation! So that weekend I called my father (my mother had died) and told him we were going to Zaire (erst while Belgium Congo) for a year. There was silence for a moment or two, and then my father said, "I have waited 45 years to hear you tell me that," and he told me of the faithful prayers of Uncle Hubert and Auntie Annie.

Allan Bloom's 1987 book *The Closing of the American Mind* was published and caused shock waves throughout academia; shortly, a book of rebarbative responses was published. I knew of it, but I didn't read it until I was on the plane to Africa. Allan Bloom got under my skin. Near the end of the first chapter, Bloom allows himself a personal reverie in which he looks back on his family history. Bloom says his grandparents arrived in America with nothing but the will to work and the love of family. They never went inside an institution of higher learning, but everything done in their home was spiritually rich, and they found reasons for the performance of their duties and the bearing of their sorrows by reference to The Book, the Old Testament. They could go to the synagogue where they heard great scholars who spoke not from an alien perspective but from a shared perspective, while simply going deeper and providing guidance. That, says Bloom, is what a community is: something that invites high and low into a common source of meaning and that practice had made them wise. In contrast, Bloom' s cousins, all of whom were MDs or PhDs, had no comparable wisdom. My question was, is it really true that without a known and loved Book, it is not possible to have a great and wise society?

The subject bothered me all year. When I got back somehow in a lecture to medical students, I told them that if Bloom is right, then you are ignorant in a deeply significant way. Today's students would immediately erupt in anger at that point, but at the end of the 1980s some courtesies remained, and it wasn't until after the lecture that a group of students came and said I owed them an apology. "But," I pointed out, "I was merely quoting Bloom. Why don't we find out whether he is right? If I read him rightly, he is saying you do not have a book that is foundational, and that you know and love. That book used to be the Bible, so here's my test. You all admire Ghandhi, and he said the greatest piece of literature he had read was the Sermon on the Mount, so why don't you tell me how it starts and a little of what it says?" They couldn't say anything. Bless them, they responded by asking me what I would do about it. Without thinking I said, "What you need is an agnostics anonymous group because you don't even know the questions let alone the answers." They agreed, and I had a voluntary extracurricular course for which the only prerequisite was that you could not claim to be a Christian, and about a quarter of the class attended. It was challenging, as each year I set out to show it is not stupid to believe that objective moral truth exists, and I succeeded.

The next act of grace involved a lot of people initially from the Canadian Christian Medical and Dental Association patiently easing me into public speaking. It was the students first. Way back, the CMDA medical students in Ontario used to organize their own conference, and on one occasion their speaker fell ill shortly before the conference. After frantic phone calls, they asked me to fill in for the speaker. Of course, it was immensely enjoyable, but more was afoot. Attending the conference was a mature student with her husband, who was a minister in Toronto Charismatic Church. They also had a conference coming up, and they just learned their speaker was seriously ill. They, correctly, had prayed about it and were convinced they were to wait, as the speaker would be provided. As they listened to me that weekend, they were sure I would be the speaker. They didn't tell me, but they went back to their church, told others what they had experienced and prayed. The next morning, they called me and said the Lord had told them I was to be their speaker for a weekend conference in a couple of weeks. My response was not as gracious as it should have been. It was winter, and I did not want to make a five-hour winter drive each way, so I would have to fly and that would be a waste of money. They were not put off but simply asked me to pray about it, because they were sure the Holy Spirit had spoken to them. I protested, "He hasn't told me. I will pray, but you can surely find a speaker in Toronto." Later that morning I was called by a representative of the milk industry who wanted me to take part in a conference on the role of milk in the human diet. They had done their homework and knew I was frankly skeptical of the demonization of cholesterol. Much of the science was either shoddy or merely correlational, and there are so many cross-correlations in dietary studies that it would not be easy to prove. Because of my interest in geographical pathology, I knew there were several societies with incredibly high fat/cholesterol diets and no significant heart disease, so any relation would be complex and related more to societal factors than was then understood. I rather cynically declined, and then they doubled the honorarium. I then found out it was to be in Toronto on the Friday before the weekend of the church conference. I asked whether my return flight could be on Sunday evening. No problem. I called the church and said it wasn't the Holy Spirit but the Canadian dairy bureau that had dealt with my quibbles. Of course, I shouldn't have said that.

However, the conference was going to teach me more about the ways of God. On Friday evening, folk were wandering in singing happy songs and quite late asked me to speak. I spoke briefly about Christian discipline and sent them to bed. The next morning, they were singing at breakfast. I was not a happy camper and went for a short walk before the first session.

As I passed a couple with their young children, the dad said, "I have met you before."

"Where?" I asked.

"British Columbia," he said.

"I don't think I have been there since the 1970s," I remarked.

"That would be about right," he said.

"That would make you a teenager," I responded.

"Yes," he said.

"Where?" I asked.

"Kitimat," he told me.

I was stunned. I had been there for two weeks. We had traveled from Jamaica to visit friends in Vancouver, and I had a cash flow problem, so I brought my documents and got a two-week locum in Kitimat. The story was lovely. We went to church and this young man's mom invited us to lunch. While she was making coffee, I did what I always do, given the chance, and looked at their bookshelves. Apparently, I was rather dismissive of their "Christian" books, but the mom immediately asked me to write a list of better books, which I did. That list changed that family; after retirement, she used it in a ministry that helped dropout young people get educated. And all because of my rude comment! And the story arrived just when I was thinking I was in the wrong place, but instead it resulted in a lovely weekend and the start of a new career.

Without doubt, it was recordings I did not know about that had the biggest impact, with Dr. David Stevens as the driving force. He had been a missionary in Kenya, where he transformed a one-doctor mission hospital into a teaching hospital. When he called me in the mid-1990s, he had recently become CEO of the U.S. Christian Medical & Dental Associations (CMDA) and realized the cultural ethos of America was no longer predominantly derived from a Protestant history. He was introduced to my talks by CMDA staff member Michael McLaughlin, and after listening several times, he asked me to come to the U.S. and make some recordings.

I had no idea what was going to happen, but within a few years I was giving hundreds of talks a year, including multiple grand rounds presentations. It was a great privilege and totally unexpected.

The next great act of grace also flowed from the Sermon on the Mount. I had taught on it for missionaries in Zaire and a few adult Sunday School groups, and my understanding of it was changing me. The act of providence was that a lady from a large downtown church somehow found out about these talks and asked me to speak to her church. I said I would need three sessions to do it reasonable justice.

After the first session, philosopher Graeme Hunter came to talk to me, and we ended our conversation by arranging a lunch date. We were both deeply disturbed by the way university was changing enrolling students whom they knew would not graduate and generally lowering standards for economic and political reasons. We hoped there were many colleagues who would share our views, but we only knew of two who would come to lunch. I knew of a few physicians, but they were all over stretched already. The group did grow, and we moved to a breakfast meeting. The phenomenon motivating us was that we had all become familiar with Christian students, particularly evangelicals, who, within a year or so, ceased to practice their faith. Some professors regularly ridiculed their faith, and they were not equipped to defend the gospel. We turned our breakfast group into a serious reading group meeting weekly to review how the Western world from the Greeks to Alasdair MacIntyre had thought about education. A core of a dozen or so academics from a range of faculties turned up regularly. There were also others, including graduate students, folk from Parliament hill and those who simply enjoyed deepening their faith. It was undoubtedly the best seminar I was ever privileged to attend, and it went on for at least a dozen years.

After at least five years of reading together, Augustine College was birthed and turned into reality through the pressure of homeschoolers and graduate students. We set about introducing Christian students (almost entirely from evangelical backgrounds) to their intellectual birthright by simply exposing them to the greatest achievements in the areas of philosophy, theology, literature, science and medicine. They rarely knew who among the great contributors to science were Christian (e.g. Nicolaus Copernicus, Galileo Galilei, Johannes Kepler, Sir Isaac Newton, Robert Boyle, Michael Faraday, and Nicholas Maxwell, to name just a very few). It was certainly a pedagogic joy for me.

Augustine College continued until the consequences of COVID, and it may fail to restart for lack of applicants. It was always a big challenge to ask students to take a year out for no immediate academic benefit. With the incredible increase in anxiety and hopelessness engendered by interactive screen, and documented by Jonathan Haidt, we face a need to rethink. However, it is good to realize 10 percent of our graduates are in the medical profession, and several are established academics in other specialties. The educational damage of masking young children will last a generation, according to several experts. How astonishing it is that to be brought up in a blue-collar Christian family was far better than what almost every child gets today.

Dr. John Patrick holds MB, BS, MRCP and MD degrees from Kings College London and St. George's Hospital Medical School in London. In his career as a researcher, Dr. Patrick did extensive work on the treatment of childhood nutritional deficiency and related diseases, holding appointments in Britain, Jamaica and Canada. He has lectured at universities in Britain, North America, the former Soviet Union, Australia, New Zealand and Africa. In Zaire/Congo, he was particularly concerned to understand the relationship between belief, culture and the treatment of severe malnutrition. He was Associate Professor in Clinical Nutrition, Department of Biochemistry and Pediatrics at the University of Ottawa for 20 years. He retired in 2002. Since leaving the university, he has been President of Augustine College. He speaks throughout the world, both to secular and faith communities, on the integration of faith and medicine, addressing issues of faith, culture and public policy. His talks, CV and recent podcasts are available at johnpatrick.ca/podcast/. John often addresses the issues of sanctity of life, abortion and euthanasia.

Notes

1. *https://www.poetryfoundation.org/poems/44370/the-pulley*
2. Polanyi, M. *Science, Faith, and Society.* University of Chicago Press (1946), p. 76.
3. Lewis, CS. "Is Theology Poetry?" originally presented at the Oxford Socratic Club in 1944. They Asked for a Paper. *Samizdat University Press* (1962).

CHAPTER 25

MEDICINE UNDER THE BANNER OF CHRIST

MICHAEL MILLER, MD

There are two symbols commonly used to represent medicine today. One is the staff of Asclepius, a single snake wrapped on a staff. The other is the Caduceus, two snakes on a staff with wings on the top. They look similar and are used interchangeably. The ancients would be shocked. Why? The ideas associated with these symbols present completely opposite visions of medicine. Studying their origin and meaning has taught me important lessons about how to practice medicine as a Christian.

The mythological god of medicine is Asclepius. He is depicted holding a rod or staff entwined by a single snake (Fig. 1). Temples of Asclepius in the ancient world were places of healing. The original Hippocratic Oath from the fifth century BC began with an invocation to Asclepius. The Oath sets the earliest ethical standards for physicians, emphasizing a selfless commitment to the patient's well-being. The staff of Asclepius represents this spirit and has been associated with the healing arts for more than two thousand years.

The Caduceus is the staff of Mercury, the winged messenger of the gods of Olympus. He carried a staff with wings wrapped by two snakes (Fig. 2). Besides serving as messenger, he was the patron of commerce- all commerce, including illicit forms such as robbery and theft. His name is buried in our language about trade and exchange. Commerce, merchandise, merchant, and mercenary are words derived from his name. He was mischievous, deceptive, and untrustworthy- a trickster. His staff, the Caduceus, is unrelated to the healing arts.

Like all the Greek pantheon, the origin of Asclepius is uncertain. The ancient Greeks were a seafaring people. Their ancestors sailed the Mediterranean, encountering different peoples from whom they imported many ideas. On the far eastern shores of the Mediterranean Sea there was a kingdom where people worshiped an object consisting of a bronze snake wrapped on a staff, believing it had miraculous healing powers. The Bible records the strange and surprising story of this object. After the Hebrews were freed from slavery in Egypt, they travelled through the Sinai to gain the homeland God promised. Several times along the way they rebelled, and God disciplined them. One time, He used poisonous snakes to invade the camp. Thousands died. The people prayed that God would remove the snakes, but God had a different plan. He told Moses to make a bronze sculpture of a snake, attach it to a pole, and hold it up for all to see. Anyone who looked at it after being bitten would not die (Numbers 21:9). So dramatic was the apparent healing power of the bronze snake on a pole that the people preserved it and eventually began to worship it! Five centuries later, a king named Hezekiah had to destroy it to stop this practice and return the people to the proper worship of God (2 Kings 18:4). If ancient Greeks had visited the Kingdom of Judah in the 8th century, prior to King Hezekiah's reforms, they would have seen the people actively worshipping the snake on the staff for its healing powers. They might have adopted these beliefs and expressed them as Asclepius, the god of healing, and his powerful staff. This seems a very reasonable explanation for how such an unlikely symbol as a poisonous snake on a staff would come to represent the healing arts.

Centuries later Jesus explained why God told Moses in the wilderness to use such a strange way to save the people from death:

"And as Moses lifted up the serpent in the wilderness, so must the Son of Man be lifted up, that whoever believes in him may have eternal life."
— JOHN 3:14,15

Moses's bronze snake modeled God's plan of salvation. Jesus Christ became sin (2 Cor. 5:21) and was raised up on a cross. All who look to Him will live. Amazingly, God supernaturally preserved this symbol through the centuries, and today it represents the healing arts. Moses' serpent is a palimpsest, an object originally made for one purpose then later reused for another. It is like a page in an ancient manuscript on which the original text has been overwritten. Yet, the original message is preserved and readable if the overwriting is pealed back. The staff of Asclepius is what cross-cultural missionaries call a redemptive analogy; an idea woven by God into the fabric of a culture that can help people understand the Gospel.

What can we learn as Christian medical professionals from these things? The contrast between the Caduceus and the staff of Asclepius reflects the tension in the minds and hearts of all medical professionals between self-interest and the needs of the patient. Physicians have significant income potential related to the volume of patients and types of procedures performed. Personal finances can be a powerful competing interest, hence the irony of the Caduceus as a symbol of medicine. But there are non-monetary conflicts as well. For me as a salaried physician working in academic institutions, financial gain has been overshadowed by other self-serving interests. Personal reputation, academic visibility, leadership opportunities, or personal convenience can sometimes tend to eclipse my dedication to the patients under my care. For example, in my clinical practice as a reconstructive surgeon, I usually have different surgical options to offer. I have been tempted to perform a more technically difficult procedure to impress colleagues or write a paper rather than the one that might be simpler and safer, but still adequately meets the patient's needs. Sometimes, I have faced the opposite problem, wanting to do something simple that allows me to finish quickly to attend a meeting, work on research, write a paper, or go home, rather than choosing a procedure that will take more time to complete and is likely to yield a better outcome. No one sees this internal tug-of-war but me.

How can we avoid practicing under the Caduceus rather than the Staff of Asclepius? How do we avoid our natural inclination toward self-centeredness as medical professionals? The tools at our disposal are no different than those that transform our character and ensure a fruitful life in Christ- the spiritual disciplines of Bible study, prayer, fellowship, and evangelism. We must work to master the scriptures with the same intensity we apply to a medical text relevant to our practice. We must cultivate our prayer life, regularly spending time with God offering worship and thanksgiving and interceding for ourselves, our families, our patients, and our colleagues. We must reserve time for consistent fellowship with believers both inside and outside of the medical profession and resist allowing professional demands to replace these times. Finally, we acquire the interpersonal skills to understand others and to discern the gaps in their lives through which the gospel can enter. We cultivate effective communication skills to have the confidence to effectively explain our faith in a professional context. Underlying these disciplines is learning to live each moment yielded to the power of the Holy Spirit, who indwells every believer in Christ.

The source of conflict we face as Christian medical professionals is not only internal but external as well. One of the most famous temples of Asclepius was in the city of Pergamum, a great center of medicine and scholarship in the ancient world. Jesus had a special message to that church:

> *"I know where you dwell, where Satan's throne is. Yet you hold*
> *fast my name, and you did not deny my faith..."*
> — REVELATION 2:13

Influential centers of academia and medicine are strategic places where spiritual forces regularly battle. As we enter universities and academic medical centers to learn and practice, we should expect to encounter powerful spiritual opposition. I was unaware and unprepared for this as a medical student and surgical resident. I often felt out of place. I thought, perhaps, I was not called to this profession. I felt unaligned with the priorities and attitudes taught in school and that I often observed in my classmates. It was liberating to realize that the source of dissonance was not medicine itself, which I loved, but this spiritual conflict with the socialization process in which education and training is packaged. The reality that "we do not wrestle against flesh and blood, but against ...the cosmic powers over this present darkness, against the spiritual forces of evil in the heavenly places" (Ephesians 6:12) became more than a curious theoretical idea. It became a real part of my daily life. I realized I needed to not only master anatomy, physiology, and surgical techniques, but also understand each element of the "whole armor of God" and how to use them to stand firm in my faith.

The Lord has blessed my professional career beyond my wildest expectations. I have been given opportunities to work in prestigious medical centers and lead elite academic programs in clinical care, research, and education. I have taught and performed surgery around the world. My career was shepherded by God and has been unfolded before me. I am living proof of what Jesus taught:

> *"But seek first the kingdom of God and his righteousness,*
> *and all these things will be added to you."*
> — MATTHEW 6:33

The cross is the most powerful symbol of Christ's work of redemption. For me, the single snake wrapped on a staff is equally potent. It predates the cross and graphically illustrates how Christ became sin, died on a cross, rose again, and redeemed my soul. God has preserved this symbol in a most remarkable way for over 3000 years. To those with eyes to see, it will remind us of the One who knew no sin but became sin on our behalf. Pray that each of us will practice the healing arts under His banner.

FIGURES AND LEGENDS

FIGURE 1.

A

B

A. Asclepius, the Greek god of healing, and his staff. (*https://commons.wikimedia.org/w/index.php?search=statue+of+Asclepius&title=Special:MediaSearch&go=Go&type=image*) (Public domain, via Wikimedia Commons)

B. Logo of the American Medical Association featuring the staff of Asclepius *https://commons.wikimedia.org/w/index.php?search=ama+logo&title=Special:MediaSearch&go=Go&type=image* (Public domain, via Wikimedia Commons)

FIGURE 2.

A. Mercury and his staff, the Caduceus. *https://commons.wikimedia.org/w/index.php?-search=greek+god+Mercury&title=Special:MediaSearch&go=Go&type=image* (Public domain, via Wikimedia Commons)
B. Flag of the Surgeon General of the U.S. Army. (Public domain, via Wikimedia Commons)

Michael J. Miller, M.D., F.A.C.S. is a practicing surgeon and Chief of Plastic and Reconstructive Surgery for Banner MD Anderson Cancer Center based in Phoenix Arizona. He graduated from The University of Massachusetts Medical School in 1982. After finishing general surgery residency, he trained in plastic surgery at The Ohio State University and then completed a fellowship in reconstructive microsurgery at Tulane University. In 1990, he joined the full-time faculty of The University of Texas MD Anderson Cancer Center and later returned to The Ohio State University in 2007 where he served as the founding Chair of the Department of Plastic Surgery for 12 years. With more than 30 years of practice, he is one of the most experienced cancer reconstructive surgeons in the country.

Dr. Miller became a Christian in high school after watching Billy Graham on television. He grew in his faith through involvement with campus student groups in college. Throughout his career he has sought to effectively integrate Christian faith and medical practice, education, and research. He has been married to his wife, Debbie, for more than 40 years and has two children and three grandchildren.

APPENDIX

Faith and Human Flourishing: Evidence for a Connection

Harold G. Koenig, MD, MHSc

This appendix is based in part on the book *Spiritual Readiness: A Survival Guide for the Christian Believer in an Age of Disbelief* (Koenig, 2024)

Human Flourishing

Reflective of optimal health overall, human flourishing has received a great deal of attention recently due in large part to the work of Tyler VanderWeele (2017). He defines human flourishing as "...doing or being well in the following five broad domains of human life: (i) happiness and life satisfaction; (ii) mental and physical; (iii) meaning and purpose; (iv) character and virtue; and (v) close social relationships." He later added financial and material stability (vi) to ensure human flourishing could be maintained over time.

Happiness and Life Satisfaction. This aspect of human flourishing includes positive emotions such as psychological well-being, happiness and life satisfaction. More broadly defined, positive emotions include feelings of optimism, hope, mastery, resilience and a sense that life is full and complete.

Meaning and Purpose. Having meaning and purpose in life means the person has a reason for getting up in the morning; feels their activities are making a difference in the lives of others; has objectives and goals to strive for; and is motivated to participate in activities that bring about the good. Meaning and purpose involves motivation toward being someone or achieving something that is perceived as life enhancing or toward fulfilling some important life goal.

Character and Virtue. The "cardinal virtues" that serve as the foundation for living a moral life and developing character are (1) prudence (practical wisdom); (2) justice; (3) courage (fortitude); and (4) temperance (self-control or self-discipline). In character formation, these virtues become habitual through regular practice, often involving a delay in gratification of needs. Having a virtuous character is strongly emphasized in all major world religions, and efforts to instill such character traits in children and adults is central to Christian education.

Close Social Relationships. Having meaningful close relationships is an essential component of a flourishing life and should be characteristic of the believer's social interactions, including those with friends, coworkers, members of their faith community and, in particular, members of their family. Having close social relationships will ensure emotional support during difficult times, painful losses and traumatic life events.

Mental and Physical Health. Mental health refers to the absence of mental health problems that might adversely affect a person's ability to function in social, occupational or recreational activities. Emotional conditions that interfere with a person's ability to function in daily life are classified as "disorders." Mental health problems that reach this threshold include depression, anxiety, addictions (alcohol, drugs, sex, food, etc.), severe trauma (post-traumatic stress disorder [PTSD], acute stress disorder) and inner conflicts over transgressing moral values that create inner emotional distress.

Physical health refers to the health of the physical body. People are physically healthy when they are physically fit and have sufficient physiological reserve to function independently and thrive in activities that require physical exertion. Good physical health reflects the absence of acute and chronic health problems that sap physical strength and vigor—these problems include diabetes, high blood pressure, heart disease, arthritis and being overweight or obese. The physical health dimension of human flourishing usually involves routine participation in activities that enhance physical health, such as regular exercise, healthy eating, sufficient sleep, not smoking and avoiding excess use of alcohol or drugs.

Financial and Material Stability. Human flourishing is not considered a momentary state that passes quickly, but one that persists over time. In order for that to be possible, a person must possess sufficient financial and material resources to maintain a state of flourishing. Being poverty-stricken or forced to live in a neighborhood where crime, addiction and physical threat are the norm, makes it difficult for a person to flourish, at least for most individuals. As important as having sufficient financial and material resources are, though, what really counts is being "content" with one's financial situation (whatever it may be). Being content with one's financial or material resources, then, is a key to flourishing.

HOLINESS

According to World War I chaplain Oswald Chambers (1935), God's purpose for people is not to make them healthy or happy, but to make us holy. According to Chambers, holiness means "unsullied walking with the feet, unsullied talking with the tongue, unsullied thinking with the mind—every detail of the life under the scrutiny of God" (September 1). Holiness results from a habit of making moral choices. The death of Jesus Christ on the cross made it possible for humans to live a holy life, or at least to strive toward holiness. Says Chambers:

> "I have a heredity I had no say in; I am not holy, not likely to be; and if all Jesus Christ can do is tell me I must be holy, His teaching plants despair. But if Jesus Christ is a Regenerator, One Who can put into me His own heredity of holiness, then I begin to see what He is driving at when he says that I have to be holy. Redemption means that Jesus Christ can put into any man the heredity disposition that was in Himself, and all the standards He gives are based on that disposition: His teaching is for the life He puts in. The moral transaction on my part is agreement with God's verdict on sin in the cross of Jesus Christ... The moral miracle of redemption is that God can put into me a new disposition whereby I can live a totally new life. When I reached the frontier of need and know my limitations, Jesus says – 'Blessed are you.' But I have to get there. God cannot put into me, a responsible moral being, the disposition that was in Jesus Christ unless I am conscious I need it... Redemption means that I can be delivered from the heredity of sin and through Jesus Christ can receive an unsullied heredity, viz., the Holy Spirit." (October 6)

Christians believe no one has reached the perfection of holiness except for Jesus Christ. However, as noted above, they also believe all should seek to be Christlike in everything they do, which is a lifelong journey. Holiness is an important part of the pathway that leads to health and well-being, and human flourishing more generally. Figure 1 describes the relationship between faith, holiness and human flourishing.

RELIGIOUS INVOLVEMENT AND HUMAN FLOURISHING

Holiness is difficult to measure and quantify. However, it is possible to measure the religious involvement that generates faith and the motivation to be holy. Scientific research has found that religious involvement is related to each of the six dimensions of human flourishing (happiness/life satisfaction, meaning and purpose, virtue/character, close social relationships, mental/physical health, financial/material stability).

Happiness and Life Satisfaction. A number of studies document the impact of religious involvement on psychological well-being. Our systematic review of the research published prior to 2010 in the 1st and 2nd editions of the Handbook identified 326 published quantitative peer-reviewed academic research studies (Koenig et al., 2001; 2012). Of those, 256 of 326 (79 percent) reported that a higher level of religious activity was related to greater happiness, more life satisfaction and improved psychological well-being; only three of those 326 studies (less than 1 percent) reported significantly lower well-being among the more religious compared to the less religious. Recent studies since 2010 support these findings (Sharma et al., 2017; Koenig & Al Shohaib, 2024; Koenig et al., 2024).

Meaning and Purpose. Questions about meaning and purpose are: Why am I here? What is the purpose of my life? Where did I come from? Where am I going after I die? Hufford et al. (2010) note that from a non-religious perspective, "...the answers are simple and obvious: the purpose of your life is what you make it, and after you die nothing happens." They then suggest, "Spiritual beliefs offer more complex, and usually more consoling answers. Belief that spirit is real, and that there is a Divine plan behind the seemingly random events of the world, gives rise to meanings with far-reaching implications, 'making sense of it all'".

In our systematic review of research provided in the first two editions of the handbook, religious involvement was consistently related to greater meaning and purpose in life (Koenig et al., 2001; 2012). In fact, 42 of 45 (93 percent) quantitative studies found greater meaning and purpose in those who scored higher on religious beliefs, commitments and practices. More recent research from the Harvard School of Public Health using larger samples and high-quality methodology reported the same finding, including studies in young adults (Chen & VanderWeele, 2018; Chen et al., 2020a).

Character and Virtue. Early Stoic philosophers emphasized the importance of character and virtue. When a person lives a life of virtue and character, the emotional casualties suffered in family life, work and life overall are far fewer. Our systematic reviews documented in the Handbooks identified studies examining the relationship between religious involvement and altruism, volunteering, gratitude, forgiveness, delinquency and crime, which might be considered indicators of character and virtue. The vast majority found that higher levels of religious involvement were related to significantly greater involvement in altruistic activities and volunteering (33 of 47 studies), more gratitude (five out of five studies), more forgiveness (34 of 40 studies) and less delinquency and crime (82 of 104 studies) (Koenig et al., 2001; 2012). Recent research within the last 10 years confirmed these findings (Koenig et al., 2024).

Close Social Relationships. Close relationships with family members and extended social networks are an important aspect of human flourishing, and they also are an important source of psychological well-being more generally. Good relationships with others are crucial for those who may need to work with others to accomplish whatever goals they may have. Because religious teachings strongly encourage mutual support and dependability, a connection here would not be surprising. The systematic review mentioned earlier found that religious beliefs, practices and commitments were associated with significantly greater social support in more than 80 percent of studies (61 of 74). More recent research in young adults supports these findings (Semplonius et al., 2016; Chen et al., 2020a).

The benefits of religious involvement also apply to marriage. Review of all quantitative research from 1948 to 2008 documented in the Handbooks identified 79 studies on the relationship between religious involvement and family/marital stability. Of those studies, 68 of 79 (86 percent) reported significantly lower rates of divorce, greater marital satisfaction, less spouse abuse, less cheating on spouse or greater likelihood of having a two-parent family among those who were more religious compared to the less religious (Koenig et al., 2001; 2012).

Those findings have been further replicated in recent studies. For example, Li et al. (2018) at the Harvard School of Public Health followed 66,444 initially married women for a 14-year period, finding a 41 to 47 percent reduction in likelihood of divorce or separation among those regularly attending religious services during follow-up (if you are a statistician, the hazard ratio [HR]=0.59, 95% CI= 0.50-0.69, for weekly attendance; HR=0.53, 95% CI=0.42-0.67, for greater than weekly). Thus, religious involvement, particularly attending religious services together, appears to make a real difference in terms of marital quality.

Mental and Physical Health. Here, I first examine the relationships between religious involvement and mental health, focusing on depression, substance use disorders, PTSD, moral injury (the inner distress from transgressing moral values) and suicide risk, and then examine their associations with indicators of physical health.

Depression. In the systematic review described in the Handbooks, a total of 444 published studies were identified on the relationship between religious beliefs/practices and depression. Of those, 272 studies (61 percent) found that religious involvement was associated with less depression and faster recovery from depression (Koenig et al., 2001; 2012). In a more recent study from the Harvard School of Public Health, researchers followed 9,862 young adults (average age 23) for up to six years, finding that those attending religious services at least weekly at the beginning of the study were nearly one-third less likely to develop a depressive order during follow-up (risk ratio [RR]= 0.69, 95% CI=0.57-0.84) (Chen et al., 2020a). In addition, randomized controlled trials have demonstrated that religious interventions such as religiously-integrated psychotherapy significantly reduce depressive symptoms (Captari et al., 2018; Koenig, 2018).

Substance Use. In our systematic research review documented in the Handbooks, we identified a total of 278 studies examining the relationship between religious beliefs/practices and alcohol use. Of those, 240 (86 percent) reported significantly less alcohol use, abuse and dependence among those who were more religious (Koenig et al., 2001; 2012). Regarding illicit drug use, the systematic review identified 185 studies. Of those, 155 (84 percent) reported significantly less illicit drug use or abuse among persons scoring higher on religious involvement.

Research conducted since 2010 confirms these findings using high-quality research methods (Koenig et al., 2024). For example, in studying a nationally representative sample of 3,151 U.S. Veterans participating in the National Health and Resilience in Veterans Study (NHRVS), researchers found that war veterans scoring high on religiosity (based on the 5-item Duke Religion Index) were 34 percent less likely to have a history of alcohol use disorder (odds ratio [OR]=0.66, 95% CI=0.46-0.93) and 72 percent less likely to have a current alcohol use disorder (OR=0.28, 95% CI = 0.19-0.41) (Sharma et al., 2017). Christian believers are fighting a war "...against principalities, against powers, against the rulers of the darkness of this world, against spiritual wickedness in high places" (Ephesians 6:12, KJV).

PTSD. Studies have also reported lower rates of PTSD among individuals who are more religious (Koenig et al., 2012; 2024). For example, in the study of 3,151 U.S. war veterans described earlier, Sharma et al. (2017) found that those scoring high on religiosity were 54 percent less likely to report a lifetime history of PTSD (OR=0.46, 95% CI=0.22-0.95) and 70 percent less likely to report current PTSD (OR=0.30, 95% CI=0.10-0.90).

Inner Conflict from Moral Injury. Those who live their lives according to moral values are at risk for moral injury when they commit acts that transgress those values (marital infidelity, engagement in pornography, sexual abuse, etc.). Despite the fact those with strong faith are at higher risk for the development of moral injury as they seek to live by high moral and ethical standards, greater religious involvement appears to be associated with lower levels of moral injury. We have reported this finding in studies of U.S. veterans (Koenig et al., 2018), active-duty military personnel (Volk & Koenig, 2019) and healthcare professionals (Mantri et al., 2021). One exception, however, has involved studies of moral injury among healthcare professionals in mainland China, where lower levels of moral injury were found in those with no religious affiliation and higher levels in those who indicated spiritual beliefs were important in daily life (Wang et al., 2021). Some religious belief systems may advocate for high moral values (such as Buddhism and Confucianism), but they have few tools for resolving symptoms resulting from transgressing those values.

Suicide Risk. The U.S. Centers for Disease Control and Prevention (CDC) recently reported that deaths from suicide in the U.S. are now at an all-time high (Rudy, 2023). In our systematic review from the Handbooks, we identified 141 research studies that examined the relationship between religious involvement and suicidal thoughts, attempts or completions (most studies in Christian-majority populations). Of those, 106 of 141 (75 percent) reported significantly fewer suicidal thoughts, attempts and completions among participants scoring higher on measures of religious involvement (Koenig et al., 2001; 2012).

More recently, studies by the Harvard School of Public Health have found that frequent attendance at religious services consistently predicts a lower risk of completed suicide and, in addition, fewer deaths from "diseases of despair" (drugs, alcohol or suicide). For example, in a 14-year study of nearly 90,000 women followed from 1996 to 2010, the risk of completed suicide was 84 percent lower among those who attended religious services at least weekly compared to non-attenders (HR=0.16, 95% CI=0.06-0.46) (Vander-

Weele et al., 2016). An even larger effect on suicide rate has been reported in the general U.S. population, where an 18-year follow-up of a random national sample of more than 20,000 U.S. adults (NHANES-III study) found a 94 percent reduction in risk of completed suicide among those attending religious services at least twice per month or more compared to those attending less than twice monthly (HR=0.06, 95% CI=0.01-0.54). These findings were independent of gender, age, size of household, previous suicide attempt and illicit drug use (Kleiman & Liu, 2014).

Deaths of despair (from drugs, alcohol or suicide) were almost 70 percent less common among frequent attendees compared to non-attenders in a 16-year follow-up study of 66,492 female health professionals (HR=0.32, 95% CI=0.16-0.62) (Chen et al., 2020b). With regard to males, Chen et al. (2020b) examined the frequency of deaths of despair among 43,141 male health professionals followed for 26 years. Researchers found that men attending religious services at least weekly at the beginning of the study were almost 50 percent less likely to die from a death of despair during follow-up compared to non-attenders (HR=0.51, 95% CI=0.37-0.70, age-adjusted).

In a meta-analysis that summarized the results of nine studies including 2,339 suicide cases and 5,252 matched controls, Wu et al. (2015) found a 62 percent reduction in suicide risk among those who were more religious (OR=0.38, 95% CI= 0.21–0.71). In regions where religious homogeneity was prominent (i.e., areas where community residents adhered to a single religion or a small number of faiths) the reduced risk was 82 percent (OR=0.18, 95% CI= 0.13–0.26).

Physical Health. Problems with mental health affect health more generally far beyond the mind only. Psychological and behavioral problems are known to have a cumulative effect on the physical body, reducing physical fitness incrementally over time beginning in the teen years. While young people have tremendous physiological reserve, it is not without limit. For example, research in teenagers and young adults has shown that the development of atherosclerosis (narrowing of the coronary arteries) begins around ages 15 to 19 (Strong et al., 1999; Tuzcu et al., 2001). Coronary artery narrowing occurs especially fast in young people with poor health habits, such as smokers and those who are over-weight (Jin et al., 2012; Aggarwal et al., 2016).

In his book *The Body Keeps the Score*, one of the world's leading experts on the effects of psychological trauma on the brain, body and nervous system carefully documented how attitudes and behaviors influence the physical body across the lifespan beginning in the teen years (Van der Kolk, 2014). If religious beliefs and practices help to improve coping with stress, alleviate emotional distress and reduce destructive behaviors, then they should also have a positive effect on the physical body and promote physical fitness.

In the systematic review of research reported in the Handbooks, we analyzed hundreds of studies examining the relationship between religious involvement and physical health. The majority of those studies found that those were more religious experienced less heart disease, lower blood pressure, lower rates of stroke, less cognitive decline with aging, increased concentration, less physical disability, better immune function, lower levels of pro-inflammatory markers, lower levels of stress hormones, lower death rates from cardiovascular disease and cancer and lower mortality overall from all causes (Koenig et al., 2001; 2012). Research published in some of the best public health journals in the world since 2010 has reported similar findings (Pantell et al., 2013; Li et al., 2016; VanderWeele et al., 2017; Chen et al., 2020b).

Financial and Material Stability. Financial problems are common among believers and nonbelievers alike. Religious involvement is strongly associated with lower socioeconomic status. In fact, greater religious activity is often an indicator of efforts to cope with financial stressors. However, if a person is religious or raised in a religious environment, the chances of completing their education are much improved (e.g., completing high school, getting good grades, entering college) (Koenig et al., 2012; 2024). Of the 11 research studies published in academic journals between 2000 and 2009 examining religious involvement and school performance (GPA or persistence to graduation), all of them (11 out of 11 studies or 100 percent) indicated that religious young people were significantly more likely to perform well in school compared to their less religious peers (Koenig et al., 2012, pp. 785-786).

Recent research conducted since 2010 confirms these findings (Horwitz et al., 2020; 2021; Horwitz, 2022a,b). For example, Horwitz (2022b) followed 3,290 Christian adolescents from 2003 to 2012 using data from the National Youth and Religion Study, which was linked to 2016 National Student Clearing-house data. She examined the effects of adolescents' religious upbringing on their education (grades and higher education attained). Horowitz found that teenage boys from working-class families regularly involved in religious activity and who strongly believed in God were twice as likely to graduate from college with a bachelor's degree compared to boys who were only moderately religious or not religious at all.

One reason for better school performance and greater academic achievement is because religious parents are more likely to instill religious values in children, as well as being more likely to monitor youth activities. Consequently, education is less likely to be interrupted by alcohol or drug addiction, teen pregnancy or delinquent behavior. Getting a good education improves the chances of obtaining a high-paying job and moving out of a bad neighborhood. Furthermore, as noted earlier, Christian beliefs promote a strong work ethic (being a responsible, dependable, hard worker) and seek to instill altruistic character traits, which will likely enhance job stability and improve performance. As a result, greater religious involvement has been associated with greater work satisfaction, higher workplace productivity and a wide range of positive attitudes toward work (Jamal & Badawi, 1993; Robert et al., 2006; Osman-Gani et al., 2013; Carroll et al., 2014; Onyemah et al., 2018). Having self-control, which religious teachings emphasize, should also influence the believer's spending habits and management of personal finances, which will likely have a positive impact on their financial stability.

In summary, active participation in religious activities appears to reduce stress, improve relationships, increase social support, enhance relationships with family members and improve mental and physical health (Koenig et al., 2024). Based on the research above, we know religious involvement has many mental and physical health benefits regardless of age or socioeconomic status.

CLINICAL APPLICATIONS

How might a clinician utilize this information when caring for patients, particularly Christian patients? The first step is to take a brief spiritual history. Five simple questions can help the clinician determine where the patient is in terms of their faith (Koenig, 2002):

1. Do your religious or spiritual beliefs provide comfort and support or do they cost stress?
2. How would these beliefs influence your medical decisions if you became really sick?
3. Do you have any beliefs that might interfere or conflict with your medical care?
4. Are you a member of a religious or spiritual community, and is it supportive?
5. Do you have any spiritual needs someone should address?

In addition to taking a spiritual history, the clinician should support the beliefs and practices of the patient. Taking a spiritual history and supporting the beliefs of patients are not controversial, and it will not get the clinician in trouble. However, with the Christian patient, the clinician may ask in certain circumstances whether the patient would like pray with the clinician; preferably, the patient would initiate this request, but many patients don't recognize this would even be possible, so the healthcare professional may need to inform the patient this is a possibility (Koenig, 2013). If the patient asks about the clinician's religious beliefs, then there is no reason why the healthcare professional should not share their beliefs with the patient. Care, however, must be taken when sharing personal beliefs with patients unless the patient asks. This is a cautious, but prudent approach to take. Prescribing religious beliefs and practices, however, must be done with extreme caution, given possible liability issues that may be raised by such actions. When spiritual needs are present, the clinician may always refer to a chaplain who may have more time and more experience addressing spiritual issues that come up in healthcare. For uncomplicated spiritual needs, however, the healthcare professional may decide to briefly address them if they have time.

CONCLUSIONS

A great deal of scientific evidence has now amassed that firmly documents that religious beliefs, practices and commitments influence virtually every aspect of human flourishing. This has been clearly demonstrated in community populations and healthcare settings. These findings support the claim that those persons with faith (have a strong relationship with God, who are seeking to be Christlike in thought, word and deed) will have the best possible chance of experiencing human flourishing in all its dimensions. Bear in mind, however, that genetic factors, adverse childhood experiences and traumatic events during adult life, which a person has little or no control over, can complicate things. The findings from research described above have a number of clinical applications, of which taking a spiritual history and supporting the religious beliefs of patients are the least controversial.

FIGURE 1

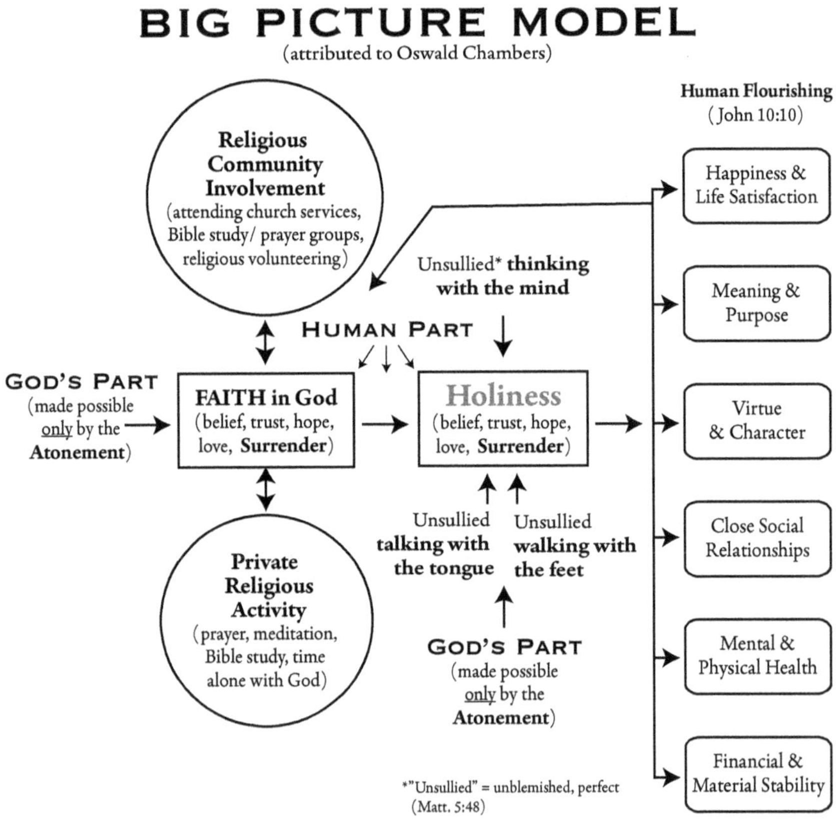

BIG PICTURE MODEL
(attributed to Oswald Chambers)

Human Flourishing (John 10:10)

- Religious Community Involvement (attending church services, Bible study/ prayer groups, religious volunteering)
- **GOD'S PART** (made possible <u>only</u> by the Atonement)
- **FAITH in God** (belief, trust, hope, love, **Surrender**)
- **Holiness** (belief, trust, hope, love, **Surrender**)
- Private Religious Activity (prayer, meditation, Bible study, time alone with God)
- Unsullied* thinking with the mind
- **HUMAN PART**
- Unsullied talking with the tongue
- Unsullied walking with the feet
- **GOD'S PART** (made possible <u>only</u> by the Atonement)

Outcomes:
- Happiness & Life Satisfaction
- Meaning & Purpose
- Virtue & Character
- Close Social Relationships
- Mental & Physical Health
- Financial & Material Stability

*"Unsullied" = unblemished, perfect (Matt. 5:48)

Figure 1. From Faith to Human Flourishing (used with permission from Koenig, 2024)

Dr. Harold Koenig is Professor of Psychiatry and Behavior Sciences and Associate Professor of Medicine at the Duke University Medical Center in Durham, North Carolina. He is also an Adjunct Professor, Department of Medicine, at the King Abdulaziz University, Jeddah, Saudi Arabia, a Visiting Professor, Shiraz University of Medical Sciences, Shiraz, Iran, and Editor-in-Chief, International Journal of Psychiatry in Medicine. Dr. Koenig is Director of the Center for Spirituality, Theology and Health at Duke, and he has published extensively in the fields of mental health, geriatrics and religion, with more than 1,000 scientific peer-reviewed articles and book chapters and more than 50 books. He is the recipient of the 2012 Oskar Pfister Award from the American Psychiatric Association and the 2013 Gary Collins Award from the American Association of Christian Counselors.

NOTES

Aggarwal, A., Srivastava, S., & Velmurugan, M. (2016). Newer perspectives of coronary artery disease in young. *World Journal of Cardiology, 8*(12), 728.

Captari, L. E., Hook, J. N., Hoyt, W., Davis, D. E., McElroy-Heltzel, S. E., & Worthington Jr, E. L. (2018). Integrating clients' religion and spirituality within psychotherapy: A comprehensive meta-analysis. *Journal of Clinical Psychology, 74*(11), 1938-1951.

Carroll, S. T., Stewart-Sicking, J. A., & Thompson, B. (2014). Sanctification of work: Assessing the role of spirituality in employment attitudes. *Mental Health, Religion & Culture, 17*(6), 545-556.

Chambers, O. (1935/1963). *My Upmost for His Highest*. Uhrichsville, OH: Barbour Publishing

Chen, Y., & VanderWeele, T.J. (2018). Associations of religious upbringing with subsequent health and well-being from adolescence to young adulthood: an outcome-wide analysis. *American Journal of Epidemiology, 187*(11), 2355-2364.

Chen, Y., Kim, E. S., & VanderWeele, T. J. (2020a). Religious-service attendance and subsequent health and well-being throughout adulthood: Evidence from three prospective cohorts. *International Journal of Epidemiology, 49*(6), 2030-2040.

Chen, Y., Koh, H. K., Kawachi, I., Botticelli, M., & VanderWeele, T. J. (2020b). Religious service attendance and deaths related to drugs, alcohol, and suicide among US health care professionals. *JAMA Psychiatry, 77*(7), 737-744.

Horwitz, I. M., Domingue, B. W., & Harris, K. M. (2020). Not a family matter: The effects of religiosity on academic outcomes based on evidence from siblings. *Social Science Research, 88*, 102426.

Horwitz, I. M. (2021). Religion and academic achievement: a research review spanning secondary school and higher education. *Review of Religious Research, 63*(1), 107-154.

Horwitz, I. M. (2022a). *God, Grades, and Graduation: Religion's Surprising Impact on Academic Success*. New York, NY: Oxford University Press.

Horwitz, I. M. (2022b). I followed the lives of 3,290 teenagers. This is what I learned about religion and education. *New York Times*. Retrieved on 5-28-22 from https://www.nytimes.com/2022/03/15/opinion/religion-school-success.html.

Hufford, D. J., Fritts, M. J., & Rhodes, J. E. (2010). Spiritual fitness. *Military Medicine, 175*(suppl_8), 73-87.

Jamal, M., & Badawi, J. (1993). Job stress among Muslim immigrants in North America: Moderating effects of religiosity. *Stress Medicine, 9*(3), 145-151.

Jin, K. N., Chun, E. J., Lee, C. H., Kim, J. A., Lee, M. S., & Choi, S. I. (2012). Subclinical coronary atherosclerosis in young adults: prevalence, characteristics, predictors with coronary computed tomography angiography. *International Journal of Cardiovascular Imaging, 28*, 93-100.

Kleiman, E. M., & Liu, R. T. (2014). Prospective prediction of suicide in a nationally representative sample: religious service attendance as a protective factor. *British Journal of Psychiatry, 204*(4), 262-266.

Koenig, H. G. (2002). An 83-year-old woman with chronic illness and strong religious beliefs. *Journal of the American Medical Association, 288*(4), 487-493.

Koenig, H. G. (2013). *Spirituality in Patient Care: Why, How, When, and What* (3rd ed.). Conshohocken, PA: Templeton Foundation Press

Koenig, H. G. (2018). *Religion and Mental Health: Research and Clinical Applications.* San Diego, CA: Academic Press

Koenig, H. G., Larson, D., & McCullough, M. E. (2001). *Handbook of Religion and Health*, 1st ed. New York, NY: Oxford University Press

Koenig, H. G., King, D. E., & Carson, V. B. (2012). *Handbook of Religion and Health*, 2nd ed. New York, NY: Oxford University Press

Koenig, H. G., VanderWeele, T. J., & Peteet, J. R. (2024). *Handbook of Religion and Health*, 3rd ed. New York, NY: Oxford University Press

Koenig, H. G., & Al Shohaib, S. (2024). Religious involvement and psychological well-being in the Middle East. *International Journal of Psychiatry in Medicine*, in press
(https://doi.org/10.1177/00912174231197548)

Koenig, H. G., Youssef, N. A., Ames, D., Oliver, J. P., Teng, E. J., Haynes, K., ... & Pearce, M. (2018). Moral injury and religiosity in US veterans with posttraumatic stress disorder symptoms. *Journal of Nervous and Mental Disease, 206*(5), 325-331.

Koenig, H. G. (2024). *Spiritual Readiness: A Survival Guide for the Christian Believer in an Age of Disbelief.* Seattle, WA: Amazon/Kindle (https://www.amazon.com/Spiritual-Readiness-Survival-Christian-Disbelief/dp/B0CP42X91N/).

Li, S., Stampfer, M.J., Williams, D.R., & VanderWeele, T.J. (2016). Association of religious service attendance with mortality among women. *JAMA Internal Medicine* 176(6), 777-785.

Li, S., Kubzansky, L. D., & VanderWeele, T. J. (2018). Religious service attendance, divorce, and remarriage among US nurses in mid and late life. *PloS One, 13*(12), e0207778.

Mantri, S., Lawson, J. M., Wang, Z., & Koenig, H. G. (2021). Prevalence and predictors of moral injury symptoms in health care professionals. *Journal of Nervous and Mental Disease, 209*(3), 174-180.

Onyemah, V., Rouziès, D., & Iacobucci, D. (2018). Impact of religiosity and culture on salesperson job satisfaction and performance. *International Journal of Cross Cultural Management, 18*(2), 191-219.

Osman-Gani, A. M., Hashim, J., & Ismail, Y. (2013). Establishing linkages between religiosity and spirituality on employee performance. *Employee Relations* 35(4), 360-376

Pantell, M., Rehkopf, D., Jutte, D., Syme, S. L., Balmes, J., & Adler, N. (2013). Social isolation: a predictor of mortality comparable to traditional clinical risk factors. *American Journal of Public Health, 103*(11), 2056-2062.

Rudy, M. (2023). Suicide rates reach all-time high in US, per CDC data: 'Silent public health crisis'. *Fox News*, August 11. Retrieved on 8-12-23 from https://www.foxnews.com/health/suicide-rates-reach-all-time-high-us-new-cdc-data.

Semplonius, T., Good, M., & Willoughby, T. (2015). Religious and nonreligious activity engagement as assets in promoting social ties throughout university: The role of emotion regulation. *Journal of Youth and Adolescence, 44*(8), 1592-1606.

Sharma, V., Marin, D. B., Koenig, H. G., Feder, A., Iacoviello, B. M., Southwick, S. M., & Pietrzak, R. H. (2017). Religion, spirituality, and mental health of US military veterans: Results from the National Health and Resilience in Veterans Study. *Journal of Affective Disorders, 217*, 197-204.

Strong, J. P., Malcom, G. T., McMahan, C. A., Tracy, R. E., Newman III, W. P., Herderick, E. E., ... & Pathobiological Determinants of Atherosclerosis in Youth Research Group. (1999). Prevalence and extent of atherosclerosis in adolescents and young adults: implications for prevention from the Pathobiological Determinants of Atherosclerosis in Youth Study. *Journal of the American Medical Association, 281*(8), 727-735.

Tuzcu, E. M., Kapadia, S. R., Tutar, E., Ziada, K. M., Hobbs, R. E., McCarthy, P. M., ... & Nissen, S. E. (2001). High prevalence of coronary atherosclerosis in asymptomatic teenagers and young adults: evidence from intravascular ultrasound. *Circulation*, *103*(22), 2705-2710.

Van der Kolk, B. (2014). *The Body Keeps the Score: Mind, Brain and Body in the Transformation of Trauma*. United Kingdom: Penguin.

VanderWeele, T. J., Li, S., Tsai, A. C., & Kawachi, I. (2016). Association between religious service attendance and lower suicide rates among US women. *JAMA Psychiatry, 73*(8), 845-851.

VanderWeele, T. J. (2017). On the promotion of human flourishing. *Proceedings of the National Academy of Sciences*, *114*(31), 8148-8156.

VanderWeele, T. J., Yu, J., Cozier, Y. C., Wise, L., Argentieri, M. A., Rosenberg, L., et al. (2017). Attendance at religious services, prayer, religious coping, and religious/spiritual identity as predictors of all-cause mortality in the Black Women's Health Study. *American Journal of Epidemiology*, *185*(7), 515-522.

Volk, F., & Koenig, H. G. (2019). Moral injury and religiosity in active duty US Military with PTSD symptoms. *Military Behavioral Health*, *7*(1), 64-72.

Wang, Z., Al Zaben, F., Koenig, H. G., & Ding, Y. (2021). Spirituality, moral injury and mental health among Chinese health professionals. *British Journal of Psychiatry (BJPsych) Open*, *7*(4), E135

Wu, A., Wang, J. Y., & Jia, C. X. (2015). Religion and completed suicide: A meta-analysis. *PloS One*, *10*(6), e0131715.

YOUR STORY

Other Featured Publications

Miracle at Tenwek: The Life of Dr. Ernie Steury
by Gregg Lewis

The account of exemplary faithfulness, spiritual wisdom, committed discipleship, lifelong obedience and genuine compassion will inspire readers to follow Ernie's example as dedicated servants of a loving God, who is anxious to show the world what great things He can accomplish with an individual totally committed to Him.

$19.99

Healthcare Missions: Devotions For Your Journey
by Trish Burgess, MD

Signing up for a mission trip is exciting! It can quickly feel overwhelming, and you can begin to second guess your mission to go. This book contains devotions to help you prepare spiritually for your mission trip, devotions for you when you arrive on the mission field and devotions for you to complete once you are back home.

$16.99

Dig In! by Bert L. Jones

This unique devotional is designed to be a tool to fuel your hunger and thirst for God's Word. As you *Dig In!* to this devotional, realize it is intended to serve more as a "shovel" than a "spoon." The author's desire is to develop a devotional that the individual reading can determine the depth of their time in the Word.

$24.99

CMDA Bookstore

Make the CMDA Bookstore your first stop for medically reliable and biblically sound resources for yourself, your patients, your colleagues and others as you bring the hope and healing of Christ to the world.

Learn more at cmda.christianbook.com

CHRISTIAN MEDICAL & DENTAL ASSOCIATIONS®
P.O. Box 7500 | Bristol, TN 37621 | 888-230-2637 | cmda.org

www.ingramcontent.com/pod-product-compliance
Lightning Source LLC
LaVergne TN
LVHW061611070526
838199LV00078B/7245